INTERNATIONAL POLITICS

International Politics

How History Modifies Theory

John M. Owen, IV
University of Virginia

Richard N. Rosecrance
Harvard University

New York   Oxford
OXFORD UNIVERSITY PRESS

Oxford University Press is a department of the University of Oxford. It furthers the University's objective of excellence in research, scholarship, and education by publishing worldwide. Oxford is a registered trade mark of Oxford University Press in the UK and certain other countries.

Published in the United States of America by Oxford University Press
198 Madison Avenue, New York, NY 10016, United States of America.

© 2019 by Oxford University Press

For titles covered by Section 112 of the US Higher
Education Opportunity Act, please visit
www.oup.com/us/he for the latest information about
pricing and alternate formats.

All rights reserved. No part of this publication may be reproduced, stored in a retrieval system, or transmitted, in any form or by any means, without the prior permission in writing of Oxford University Press, or as expressly permitted by law, by license, or under terms agreed with the appropriate reproduction rights organization. Inquiries concerning reproduction outside the scope of the above should be sent to the Rights Department, Oxford University Press, at the address above.

You must not circulate this work in any other form
and you must impose this same condition on any acquirer.

Library of Congress Cataloging-in-Publication Data

Names: Owen, John M. (John Malloy), 1962- author. | Rosecrance, Richard N.,
    author.
Title: International politics : how history modifies theory / John M. Owen,
    IV, University of Virginia Richard Rosecrance, Harvard University.
Description: New York : Oxford University Press, [2019]
Identifiers: LCCN 2017035278 | ISBN 9780190216092 (softcover : alk. paper)
Subjects: LCSH: International relations. | International relations—History.
    | International relations—Philosophy. | World politics.
Classification: LCC JZ1305 .O94 2019 | DDC 327—dc23 LC record available at
https://lccn.loc.gov/2017035278

9 8 7 6 5 4 3 2 1
Printed by Sheridan Books, Inc., United States of America.

To the ever-present memory of Barbara.

—R.R.

To Trish.

—J.O.

CONTENTS

PREFACE

A few decades ago, only a small number of textbooks were available to introduce students to the study of international relations. Today, the number is large. Some stress theories and paradigms; some explore the choices available to states and their leaders; some focus mostly on recent events and current problems. Some emphasize war and peace; others, trade and investment. Some focus more on powerful and rich countries; others on the less powerful and the particular challenges they face.

Such books often contain historical material—for example, on the Cold War, the World Wars of the twentieth century, even some European history and imperialism prior to that. But the book you hold in your hands, or see on your device, is different: it takes seriously history that is more distant in time yet is vital to understanding where world politics is today and where it likely is heading.

Much theorizing about international relations—particularly that of the *realist* school of thought—asserts that the world never really changes, that sovereign states are the units, there is no world government to enforce their agreements, they must always be ready for war against one another, and there is no escape or even relief from this tragic situation. *International Politics: How History Modifies Theory* takes a different view: certain states, which we call trading or commercial republics—later to become liberal democracies—have found relief from this ruthless realist world. They win through cooperation, not war, and their numbers have increased in fits and starts over the centuries.

This book, then, takes the past very seriously, because history is the story of the transformation of world politics. Most of the land surface on planet earth today is divided into sovereign states, but that has not always been the case. Indeed, for the greater part of human history most of the world was made up of large empires and smaller territories ruled by tribes. The system of sovereign states began in Europe half a millennium ago and spread over the world in two stages: European imperialism brought ideas about states to the Americas, Asia, and Africa, and, later, peoples in these regions decided they wanted states for themselves and threw off European domination. It clearly is not the case, then, that world politics never changes.

But another large historical transformation was happening even as states were populating the world—the ways those states interacted changed gradually. That kind of change is the main subject of this book. The original international system in early modern Europe was marked by frequent wars and even more frequent threats of war. Most states were ruled by kings bent on centralizing power at home and expanding it abroad. Wealth came mostly from agriculture and from precious metals, and so power came from controlling land in Europe and overseas. One king's gain was another's loss. Realist writers at this time called this situation a "state of war": even when kings were not fighting, they were aware that war could break out at any time and constantly had to be ready for it. But even while this dangerously competitive system was emerging 500 years ago, some people were more interested in making money by trading than by raiding. Eventually commercially minded people in the Netherlands set up a republic that began to outshine the neighboring powerful monarchies of Spain, France, and England. The Netherlands fought and won wars, to be sure, but its population became increasingly middle class and preferred commerce to combat. By the end of the seventeenth century the English had begun to do the same, and there began to take shape an international subsystem of states that decentralized power at home (away from kings) and excelled at trading abroad.

This took many more centuries and crises and massive wars that nearly wrecked the ambitions of trading republics. But by the late twentieth century, aided by the power and leverage of the United States, the liberal international subsystem had become globally predominant. The defeat of fascism in World War II and communism in the Cold War yielded an age of globalization in which former holdouts—including the giant states of China, India, and Brazil—decided that the route to wealth and stability was through joining the liberal international system of markets, trade, and finance.

The story is not a simple one of good guys and bad guys, however. Liberal democracies, including the United States, coerce others and violate their own principles, and realism can help us understand why. World politics is no utopia. Indeed, the liberal international system that took centuries and countless struggles to establish faces serious challenges today. China has become the world's second leading economy by participating fully in the global economy but is no liberal democracy, and its ruling Communist Party has made clear that it intends to hold onto its monopoly of power. Russia retains a large nuclear arsenal, has upgraded its conventional military force, and seized in 2014 part of a neighboring state's sovereign territory (Crimea, in Ukraine). In the Middle East, the liberal international system has at best a foothold; it is far from dominant, and regional power Iran sees in the liberal system a sign of American imperialism. Even within Europe and North America, where commercial republicanism first emerged in the modern world, some have become skeptical, if not of democracy, then of having an economy open to foreign trade, investment, and immigration.

That is the situation facing the world today. The past 500 years of history illuminate this situation by showing what forces have been at work. That history also shows that people—governments and citizens—have the freedom to choose. It is our hope that this book will show students that the future of world politics is no more set in stone now than it was in 1600 or 1800 or 1945 and that, like leaders and ordinary people who came before, they can shape the future in gradual but consequential ways.

ACKNOWLEDGMENTS

The authors of a book of this scope and ambition are bound to incur too many debts to recall and mention. Over the years we both have learned a great deal from mentors, colleagues, students, and indeed from long-dead scholars, many of whom we cite in this book, many of whom we do not. We thank Jennifer Carpenter at Oxford University Press for seeing potential in our idea for a new international relations text that takes history seriously. The staff at OUP have been extremely helpful in bringing the project to fruition. For research assistance and for help in compiling illustrations and data we thank Malloy Owen.

We are grateful to the following reviewers for their comments on the manuscript: David Bachman (University of Washington), Ewan Harrison (Rutgers University), Donald S. Inbody (Texas State University), Rita Peters (University of Massachusetts, Boston), Jim Rogers (Louisiana State University, Alexandria), Michael Holm (Boston University), Matthew Crosston (Bellvue University), Mai'a Cross (Northeastern University), Steve Chan (University of Colorado, Boulder), Felix E. Martin (Florida International University), and Steve Yetiv (Old Dominion University).

For their support, indulgence, and inspiration, we thank our families: Trish, Malloy, Frances, and Alice Owen and, for her special help and love, Richard Rosecrance would like to thank the late Barbara Rosecrance.

INTERNATIONAL POLITICS

1

INTRODUCTION

Why Study International Politics?

We study international politics because it affects us. Many important influences on our daily life come from outside the country we live in. The food we eat, the cell phones and computers we purchase, the clothes we wear, the news we receive (via Twitter or Google), our music, television, or movies may well originate elsewhere. In America, fresh fruits often come from Mexico; coffee from Indonesia, Colombia, or the Ivory Coast; timber from Indonesia and Thailand; newsprint, electric power, and water from Canada; flowers from a consortium originating in the Netherlands; oil from the Middle East or Venezuela; iron from Brazil and Australia. Even American goods like the ever-present iPhone are assembled by Taiwanese companies working in China. Investment capital is as likely to come from Europe or China as from Wall Street. Large numbers of components for American cars are produced in Mexico, Germany, Japan, South Korea, and Thailand.

Any interruption of trade, communication, or travel would leave the United States bereft of vital sources of well-being. Unthinkable, you say? Such disruptions have occurred in the past. When Napoleon Bonaparte, the French emperor, cut Great Britain off from Europe, the British nearly starved in 1811 and faced economic collapse.

In response, the British navy severed French trade with the outside world. As British historian G. M. Trevelyan said, Britain "won the race of starvation by a neck."[1] In the 1930s world trade plummeted as the United States and then other countries tried to protect workers and industries from foreign competition. The result was the opposite of what governments intended: they made the Great Depression deeper and longer.

Today the economies of China and the United States are highly interdependent, and any large repatriation of Chinese investments would undermine the New York money market, which now hosts more than $1.3 trillion of Chinese assets in U.S. bonds and corporate securities. If these funds went back to China, interest rates in the United States would rise, slowing American economic growth. For China, the American market is equally crucial. With large export surpluses, China needs to put these sums where they can be protected and receive interest payments. There is no other place—not Germany or Japan, for example—that can absorb such large amounts of Chinese capital.

Likewise, America would be grossly affected if it could not invest elsewhere. U.S. "production chains" make and assemble the components of American products in other countries including Mexico, China, and the nations of Southeast Asia. These chains use lower-cost labor and permit imports into the United States of finished cars, cell phones, television sets, machines, and electrical devices of all types. In fact, U.S. industry would not be competitive with European or Japanese firms if it could not save money by manufacturing more cheaply overseas. We live in a globalized era, in which national economies are more integrated and interdependent than ever before. Globalization is a result of political decisions by governments that, in effect, trade increasing amounts of national autonomy for even more increasing amounts of wealth. Globalization comes at a cost; for one thing, not everyone in every country wins from all of this international trade and investment, and there are signs that many of those who have lost factory jobs in recent years in North America and Europe are pushing back. But that just makes the point even clearer: international politics affects everyday life in profound ways.

Economic influences and impingements, however, are not the only reason for paying attention to what goes on in the outside world. A perfectly peaceful nation may be drawn into war or directly attacked by a foreign country or even a transnational terrorist network. This has been the case for many centuries. In 1914, neutral Belgium did not expect to be involved in war, but German military plans dictated an offensive to take the hub of Liege, from which the great encircling movements of the Schlieffen Plan would thrust German forces behind French lines, engulfing (so the Germans hoped) Paris. German armies crashed

---

1. G. M. Trevelyan, *British History in the Nineteenth Century and After* (London: Longmans, Green 1922), 130.

into Belgium on August 4, 1914, and it was this violation of an innocent nation's neutrality that brought England into the war. In 1941 President Roosevelt was still formally negotiating with Japanese emissaries as Japanese Zeroes, taking off from Admiral Yamamoto's aircraft carriers in the Eastern Pacific, sank U.S. battleships moored in Pearl Harbor. Roosevelt and others thought the Japanese might strike south, toward the Philippines, but they did not imagine in their wildest dreams a Japanese attack on American bases in Hawaii.

As it turned out, the German warmachine did not breach allied lines or take Paris in 1914. After four years of trench warfare, the allies, spearheaded by U.S. tanks and fresh infantry, prevailed in November 1918. Japanese attacks on the U.S. Navy in 1941 hit battleships but entirely missed the aircraft carriers, which were out of port. Axis forces (Japanese, German, and Italian) enjoyed some successes and as late as 1943 it appeared that Germany might still win the war. But by 1945 British, American, and Russian armies had vanquished Germany, and Japan surrendered on August 14 after two U.S. atomic attacks. It might seem reasonable to conclude from these catastrophic defeats that it is irrational to start a war. But countries still threaten each other and sometimes engage in military actions even in the twenty-first century.

Military factors thus cause nations to pay attention in foreign affairs. World War II and the Cold War are over, but nuclear weapons have spread to nine nations—the United States, Russia, China, India, Britain, France, Pakistan, Israel, and North Korea. Fears that Iran would develop nuclear weapons tempted Israel and the United States to attack until an agreement was hammered out in 2015. One cannot be sure in dire circumstances that all of these nuclear-armed states will be deterred from use of their warheads. So we study international politics for very good reasons. International relations represent an unsolved problem.

Theory and History

These two areas deeply affected by international politics—economic and military—are sometimes treated separately, as if they have nothing to do with each other. Scholars who study international relations often do so in their writings. Most, however, agree that in fact trade and investment, on the one hand, and wars and threats, on the other, do relate in some ways. One school of thought, called *realism*, holds that the military always dominates the economic—for example, that trade never makes war less likely but that war can cause disruptions in trade. More generally, realism teaches that international politics is always bound to be dangerous. There will always be another war; might makes right; and efforts to pull states or the international system out of this situation will only make things worse.

As you will see throughout this book, we recognize that realism has value in pointing to the ever-present possibility of violence and war, even by countries that prefer peace and commerce. We also acknowledge that there have been periods in history and even today where regions act in accord with realism. But we also will argue that realism misses some very important facts about international politics. Looked at one way, the basic problem with realism is that it is "ahistorical"—that is, does not take into account transformations over time in ideas, institutions, and technology and how changes in these three things have combined to make war among a growing number of countries less likely. Several hundred years ago in Europe, a new kind of society began to emerge, one in which growing numbers of people valued commerce more than conquest, cooperation more than coercion. We will call these countries by various names, including *commercial republics*, *trading states*, and *liberal democracies*. In these countries, over decades and centuries, power became more dispersed and rulers became more constrained by law and the popular will. Commercial republics were more likely to grow rich through trade; later, they began to build up international law and organizations to foster cooperation among countries. This international architecture, in turn, gave commercial republics space to develop and deepen their institutions.

Such countries could sometimes be as warlike as their more despotic neighbors, partly because they had to compete with those neighbors and partly because they still had powerful people who retained an interest in conquest. But gradually commercial republics showed themselves superior at generating wealth and stability, and at international cooperation, and they inspired imitation. As the number of republics grew, so did global trade, technological innovation, prosperity, and even peace.

International history, especially since World War II, shows that realism is woefully inadequate as a universal theory of international politics. Instead, what is usually called *liberalism* has a great deal to add to our collective understanding. By liberalism we do not mean what Americans mean in everyday language—"big government" or "caring government"—but instead what classical political theory means: a commitment to individual liberty and the governmental institutions that serve it. As concerns international relations, liberalism is more hopeful than realism that (1) liberal, democratic, commercial states can sustain cooperation for very long periods of time, to the point where they can plan in the long term for peace with one another, and (2) there are pressures on states to become liberal, democratic, commercial states—that is, broadly speaking, the number of commercial republics has and will likely continue to grow over time.

What is realism then, and where did it come from? What about liberalism?

Realism

For realists, politics within a state may proceed on a peaceful basis, because well-functioning states do have a central government to deter aggression and enforce agreements. But between states the arts of violence have led to increasingly destructive wars. In the twentieth century, over 50 million were killed in World War II and 30 million in World War I out of a population of 4 to 5 billion worldwide. There have been a further 41 million war-related deaths since 1945.

Going further back into history, states used to take territory, steal hostages or slaves (principally women and children), and destroy an opponent's army, sometimes killing soldiers to the very last man. They did this because, looked at purely in terms of efficiency, it often paid to do so. In the twelfth century Genghis Khan's army raped and pillaged as it plundered villages and walled cities along the Silk Road between Europe and Asia. Many centuries earlier, Thucydides, the Greek general and historian, claimed that war was "inevitable" and saw his theory vindicated in the Peloponnesian Wars of Ancient Greece. Sparta went to war with Athens not because Athens had attacked it but because it feared Athens's rising power. War then became unavoidable.

To Niccolò Machiavelli, an Italian diplomat of the Renaissance, it was the absence of a sovereign over the Italian peninsula that led powerful European dynasties of Habsburg and Valois to fight for control of Italy. A century later during the Thirty Years' War, the opposition between Catholic and Protestant princes devastated Germany and Europe. This pessimism is seen also in the political theory of English philosopher Thomas Hobbes. Reacting to the civil war in England between Parliament and the king that led to the latter's beheading in 1649, Hobbes claimed in his masterpiece *Leviathan* that the only sure way to safeguard people from violent death was to concentrate all power in the hands of a central government.

Of course, it is possible to do that within a state, but there is no world government to safeguard states from one another, and the prospects for getting world government are always slim. In the twentieth century, Hans Morgenthau, a German refugee observing the ravages of the First and Second World Wars, concluded that states would aim for all the power available. If they did not do so, he thought, they would be dominated by other countries. This longstanding pessimism, which stresses power seeking, insecurity, and the lack of world government, is summed up in the term "realism."

Realists past and present are not identical, but they generally hold in common the following tenets:[2]

1. The only important political units are sovereign states (nation-states or city-states).
2. One of the most important facts about sovereign states—perhaps the most important fact—is that there is no world government above them to enforce agreements or punish aggression. That is, the international system is *anarchical*.

---

2. See, e.g., John Mearsheimer, *The Tragedy of Great Power Politics* (New York: Norton, 2001).

3. Each state thus must worry constantly about all others' gains in power, and must take steps to ensure its own security, including by arming itself, forming (temporary) alliances, and acquiring more territory.
4. This situation among states is permanent. It cannot be changed by:
   a. institutions, either international (such as the United Nations or World Bank) or domestic (such as democracy)
   b. international interactions such as trade, investment, or population movements
   c. peaceful ideas or moral or psychological improvement
5. Realist conflicts are frequently expressed by demands to control greater territory.

The Genesis of Realist Theory

Realism purports to be a timeless theory, but it arose at particular times and in particular places. International ideas do not emerge from thin air. They arise to explain, modify, or ratify existing practice. And historical practice of a given time tells us what is feasible, possible, or needed. In ancient China, realist thinking and advice is evident in *The Art of War* by Sun-Tzu (ca. 544–496 BCE), who lived during China's Warring States period. In ancient Greece, the historian Thucydides (ca. 460–ca. 395 BCE) wrote his *History of the Peloponnesian War* during and after a long and catastrophic war between the cities of Athens and Sparta; the book is brimming with realist thinking, including the proposition that the rise of Athenian power created fear in Sparta and made war inevitable. In ancient India, Kautilya (ca. 370–ca. 283 BCE) wrote in his *Arthashastra* (*Economics*) that states are prone to have bad relations with near neighbors and better relations with farther neighbors, because near neighbors are more dangerous. Kautilya wrote to help the Mauryan emperor conquer other Indian kingdoms.

Let us consider Thucydides. He believed war was inevitable because states must fear each other's gains in power. But states benefited from using power to gain additional colonies, farmland, slaves, taxes, and tribute. Pericles, the 60-year-old military leader of Athens at the beginning of the second Peloponnesian war in 433 BCE, encouraged his followers, saying:

> All who have taken it upon themselves to rule over others have incurred hatred and unpopularity for a time. . . . [But] this burden of envy must be accepted. . . . Hatred does not last long . . . present brilliance will become future glory . . . in the memory of mankind.[3]

---

3. Perhaps Vladimir Putin believed this as he moved Russian troops into the Crimea in 2014.

Athens formed the Delian League, a closed trading as well as defense network. Sparta responded with its own Peloponnesian League. Each sought to expand its network to maximize trading gains as well as military power. Independent Greek settlements that wished to remain neutral between the two competing leagues were blockaded or invaded by Athens or Sparta. In fourth-century Greece, trade was governed by political control; it was not an autonomous field of endeavor. Cities with large navies could cut off other cities from trade, virtually strangling them. When Athens punished Megara, a Spartan ally, by prohibiting it from trading with the Athenian empire, Pericles helped bring on general war. Athens and Sparta were involved in what game theorists call a "zero-sum game," in which the gains of one equaled the losses of the other. It was not surprising that Thucydides believed war in such circumstances was likely, even inevitable.

Nineteen centuries later Machiavelli, a military diplomat and adviser to the government of Florence (in Italy), reasserted Thucydides's pessimism and realism. He shared the belief that states are condemned endlessly to repeat contests over power, leading frequently to war. He learned from recent history: in the 1490s, France had invaded Italy and was threatening the independence of Italian city-states like Milan, Naples, and Siena. No central authority existed to halt the attack. The Catholic Church was corrupt and venal, and the horizontal band of Papal States that stood athwart Italy hampered any collective Italian resistance to foreign invasion by France or Austria. Individuals like Lorenzo di Medici (in Florence) were left to respond on their own. How could they do so? Machiavelli recommended that Lorenzo concentrate his forces, get allies in other city-states, and trick his opponents into cooperative submission. Cesare Borgia, one of Machiavelli's heroes, knew how to poison or have Lucretia Borgia, his sister, seduce rival commanders. The point is not that Machiavelli was a particularly immoral practitioner of malign arts in world politics; rather, he learned from his historical situation and devised strategies that might work in the Italy of his time. Jacob Burckhardt, the Swiss historian, commended Machiavelli for taking the widest possible view and creating the state as "a work of art," using any material or devious instrumentality that might serve that broader aesthetic as well as political purpose of glorifying the state and unifying it against powerful enemies. Thus theory emerges from a contingent historical situation.

This was true also of Thomas Hobbes, who was the first to translate Thucydides's masterwork into English. He devoted attention in *Leviathan* and *Behemoth,* his two great books, to the creation and design of stronger states that would prevent another English civil war. Hobbes believed that the state needed to be big and strong enough to survive the clash of rival parties. He had been tutor of King Charles I, and he witnessed up close the rise of republican Oliver Cromwell, whose victory led to Charles's execution in London in January 1649. Hobbes worried about the collapse of royal authority. Men in a "State of Nature" could never work together or trust one another unless, according to Hobbes, they were under a sovereign, a Leviathan capable of enforcing peace. In the state of nature, domestic cooperation could not exist and individuals would languish in fear of violent death. Once a social contract had been formed among them and a sovereign installed, however, domestic peace could be assured.

Before the establishment of sovereign power over men, war existed within local communities because each man was strong or devious enough to kill another man. But among sovereign countries, this was not true. A country could not usually be eliminated by a single blow from another state even though its leader might be killed. Hobbes wrote that sovereigns (heads of state) stood in a perpetual state of war with one another: Why otherwise would they not sign a contract to outlaw war as individuals had done (so he claimed) within domestic society? It was because states were much stronger than individuals and did not need such protections. So although states would always fear one another and wars would always happen, world government would never be required for states to survive, nor would it emerge among countries. Without directly saying so, Hobbes was implying that the most powerful states—which international relations scholars call great powers—would ensure that no world government would ever emerge. In his time the great powers included Austria, Russia, England, France, and Prussia. One hundred and fifty years later in the early nineteenth century, Friedrich von Gentz, the Prussian theorist, defined a great power as a state that could hold its own against a collection of other states. Smaller states, in contrast, were vulnerable to conquest and partition. Gentz's realist corollary was likewise a product of his time and place: Germany was not a unified state but a collection of principalities and cities. He was warning small German polities about Napoleon's ambitions along the Rhine that might jeopardize their territorial independence.

The realist doctrine that all states are perpetually insecure leads to the next question: What then would a state under threat do if its own efforts were insufficient? It would ally with others in hopes of constructing a balance of power against a potential aggressor. In this way Hobbes's approach and Gentz's additions melded together to form the most common strand of realism: balance-of-power theory. The theory says that the great powers will seek to counterbalance one another's power and that the typical or equilibrium situation among these states will be a balance of power that prevents great-power war. Thus, if there are two great powers in the international system (think of the United States and Soviet Union during the Cold War), they will balance one another so that power will be equally distributed between them. If there are five great powers (think Europe in 1914) in equilibrium, those five will have roughly the same amount of power. If two of those great powers form an alliance, at least two of the others will form a counteralliance. Each coalition of states will form so as to safeguard itself from attack by the other.[4]

Realism and balance-of-power theory have a great deal of value. Yet, if one examines actual historical practice, a mere balance of power has often neither safeguarded a state's security nor prevented major war. States did occasionally form coalitions to restrain an aggressor, but generally allied states had to go to war to actually defeat that aggressor to construct that balance. During the sixteenth century Hapsburg and Valois kings clashed in Italy, each balancing the other, but they did so by making war. The Kaunitz Coalition (France, Austria, and Russia), created in 1756 to restrain Frederick the Great of Prussia, did so by attacking him, at a cost of a half a million killed.[5] Napoleon, the French emperor, eventually confronted a strong coalition aligned against him after his defeat in Russia in 1812, but he was obliged to fight against that coalition; peace did not emerge naturally on its own. The balance of power created through the formation of the Triple Entente against the Triple Alliance after 1907 did not prevent war, it merely allocated the Great Powers to different camps that would then make war against each other in World War I. After 1945, the gradual accumulation of Western power against the Soviet Union did not assure peace until the West achieved what we call an "overbalance of power" and the USSR sought to join with Western democracies in 1991.[6] In much the same way a Western balance against China will not achieve peace or harmony unless and until that balance becomes an overbalance, attracting Beijing toward the West.

As we shall discuss later, a minority of realists—sometimes called power-preponderance or hegemonic realists—agree that imbalances of power are more common and stable than balances of power. But even these realists focus chiefly on international anarchy and power and therefore miss the most important developments in recent international history, developments that make liberalism a better overall theory.

Liberalism

The chief problem with realism may be that war is no longer likely among most of the states that fought the most destructive wars over the past 500 years. The preponderant historical tendency toward greater restraint and a larger environment

---

4. For more on balance-of-power theory, see Kenneth N. Waltz, *Theory of International Politics* (New York: McGraw-Hill, 1979).

5. Prussia's defense of its newly acquired territories in the Seven Years War does illustrate Gentz's dictum that one great power might hold its own against powerful other states.

6. They failed to do so because of Russia's undemocratic and unstable character.

of peace has contrasted with traditional realism for two basic reasons. First, realist theory owes its origin to authoritarian and princely states where peoples played little role in the struggles between countries. Second, for most of recorded history, reasonably self-sufficient political units (states or cities) relied on local or internal trade for their livelihoods. Even as the early modern international system for war-making was taking shape, some of those states—Venice, Portugal, Spain, and then the Netherlands—were taking early steps to undermine that system by engaging in *international* commerce. In doing this, they began modifying the nature of competition among them and took the first steps toward undermining the relevance of realism. As new ideologies, growing political participation, and stronger administrative units ascended the political staircase, international relations gradually changed. Less and less were power and territory the dominant objectives of the new more popular polities. Instead, new domestic ideologies, institutions, and economic modes of action came to the fore. These influences gave rise to the liberal notions of John Locke and Immanuel Kant, the great English and German philosophers who, along with the Scotsman Adam Smith, prescribed life, liberty, and property together with peaceful commerce as the best means to national fulfillment.

Liberal theories of international politics come in various forms, but most would agree with the following:

1. The most important political units are individuals. Individuals form groups, including sovereign states (nation-states or city-states), with different institutions (democratic, authoritarian, etc.) depending on the ideas they hold.
   a. As realism says, those states exist in an anarchical situation, meaning that there is no world government to enforce agreements or punish aggression.
2. States that have liberal-democratic institutions conduct themselves differently from other types of state—namely, they tend not to fight one another, but to trade with and invest in one another; they also join and abide by international institutions. They form what we call a *liberal international subsystem.*
3. Liberal democracies generally interact with non-democracies as realism would expect: they fight with them more and trade with them less.
4. Expanded territory is not necessary for economic success.

Many liberals also would agree with the following:

5. The gradual rise of liberal commercial classes in early modern Europe, new ideas about liberty and democracy, and technological innovations explain the emergence and persistence of liberal democracies.

6. Under broad conditions, liberal democracies enjoy advantages over non-democracies, and so, over time, more countries have become liberal democracies.
7. Thus, the liberal international subsystem has spread around the globe, and more and more countries pursue their interests through commerce rather than war.
8. Shocks such as economic depressions or great-power wars can cause liberal democracies and the subsystem itself to backslide.

Unlike realism, liberalism is attuned to history, particularly historical changes in ideas, institutions, and technology. Realism is correct about some states and about some periods and regions in history—for example, much of Europe in the seventeenth century, or some of East Asia today. But realism claims to be a timeless, universal theory, and that is where it goes wrong. Liberalism highlights changes that have shifted international politics.

The shift has been gradual and complex, partly because the empowerment of peoples within countries brought with it nationalism—the ideology that glorifies the country. Nationalism has sometimes been a spur to conflict. On the whole, however, the coming of popular sovereignty and the rule of law within countries has pacified relations among countries. While colonies have shrugged off imperial controls, gaining independence from the empires of the past, the underlying theme has been the gradual organization of the planet in economic terms, creating a voluntary empire of trade and increasingly a transnational engine propelling factors of production (labor, technology, and capital) from one place to another. In response to this powerful movement, living standards, life expectancies, and literacy have risen across the globe. This growth could not take place without a broad background of peace most of the time among most nations. Peace and economic growth have been mutually reinforcing.

Figure 1.1, constructed from data from the economic historian Angus Maddison, depicts global wealth per capita over the past 2,000 years. Note that steep, sustained growth only began in the late nineteenth century. These changes suggest that while modern states might fall apart or become captured by a destructive religious or secular ideology, they might also achieve their goals in purely peaceful terms by organizing trade and capital flows with their brother states that are becoming democratic in character. Leading members of the system were once absolutist monarchies; now, most (but not all) are decentralized liberal republics whose objective is the welfare of their populations. These liberal states still compete, but they have tools at their disposal, including trade and financial sanctions, institutions to mobilize group activity, and widely held norms or rules about acceptable behavior to guide them. Liberal trading republics still worry about power and prepare for war. But they do this because not all states are liberal

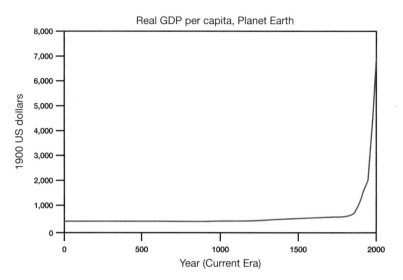

FIGURE 1.1 Growth in real GDP per capita, 0–2000 ce.
Source: Angus Maddison.

democracies. Figure 1.2 shows the growth in the number of countries to become democracies since 1800 (the solid line).

Finally, Steven Pinker asserts that a trend against violence has emerged in both domestic and external realms.[7] Fighting in international relations has also declined at least as a percentage of the now much larger world population. His graphs demonstrate a decline in homicides but also in war deaths. In primordial societies war deaths per 100,000 people averaged about 550 per annum. In modern societies—even in the violent nineteenth and twentieth centuries—war deaths average less than one hundred people.[8] (It is important to note, however, that part of the decline in war deaths is due to improvements in medical and emergency transportation technology, improvements that save the lives of more battle-wounded combatants than ever.[9])

The Genesis of Interdependence and Peace Approaches

Hand in hand with these trends over the past two centuries, liberalism, institutionalism, economic interdependence, and domestic theories of foreign policy have emerged to contrast with realism. Realism is fundamentally a "territorial"

---

7. Steven Pinker, *The Better Angels of Our Nature: Why Violence Has Declined* (New York: Penguin Books, 2011).

8. Pinker, *Better Angels*, 53.

9. Tanisha Fazal, "Dead Wrong? Battle Deaths, Military Medicine, and Exaggerated Reports of War's Demise," *International Security* 39, no. 1 (Summer 2014): 95–125.

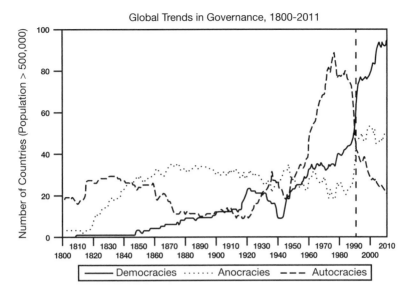

FIGURE 1.2 Change in global distribution of regime types since 1800.
Source: Center for Systemic Peace.

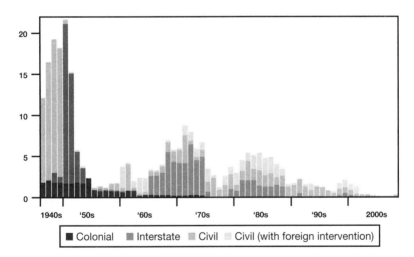

FIGURE 1.3 Decline in battle deaths since the 1940s.
Source: Human Security Resource, the Uppsala Conflict Data Project, and the Peace Research Institute of Oslo.

theory. It applies when states view territory as the ultimate resource that could be easily acquired. The more one state conquers, the stronger it becomes and the less another state possesses. In the old days resources and land were the main constituents of power and welfare. Agriculture and minerals were important long before industry took hold. The taking of territory was often cost-effective during the medieval and early modern periods. Domestic groups had not formed a consciousness of national identity or generated an active nationalism and patriotism to resist foreign attack. They would obey a conqueror. And until the American Revolution in 1776, colonial territories remained quiescent within the imperial fold, and conquests were usually definitive. After 1776,[10] the principle began to spread that foreign rulers could not compel obedience, and one by one colonies broke away from their mother countries. The trend accelerated after 1945. Countries resisted attack and continued to resist after being occupied by enemy forces, as most Ukrainians did when invaded by poorly disguised Russian troops in 2014.

Throughout the nineteenth century populations were becoming increasingly literate, urban, and mobilized for political activity against a conqueror. In the second half of the twentieth century, populations rebelled and imposed costs on territorial empire, reducing the fruits of imperial rule. Given colonial uprisings, 100 new states became independent following the breakup of the Dutch, British, French, Portuguese, Belgian, and Spanish empires. Second, economic growth gave the potential aggressor another outlet for its energies. A government could use foreign trade to improve its country's economic position without expanding militarily. The strength and power of a country could increase without any increment in territorial size.

Just as realist thinking emerged in times of insecurity, war, and conquest, liberal thinking has tended to emerge in countries that are democratizing and seek peace through commerce. Immanuel Kant, the great Königsberg philosopher,[11] emphasized that the spirit of commerce was incompatible with war between states. Contending parties would be better off trading freely with one another than fighting for spoils or riches, which killed people and left provinces devastated. Kant's Scottish contemporary, Adam Smith, concluded that an "invisible hand" united the interests of consumer and producer (manufacturer) so that both benefited from the perfectly unconscious actions that led to trade between the two. So in international relations, one country could buy or sell freely and peacefully to another, leading to mutual benefit. Liberal ideas about international relations have continued to develop in the twentieth and twenty-first centuries. Modern international trade theory underscores the conclusion that two nations can gain from opening free trading relations with each other. As money is transferred from an importing to exporting nation, the latter has an increased money supply, raising prices. In the country receiving imports (and having to pay for them), the money in circulation declines, depressing prices, giving advantage to the now lower-priced exports of the purchaser. In free trading conditions, higher exports lead

---

10. See Carl Kaysen, "Is War Obsolete? A Review Essay," *International Security* 14, no. 4 (Spring 1990): 42–64.

11. Cut off from the West, Kant's home city is now ensconced in Kaliningrad Oblast, Russia.

to higher imports, re-establishing equilibrium.

Realism does not capture or explain relations among states in large areas of the globe—in, for example, most of Europe, most of the Americas, and the democratic parts of Asia and Africa. We have already noted that large numbers of countries do not react to one another's material gains with fear or power balancing. Instead, these states—many of which fought wars with one another in the past—welcome a neighbor's increase in wealth because they all benefit. German economic gains in Europe are shared by France and Benelux today. These interdependent countries tend to belong to robust international institutions that facilitate cooperation,

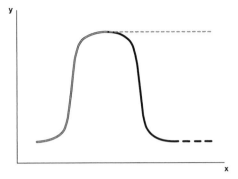

FIGURE 1.4 Ideas emerging from power relations. Ideas emerge out of history and then are projected to continue partly autonomously of historical changes. Realism emerged out of rising international conflict (gray line); it then continued even after trading relations partly substituted for military attacks. Equally, notions of the "value of trade and interdependence" (black line) emerged amid peaceful relations in the eighteenth to mid-nineteenth centuries and continued regardless of the subsequent rise in military conflict at the beginning of the twentieth century. Ideas and violence are on the y-axis; time is on the x-axis.

like those of the European Union (EU) or the International Monetary Fund (IMF). They also tend to be liberal democracies with free-market economies.

Recognizing this development, individual scholars have developed new theories emphasizing how liberal trading strategies can change international politics. Others have stressed the institutional network that facilitates such changes. Some of the theories are called constructivist because they stress that these institutions are not naturally formed but are built by people acting in large groups over a considerable period of time.[12] As realism comes in different versions, so do non-realist theories.

In this book we use the term "liberal" to denote those approaches, but we agree with constructivist scholars that people have the ability, at least under some conditions, to formulate ideas and build institutions that can mitigate the problems that realism says are permanent. Liberalism does not deny the continuing threat of war or indeed the importance of power in international relations. Liberalism does not claim that humankind can banish power and self-interest, much less war or the threat of war. It does claim that self-interest and competition can take less lethal forms among liberal democracies and that governments and peoples understand this.

---

12. The most influential work of constructivist international relations scholarship is Alexander Wendt, *Social Theory of International Politics* (New York: Cambridge University Press, 1999).

The development of theory as a response to history did not mean that theory was endlessly changing in response to historical events. At critical periods, theory congealed and continued almost irrespective of historical change. The realism of Thucydides, Hobbes, and Machiavelli is still with us, even though historical conditions are not the same as when these giants were writing their works. In face of Vladimir Putin's ambitions to recreate the Soviet empire on the fringes of Europe, realism accurately characterizes military incentives in particular parts of the world even today. In Putin's case, it reflects Russia's technological backwardness. Russia's attempt to gain territory and to re-establish the old Soviet Empire is a negative means to regain growth and influence in world politics that Russia could not achieve solely through economic means.

The Persistence of Power and War

Despite the encouraging trends shown in Figures 1.1, 1.2, and 1.3, we should not conclude that war, even among major powers, has been banished from the earth. New countries like North Korea and Iran either sport nuclear weapons or are developing such capacities. The Middle East is rife with conflict between Sunni and Shi'ite Muslims, as well as between Islamist and more secular societies and groups within societies. The Palestinians and Israel have not reached peace with one another, and al-Qaeda franchises spring up in Yemen, Syria, and Iraq. The Sunni group ISIL (Islamic State in the Levant), which has been dominant on the frontier between Iraq and Syria, beheads its Christian captives. The United States is seeking to limit its role in Iraq and Afghanistan, but the struggle against ISIL may represent a new chapter in Middle East conflict, occasioning new American involvement.

Two of the world's largest nations, Russia and China, remain exceptions to the liberalizing trend: they have market economies (with heavy state intervention) and rely on exports for wealth but are neither democratic nor liberal in character. Furthermore, Middle Eastern pashas still redistribute favors among royal families and henchmen with little regard for the wishes of their countrymen. As we discuss below, the world is far from being a Kantian paradise.

Furthermore, national power still matters a great deal: it is important, for example, that the liberal-democratic United States is far and away the world's leading military state, and it matters for the future of international order that China is poised to become the world's leading economy. But in many domains, states—especially liberal democracies—find they have non-lethal instruments of power to deal with differences that may arise. As a result there are large areas of cooperation and peace that did not exist in past centuries when realist theory prevailed. Western Europe has become the hub of peace and economic transformation in regional terms.

How much comfort, then, should we take from detached and disembodied statistics about the decline of poverty, authoritarianism, and war deaths? Sometimes terrible wars were avoided by the narrowest of margins. In October 1962 the United States and the Soviet Union came far too close to nuclear war. Many have credited President John F. Kennedy and, to a lesser extent, Chairman Nikita Khrushchev for ending the Cuban missile crisis on October 29, 1962, with a public agreement to remove Russian missiles (and warheads) from Cuba and a secret protocol to remove U.S. missiles from Italy and Turkey. The United States pledged not to invade Cuba. Whatever the wishes of the two leaders, however, their subordinates nearly went to nuclear war. On October 27, U.S. destroyers were sending depth charges toward a Soviet submarine on the floor of the Caribbean. They did not know that that submarine possessed nuclear torpedoes. Facing destruction, the Soviet submarine was tempted to fire its torpedoes at the attackers. One of three officers on that ship, Vasili Arkhipov, refused to do so (despite standing orders to the contrary) without first getting permission directly from the Kremlin. By his single action, he prevented the onset of nuclear war between the United States and the Soviet Union. Reviewing the episode, the historian Arthur Schlesinger Jr. wrote: "This was the most dangerous moment in human history."[13] The United States emerged intact, but it was very, very lucky. Could one count on such good luck on every future occasion of crisis? Very likely not!

What accounts for the persistence of conflict between nations? Realists say that it is because all states seek to increase their power and are bound to conflict with one another as they do so. States are not a united family or household, nor do they act under the benign suzerainty of a hegemonic leader or an all-powerful father figure. If things go wrong, as one student pointed out, a nation cannot dial 911 to get help.

A liberal view, however, begins by noting that the most serious international conflicts usually involve at least one state that is authoritarian and not yet a full participant in the liberal international order. This view distinguishes among types of states and varieties of international relations and holds that separateness can be modified by economic and political closeness and interdependence among nations. Trade among countries, which is increasing more rapidly than GDP on a worldwide basis, is one important example. States can also become more "simpatico" in economic and cultural terms as their people interact with one another; they can construct similar democratic governments with migrants and tourists roaming freely between neighbors and joining in their media, music, sports, and arts. Over time, as Canada and the United States have done, they can develop kindred feelings about political and economic matters. Members of the EU have

---

13. Quoted in Marion Lloyd, "Soviets Close to Using A-Bomb in 1962 Crisis, Forum Told," *Boston Globe* (October 13, 2002).

come closer together and given up some measure of sovereignty in the process. War between members of the EU has become virtually unthinkable. Despite occasional claims to the contrary, the existence of separate states does not by itself dictate conflict. State relations can improve to the point where war between them becomes highly unlikely, if not, indeed, impossible. In these realms, international competition is mostly limited to commerce and sports.

Further, as noted above, war, conflict, and death by violence were worse in past ages, at least as a percentage of the world population. In hunter-gatherer societies, people killed almost anything to eat it, and fighting over food was legendary. Burial records suggest that 15 percent of skulls in such premodern periods had axes imbedded in them. Life spans were brutal and short, and the probability of a violent death was high. People had to fight to preserve themselves. But when modern states emerged, violence within domestic communities declined. Today, while there are pockets of unsafe streets and drug-infested neighborhoods within a society, most people in developed countries live a much more relaxed and peaceful life than their forebears experienced in the sixteenth century.

This is because within organized states a kind of political Leviathan (government) exists to ensure order, punishing those who kill, rob, rape, steal, and destroy the property of others. A Leviathan—Thomas Hobbes's term for centralized rule—enforces law, levying a heavy penalty on violence. Seeing this, perceptive citizens act to remain within the law, seeking economic gains through hard work, investment, education, and savings. They prosper as their society grows. This does not diminish competition among domestic persons or organizations, but it does direct that competition into largely peaceful channels.

A purely Hobbesian account fails to distinguish liberal democratic states from other types. A liberal democratic state possesses coercive power, to be sure. But that power is administratively dispersed across branches of government and sometimes across states or provinces. It is also dispensed differently over time, thanks to regular competitive elections. Control of power is codified and institutionalized so that it is difficult for the executive branch to amass power and tyrannize the population. Authoritarian states come in different types, but what they have in common is that power is concentrated usually in the hands of a dictator, central committee, or small cohort of military officers. To hold on to their power, such states eventually require a heavy direct coercion, including secret police and courts and legislatures that are under the executive's thumb. The citizens of authoritarian states are usually well behaved and indeed typically enjoy low crime rates, but that is because people are so fearful of the regimes under which they live. An extreme example today is North Korea; more moderate examples are China and Russia. These are states that would please Hobbes.

So war always will remain possible. Most wars, however, are not accidents and are fully intended by at least one of the parties. That means that if a state really does not want war, it is less likely that it will start one. If they think that war is a game not worth the candle because it is too expensive and not necessary, they will seek to avoid it. In areas of the world where this is true, liberal international relations theory has developed in recognition of that fact.

Power and the Spread of Peace

We have noted that members of the liberal-democratic club of states generally have less friendly relations with non-democracies. That sounds like a form of realism, and in fact liberalism does not ignore the role of power. Growing zones of peace and prosperity have emerged over the centuries under the leadership or hegemony of a few liberal states. In the nineteenth century Great Britain helped to open the international economy allowing others to trade. Britain's navy and large economy gave others incentives to venture outside the conflict-ridden state of nature depicted by realism. Britain also inspired other countries to imitate its internal institutions, including parliamentary democracy and civil liberties. In the twentieth century the United States played a similar role opening the global economy and setting up and defending successful liberal democracies in many parts of the world. This inspired imitation even from the authoritarian Soviet Union as the Cold War came to an end.

Furthermore, the cohesiveness of liberal democracy actually benefited from authoritarian opposition. As we shall see, one of the most potent tendencies in democratic states has been to extend the democratic flag to new standard-bearers waiting outside to join. Authoritarians resist this intrusion and a pattern of opposition between the two forms emerges. Vladimir Putin and the late Hugo Chavez—two authoritarian leaders— piqued democrats in many countries to take action on behalf of democratic causes and to resist Russian encroachments in the Ukraine.

Shifts in power toward the middle or commercial classes and the states they governed, in fact, were integral to the growth and spread of liberal democracy and trade. The story is not simple or linear. After the defeat of Napoleon in 1815, a reconstructed France rejoined the other members of the Quadruple Alliance (Britain, Russia, Prussia, and Austria), establishing the Concert of Europe, which informally governed international relationships from 1815 to 1848. The club was called a "concert" because its members did not fight one another during this period, but met regularly and "played" in unison so as to keep power regulated among themselves. They achieved what might be called an *overbalance* of power. Peace helped the societies grow wealthier as they industrialized and developed middle and working classes. International trade began to grow after 1815 (Figure 1.5).

Notwithstanding peace and growing trade, it would be a mistake to call the Concert of Europe liberal or democratic. Russia, Austria, Prussia, and sometimes

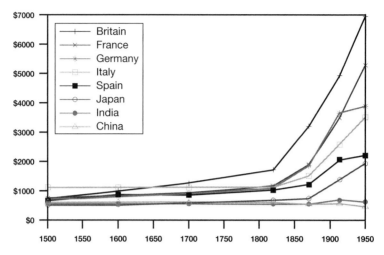

FIGURE 1.5 Trade growth since 1500.
Source: After Maddison, 2007.

France were ruled by absolute monarchs and were held together by a common interest in quashing liberalism in Europe. They intervened many times in weaker countries to suppress revolts and revolutions. Liberal Britain opposed these interventions. In 1848 a wave of liberal and radical revolutions rolled across most of Europe, toppling governments and threatening monarchism itself. Most of the revolutions were suppressed by Concert intervention.

Still, beginning in the 1850s, all states but Russia began to democratize in limited but real ways. Under the hegemony of Britain, which had the world's largest economy and navy and began to practice free trade in the 1840s, international trade increased dramatically (see Figure 1.5). Political scientist A. F. K. Organski argued that hegemons or dominant states—those that enjoy the most power and prestige—set up the rules of the international system and maintain order.[14] Hegemons have included Portugal in the sixteenth century, Holland in the seventeenth, Britain in the eighteenth, France in the early nineteenth, Britain again until World War I, and finally the United States. Of these, only Britain and the United States have been liberal hegemons—i.e., only they have set up international rules encouraging free trade.

All of these hegemons gained their top status through defeating the preceding hegemon in a major war—except for the United States, which did not fight nineteenth-century Britain for leadership. Indeed, the United States, while clearly mindful of power and national security, was invited by European nations

---

14. A.F.K. Organski, *World Politics*, New York: Knopf, 1958.

to become hegemonic. After the First World War America refused, but after the Second, the United States acquired what Norwegian historian Geir Lundestad calls an "empire by invitation."[15] The Europeans were not threatened by America because they knew that it sought no new territory and was not interested in making their nations into colonies or satellites.

Nor did U.S. power erase the autonomy of its coalition's member nations. Indeed, as historian Paul Schroeder has shown, restraints within such a coalition could achieve what was missing outside.[16] To retain and keep state participants within the coalition, central leaders of the group would have to respect their wishes and distribute benefits accordingly. Otherwise, dissident states would leave. Acting as such a leader, the United States built and maintained the Western coalition after 1945. Dissatisfied states could always have switched to the Soviet Union, but they did not do so because Western economic and political rewards were so favorable and Soviet alternatives so grim (including occupation by Soviet armies). At the end of the war, Soviet dictator Josef Stalin was determined to build an empire at least to counterbalance the West. Beginning in 1939, the Soviets had shifted the boundaries in Eastern Europe—rewarding themselves with additional land in Poland, Rumania, and the Baltic countries (Estonia, Latvia, and Lithuania), and they sought to do the same with Turkey in 1945. In the last attempt, however, they were stopped by Western resistance. Still, the Soviets had gained a great deal of territorial power as a result of World War II (Figure 1.6). In February 1946, Stalin and his foreign minister, Vyacheslav Molotov, gazed at a world map in the Kremlin and enthused over Russia's territorial increases:

> "Let's see, what is the result for us [Stalin asked]? In the North everything is in order, fine. Finland committed a great offense against us and we have moved the border back toward Leningrad. The Baltic Coast—an age-old Russian territory is ours again, the Belorussians are all now living together with us, the Ukrainians are together, the Moldavians are together. In the West everything is fine." At once he went to the Eastern borders. "What have we here? . . . the Kurile islands are ours now, all of Sakhalin is ours, see how good it is! And Port Arthur is ours and Dairen is ours.—Stalin drew his pipe across China—"and the Chinese Eastern Railway is ours. China, Mongolia—everything is in order. But here I don't like our border" said

15. Geir Lundestad. The American "Empire": And Other Studies of U.S. Foreign Policy in a Comparative Perspective (New York: Oxford University Press or Norwegian University Press, Oslo. 1990.)

16. "Alliances, 1815–1945: Weapons of Power and Tools of Management," in Klaus Knorr, ed., Historical Dimensions of National Security Problems (Lawrence: University of Kansas Press, 1975).

FIGURE 1.6 Map of Soviet territorial accessions in World War II.

Stalin pointing south to the Caucasus. [Stalin wanted to put troops into northern Iran.] Later Molotov said, "I saw it as my task as Minister of Foreign Affairs to extend as much as possible the bounds of our Fatherland."[17]

---

17. David Holloway, *Stalin and the Bomb* (New Haven, CT: Yale University Press, 1994), 152.

The violent seizure and retention of control over foreign territory by authoritarian states such as the Soviet Union is consistent with realism. It is no surprise that these nations are less democratic and less liberal. More recently, Russia has seized and annexed Crimea and threatened Eastern Ukraine and taken Abkhazia and South Ossetia from Georgia. Some of China's ambitions embody realist notions where they involve creating exclusive defense identification zones to keep foreign warships out of the East China Sea or planting oil rigs in the Vietnamese economic zone. Iran may be tempted to expand its influence in Iraq and Afghanistan through ostensibly military means as the United States withdraws.

But this is not the whole, or even the principal, story in world politics. Brazil, India, Indonesia, Japan, Germany, Korea, Australia, Canada, South Africa, and most of the nations of Europe and East Asia have used economic development and trade to peacefully improve their positions in international politics. Expanding territorially creates a zero-sum game because one country's gain is another's loss. But greater economic prosperity obviates such outcomes because it is a gain of increasing sum. Through greater trade and economic demand, higher wealth in one country usually leads to greater prosperity elsewhere.

Equally, the spread of liberal-democratic political institutions does not injure anyone, although it does redistribute power away from despotic individuals and groups. Through emulation effects, liberal democracy may spread the region of peace to more countries, benefiting them all.[18] Democratic states rarely attack one another, and their relations seldom reach the point where either even contemplates attacking the other. Thus, the net outcome of Western history at least has been the creation of economically oriented democratic states, eschewing the use of military force. Emulating one another, these states have populated Europe and are in the process of spreading democracy to East Asia and Latin America as well. It is not clear that Russia and China, over time, will be able to maintain domestic authoritarianism in face of liberal influences intruding from every quarter. Russia did not liberalize after the breakup of the Soviet Union in 1991, but Russia's attempts to spread authoritarianism (and win back previous members of the Soviet system) are likely to lead to a strengthening of the West, an economic weakening of Russia, and an even more concerted effort to reform that country.

Under the influence of trading relationships, balance-of-power factors could thus be disciplined to achieve an overbalance if they were acquired peacefully. This is a lesson that China will have to learn as her power rises in the years to come.

---

18. As to the means by which democracies may lead to peace internationally, see particularly Michael W. Doyle, *Ways of War and Peace* (New York: Norton, 1997).

The Spread of the Liberal Peace: Likely but Not Inevitable

This liberal-democratic effort, however, is not guaranteed to succeed. In the 1990s, some liberal scholars believed, like Kant, that the league of liberal states was expanding and might even incorporate the entire world, bringing with it perpetual peace. The most persuasive version of this view was articulated by Francis Fukuyama, who argued that "the end of history" had been achieved because there were no new ideas or historical tendencies currently afoot. The age-old struggle over regnant ideas had been definitively won by liberalism. Authoritarianism had no real future.[19]

At this point a reader might protest: "Yes, but what about all the conflicts in the Middle East and the ever-present threat of international terrorism based on continuing sectarian and ideological disagreements between Islam and the Western world? Won't these continue, further disrupting peaceful trade and economic intercourse and preventing any universal tendency to democracy?"

The reader is right to raise such questions, and Fukuyama himself has backed away from his strongest statements. Liberalism and democracy are neither inevitable nor necessarily permanent outcomes. Economic crises and domestic political revolutions have turned back the clock at many periods and geographic locations in past history. The French Revolution—to take but one example—did not immediately spread to all other European countries. Indeed, it degenerated into despotism in France itself, and in most of Europe authoritarian leaders regained their poise and leadership for much of the nineteenth century. After the ravages of the First World War, which should have awakened the world to both the dangers of war and of authoritarian politics, humankind let right-wing and left-wing authoritarians back into power. They were ready to fight wars again, and the temporarily weaker remnants of liberal democracy—in Britain, France, and the United States—were resolved in the 1930s not to use force for any purpose.

The answer is that Islamic terrorism and opposition between Sunnis and Shi'ites will not last forever. Western history has a remarkable analogue: the so-called wars of religion from the 1520s until 1648. From October 1517, when Martin Luther pounded his 95 theses denouncing the sale of indulgences by the Catholic Church into the church door in Wittenberg, Saxony, until the end of the seventeenth century, Europe was ravaged by a political and military struggle between Protestant and Catholic rulers, culminating in invasions and counterinvasions during the Thirty Years' War. Protestant Sweden and the Protestant princes of Germany fought against Austria and the Catholic powers (though the Protestants were sometimes assisted by Catholic France). The Protestant Reformation led to a whole new series of anti-Catholic states—Sweden, north German

---

19. Francis Fukuyama, *The End of History and the Last Man* (New York: The Free Press, 1992).

states, Prussia, Holland, and Calvinist parts of Switzerland. England became more and more important as a Protestant stronghold. Meanwhile, Austria, Spain, and Italy remained Catholic, and the French waffled between the two.

Nonetheless, by the end of the seventeenth century, the recognition of state sovereignty and the principle of toleration began to reduce ideological conflict in European international relations; it breathed new life into moderate world politics. Seeing the disastrous religious wars, Jean Bodin stressed the need to combine internal sovereignty with toleration of different religious views. This change did not happen right away. Sovereignty (a doctrine challenged by Church authority) was not yet fully embraced by states, though princes began to seize on the advantages of enjoying technically supreme power. In practical terms, the safeguarding of domestic populations awaited the 1648 Peace of Westphalia (signed at Osnabrück and Münster in northwestern Germany, on October 24, 1648). It was a reaction to the excesses of the Thirty Years' War, which saw the destruction of perhaps one-third of the German population.

But Westphalia also reinforced political boundaries, legitimized sovereignty, and pledged princes and monarchs not to intervene within an opponent's towns and villages or to devastate populations and countrysides. From then on, kings would fight their battles mostly on the frontiers. It was more or less agreed that the civil population should not be punished because of the malevolent designs of princes. Sovereignty thus extended a public and protective benefit to peoples, who had been the everlasting victims of the Thirty Years' War.

At the end of the seventeenth century, wars certainly did not come to an end, but there were no more wars to defend one branch of Christianity against another.[20] Within European societies as well over the next two centuries, beginning in Holland and spreading to Britain and elsewhere, the principle of toleration of opposing religious views extended throughout Europe. In addition, the Reformation lent greater strength to Protestant and even Catholic princes in their struggles for independence from both pope and (Holy Roman) emperor. The structure of late medieval authority was broken.

The analogy with today's Muslim world is not perfect. The Islamist revival is partly a reaction to twentieth-century attempts by Muslim elites to build secular sovereign states like Europeans had. Atatürk in Turkey, the shahs of Iran, Jinnah in Pakistan, Nasser in Egypt, and others all tried to imitate the secular state builders

---

20. Paul Schroeder writes: "religion ceased in the latter half of the eighteenth century to be a central cause of war and disorder not because it declined in importance and influence or was dethroned by other concerns or changed its nature, but because it was defused and de-fanged as a source of interstate conflict through a long, painful quest for order carried out in both domestic and international politics"; "Not Even for the Seventeenth and Eighteenth Centuries: Power and Order in the Early Modern Era," in *History and Neorealism*, ed. Ernest May, Richard Rosecrance, and Zara Steiner (Cambridge, UK: Cambridge University Press, 2010), 87.

of early modern Europe. They were far less successful than their European forerunners and generated fierce and powerful religious opposition. It also is important to note that Europe from 1648 through the late eighteenth century was Exhibit A for realism—not for liberalism. In depoliticizing religion, Europe's rulers were grabbing power for themselves from the Church, their own aristocrats, and from one another; these efforts usually involved war. The answer for the Muslim world is not in Machiavelli or Hobbes, although their countries may need to continue to go through a realist state-building phase as Europe did. The answer to continuing terrorism and jihadism is the same competitive pressure that caused toleration to spread in Europe. Rulers and aspiring rulers in the Middle East must be convinced that stability and wealth are best ensured in states that are open to foreign ideas, goods, capital, and people. This has already begun to happen in Southeast Asia. Indonesia, the world's largest Muslim state, embraces electoral democracy and trading strategies of national advancement.

The Future of Conflict

This does not mean a future of peace is with us for all time. When the Cold War came to an end in 1991, all states did not become democratic, nor did they universally endorse purely economic modes of advancement. Popular ideologies of nationalism and anti-immigration could reject international influences. Economic crises (as did in fact occur from 2007 to 2012) could undercut the structure of cooperation, commending as they did internal rejection of the volatility of international capitalism. New ideologies of Islamic resurgence might then claim that democratic liberalism and capitalism had lost their historical relevance and perhaps would give way ultimately to an Islamic caliphate. Where weak democratic governments remained, they were apparently incompetent to offer Middle Eastern states a more progressive alternative to unalloyed Islamic rule. It would take much greater democratic activity and economic power to bring a change in the popular acceptance of capitalist bankruptcy.

Yet that change was likely to come, especially with the revolution in energy that shale, solar power, wind and tides held out to buffeted Western and Eastern economies. With agreements on reduction in the spread of carbon dioxide emissions, new stimuli to conservation (higher gas mileage requirements for cars and trucks), and a further reduction in the dependence of GDP growth on the expenditure of energy, the relevance of economic growth can once again be seen as a viable alternative to the use of military force to advance national agendas. Giant solar-produced batteries can emancipate humankind from the limitations of fossile fuels. In Eastern Europe, a patient rejection through economic sanctions of Russian expansion in the Ukraine and elsewhere in East Europe, together with the weakness of the ruble and the collapse of oil prices, will put paid to Russian demands for additional territory. In the end Russia will be dependent on incoming Western funds and technology to find its feet. Russia will prosper much more by becoming a reliable part of the West than it can ever do acting purely on its own.

One can look at world politics today in terms of the trade-off between military and economic strategies. If economic strategies succeed—bringing increasing returns to countries and populations—there is no need for military expansion. But a country bested or threatened in economic terms may well seek military means to redress its position. Conversely a country which fails to assert dominance militarily may shift to economic strategies to improve its outcome. In the second half of the nineteenth century, Japan viewed the technological and naval development of other powers like the United States and European nations as a major challenge. So Japan first developed local industry and then turned to the military arts. It emerged as an Eastern imperial power, seeking territory in Korea and China, eventually even challenging Russia's hold on the Far East. In the 1930s, as the Great Depression led Western countries to raise high barriers to trade, Japan aggressively reached for empire in China and Southeast Asia. But Japan's burst of militarism did not last. Defeated in Second World War and pressured and enabled by the United States, Japan turned to economic strategies to advance its goals, and it has prospered in doing so.

In the chapters that follow, you will see how the international system of sovereign states emerged in Europe around 500 years ago. You will see how realist ideas arose at the same time, and how young states and their powerful rulers generally acted in accord with realist principles: centralizing power, valuing territory above all, and suspecting one another. You will see how some people, starting in northwestern Europe, saw a different and better route to wealth and power, involving the decentralization of power at home and trading with foreigners. You will see how that latter, liberal system spread, in fits and starts, within and across countries. The story involves imperialism and war as well as trade and peace. The liberal international system spread partly because its ideas proved attractive, but partly because commercial republics proved the most competitive states. Since 1990 the liberal system has been globally dominant, but it faces new challenges that require fresh thinking and reform. That, too, is always part of the liberal story.

CONCLUSION

As long as individual states exist, there will always be uncertainty about the relations between them. But if countries seek to improve their positions through trade and commerce (not military expansion), a tolerable peace can be maintained. Some authoritarian countries seek their fulfillment through economic growth and technological development. Most southeast Asian states have done so, irrespective of political form. Korea did so; so did Taiwan. Indonesia and Thailand are seeking to improve their positions through commerce with others. China has prospered through trade. This does not mean that an economic crisis or universal depression could not reverse this trend. It did so in the 1930s. But abetted by the IMF and the World Bank, countries now have access to capital to "ride out" such crises, as they did after 2009 when growth resumed.

A commitment to trade and commerce as the means to development reassures others and fosters common aspirations. This does not mean that all states become democratic. We are far from that point in Russia, China, and the Middle East. But for capitalism to continue, countries must protect property and ensure property rights. Technological advances cannot be stolen from others but must be negotiated freely. In China's case, the renminbi (China's currency) will not be held or used by others if it is manipulated in Beijing. It will have to be freely fluctuating, both up and down. If Chinese authorities do not wish to see their undervalued renminbi sold abroad, they will have to increase interest rates. This will in turn reduce China's rate of growth. Thus a commitment to trade may ineluctably create flexible currencies that will be more easily sustained by democratic governments enjoying easy access to debt instruments to pay their way. France and England became democratic by creating legislatures that underwrote the debt of sovereigns. At some point China and Russia will need such institutions if Beijing and Moscow are to develop over the long term.

War may, of course, occur, and crises will happen. But perhaps gradually, international pressures will come to favor democracy as a political and development unit. The bases of realism then will come into question, though they will never be abolished.

FURTHER READING

Brooks, Stephen G. *Producing Security: Multinational Corporations, Globalization, and the Changing Calculus of Conflict.* Princeton, NJ: Princeton University Press, 2005.

Doyle, Michael W. *Ways of War and Peace: Realism, Liberalism, and Socialism.* New York: Norton, 1997.

Fukuyama, Francis. *The End of History and the Last Man.* New York: Free Press, 1992.

Mearsheimer, John J. *The Tragedy of Great Power Politics.* New York: Norton, 2001.

Owen, John M. *Confronting Political Islam: Six Lessons from the West's Past.* Princeton, NJ: Princeton University Press, 2015.

Rosecrance, Richard. *The Rise of the Trading State: Commerce and Conquest in the Modern World.* New York: Basic Books, 1986.

Waltz, Kenneth N. *Theory of International Politics.* New York: McGraw-Hill, 1979.

2 THE REFORMATION AND THE ABSOLUTIST STATE

Realism and Early Modern Europe

Realist international relations theory has existed for thousands of years. In ancient China, realist thinking and advice is evident in *The Art of War* by Sun-Tzu (ca. 544–496 BCE); in ancient Greece, in the *History of the Peloponnesian War* by the ancient Greek historian Thucydides (ca. 460—ca. 395 BCE); and in ancient India, in *Economics* by Kautilya (ca. 370—ca. 283 BCE).

Realists past and present are not identical, but as noted in Chapter 1, they generally hold in common the following tenets:

1. The only important political units are sovereign states (nation-states or city-states).
2. Those states exist in an anarchical situation, meaning that there is no world government to enforce agreements or punish aggression.
3. Each state thus must worry constantly about all others' gains in power and must take steps to ensure its own security.
4. This situation among states is permanent, and cannot be changed by:
   a. Institutions, either international (such as the United Nations or World Bank) or domestic (such as democracy)

    b. International interactions such as trade, investment, or population movements

    c. Peaceful ideas or moral or psychological improvement

There are good reasons why realism has survived as a theory: it is simple and it can explain much of what happens in world politics. When Russia seized Crimea, a region of Ukraine, in 2014, realists such as John Mearsheimer claimed that Russia feared the eastward expansion of the European Union and NATO, because behind that expansion lay the power of the United States, the world's only superpower. Thus, Russia annexed Crimea as a way to protect itself.[1] It did not consider democratic reform as a means of currying favor with the West.

But realism is not the universally valid theory that its proponents claim it to be. Consider the following fact: all three ancient writers—Sun-Tzu, Thucydides, and Kautilya—lived in times and places when groups of states were fighting one another for predominance. The modern theory of realism also was born in a violent time and place: early modern Europe, when sovereign states were forming, gathering power, and competing ferociously. In times and regions where there are no sovereign competing political units, or where the units exist in relative peace, however, thinkers and scholars tend to be more liberal and constructivist.

In this chapter, we open with a brief history of political development in early societies in various parts of the world, a history that helps make sense of the realist approach. We then discuss modern realism—the version that arose several hundred years ago in Europe and is still widely used in modified form. It is crucial to look at Europe several centuries ago, because the system of sovereign competing states that developed there has in subsequent centuries spread to encompass the entire globe. We then discuss why that version of realism arose when and where it did, and how it was indeed the best theory for Europe between 1500 and roughly 1780. In doing that we analyze the medieval political system that preceded it in Europe—a system that had no sovereign states and where realist theory was nearly unknown. We then discuss how sovereign states emerged and how their intense fear, competition, wars, and empire-building fit realist expectations.

Early Political Order

The species *Homo sapiens* inhabited earth 500,000 years ago, but its brain was smaller than those of modern men and women, and it took another 400,000 years for humans to develop the use of fire for heating and cooking. Even then, human development was not rapid. New Guineans did not come to accept settled

---

1. John J. Mearsheimer, "Why The Ukraine Crisis Is the West's Fault: The Liberal Delusions That Provoked Putin," *Foreign Affairs* (September-October 2014): 77–89.

cultivation in one spot but remained foragers for food and protection, roving far and wide within their land mass. Hunting and gathering were the activities of the Aboriginal population of Australia until very recently. In the Fertile Crescent (in the riverine Middle East), a form of settled cultivation (agriculture) emerged 11,000 years ago and has persisted since.

The itinerant existence of our early ancestors affected politics as well. Overarching political organizations did not quickly emerge above the village level. Rather, villages sometimes fought each other as enemies over a long period of time. Some inhabitants may not have believed in uncaused death and continued to think that individuals from enemy villages had killed their comrades, leading ultimately to revenge being sought against the offending village. (See the work of Robert Boyd for this anachronistic result.)

But settled agriculture and larger political units arose more or less together, since one could not occur and establish itself without the other. Agriculture needed protection that isolated villages could not fully provide. Larger political units required revenue or tribute from larger areas to provide such protection. As this occurred, chiefdoms emerged first, and states only later (states emerged in the Near East around 3700 BCE). Fighting of course occurred between states, but even villages had many murders and violent deaths.[2]

To operate, however, states needed a ruling group or functional king. This in turn allowed the king (in return for his services) to acquire large new resources and valuables not given to the rest of the society. King Midas was no exception to the royal trend. Kleptocracy—a society based on predation or stealing—became typical, with higher-ranked individuals seizing valuables. (Transparency International, based in Berlin, reports that kleptocracy remains a problem in many countries today.)

Thus, larger authoritarian polities emerged, but stability could not be maintained within or among them. This defect entailed violent transfers of power but later gave rise to the possibility of politics in which people participated in legitimate shifts in governance. Not surprisingly, development did not proceed at uniform rates across the globe. In many regions, hunter-gatherer societies dominated until relatively recently. There was no cultivation of crops, and humans from nearby villages fought to seize food and animals to eat. There was no regular authority structure: the self-sufficient micro-towns had little trade, though occasional warfare occurred.[3] Such isolated villages were also vulnerable to germs coming from outside, as were Latin Americans to diseases brought in

---

2. Jared Diamond, *Guns, Germs, and Steel: The Fates of Human Societies* (New York: Norton, 1999), 277.

3. E. E. Evans-Pritchard, in *The Nuer: A Description of the Modes of Livelihood and Political Institutions of a Nilotic People* (New York: Oxford University Press, 1940), writes about the Nuer versus the Dinka.

from Europe in the sixteenth century. Equally, the early villages did not have iron weapons, and their Stone Age or pottery technologies were no match for guns, lances, and horses wielded by Spanish and Portuguese invaders, as Cortez demonstrated in his conquest of the Aztecs in Mexico.

The outcome in these traditional societies was either chronic fighting or submission to empire. The former characterized the "warring states period" in China between 403 and 221 BCE. The latter includes European conquest of the Americas, pioneered by the Spanish, Portuguese, English, and Dutch. In Africa, Britain, France, Germany, and lesser states like Belgium and Portugal established large colonies. Much earlier (in the twelfth century), Genghis Khan's Mongolian Empire tyrannized along the Silk Road from the Mediterranean to China and forced absolute obedience. In the thirteenth century, under Kublai Khan, the family ran China. In India, France and Britain competed for dominance until England won out in the 1750s.

Medieval China was a technological innovator. It discovered gunpowder (from fireworks), wove silk, fashioned tableware, shaped porcelain, and devised irrigation systems. But it did not engage in regular trade with other states to profit from its inventions. The Chinese had no regular interaction with the outside world, nor did they believe they needed any. They did not fight against a foreign power until the nineteenth-century Opium War, when Britain attacked China to induce it to purchase opium from poppies grown in India (see Chapter 6).

In another instance, Moguls (from the Persian spelling of Mongol) came to India in the fourteenth century. They were acolytes of Genghis Khan and traversed from Iran to India. The Moguls had converted to Islam but ruled largely impartially over India's Hindus until the eighteenth century, when they were deposed or diverted by the extension of British rule over the entire subcontinent.

This brief sketch of early history shows that across the world people self-organized into political units and that the process entailed coercion and war. When no one group or ruler prevailed, a set of roughly equal political units or states—typically suspicious of one another and often at war—was the result. Sets of states produce theories that justify the sovereignty of each state and explain why war and suspicion are necessary. Thus, the writings of Sun-Tzu, Kautilya, and Thucydides. When one group or ruler prevailed, an empire was the result. Empires produce theories that justify the emperor's rule and the subordination of defeated communities. That brings us to medieval and early modern Europe, birthplace of both the modern states system that now covers the globe, and of modern realism.

Early Modern Realism

In the Western world, realism was dormant for many centuries. Medieval Europeans had never heard of Sun-Tzu or Kautilya, and historian Marianne Pade notes that even the Greek Thucydides's realist masterwork was nearly unknown in Europe; scholars had a few quotations in other works, but not the original.

Realism would have made little sense to medieval Europeans in any case. At the time, they had a very different type of political theory, one that is strange to us today but reflects the loose imperial order of that time and place. One example comes from the Italian poet Dante Alighieri, famous for his epic *Divine Comedy.* Around the year 1312, Dante, in exile from his home city of Florence, Italy, published *On Monarchy.* The book argues that there should be one ruler over the whole human race and that that ruler is the Holy Roman Emperor. The fragmentation, disputes, and disorder that afflicted medieval Europe would end, if only everyone would submit to the emperor's authority. Just as God is sole ruler of the universe, the world needed—and could have—a single ruler.

On Monarchy is much like other political theories of that time and place. Indeed, Dante was responding to a document published a few years earlier, *Unam Sanctam*, by Pope Boniface VIII, declaring that he, the pope, was and ought to be the supreme ruler of the world. Boniface and Dante agreed that strife and violence were caused by the absence of a world ruler—analogous to God—and that humankind could fix the situation. They just disagreed on who the universal ruler should be.

Around 200 years later Niccolò Machiavelli—a native of Florence, like Dante—wrote a radically different kind of book about politics. Titled *The Prince,* the book repudiated the idea that earth can be like heaven. "[F]or how we live is so far removed from how we ought to live," wrote Machiavelli, "that he who abandons what is done for what ought to be done, will rather learn to bring about his own ruin than his preservation." Looking at the Europe of his time and ancient Greece and Rome, Machiavelli saw a ruthless competition among men of war, in which the strongest and most ruthless win and those who try to be good lose. The successful prince will look after himself, because others will only betray him. The goal was not to submit to a universal holy empire, but to dominate others so as to avoid being dominated.

The Prince is the first modern realist text. In the 200 years between the two Florentine writers Dante and Machiavelli, Europe had begun to change in profound ways. In Dante's time, European states were not sovereign. Territory and the people who lived on it had multiple overlapping political loyalties. Ask a peasant living in 1312 in what is now France what his nation was, he probably would have given you his region—Brittany, Burgundy, Gascony, as the case may have been—and his region would not have had his primary loyalty. There were powerful men with armies and money, to be sure, but none of them completely controlled any territory. Even kings in 1310 did not enjoy sovereignty. They shared territory with dukes, barons, and other nobles. Some nobles were loyal to (or vassals of) more than one king; some nobles had more land, money, and soldiers than their kings did. Some bishops of the Catholic Church ruled territory. A king was not truly sovereign over his territory. That meant that medieval Europe did not have consolidated states or unified political entities.

When *The Prince* was published in 1532, it scandalized Europe and was placed on the Catholic Church's *Index of Prohibited Books* (remaining there until the *Index* was abolished in 1966). But rulers and would-be rulers read it and put its ideas into practice. And subsequent European writers were to develop realism over the next two centuries. The French legal scholar Jean Bodin (1530–1596) did not like Machiavelli's evident secularism; he put a more religious grounding beneath the theory. But Bodin, too, argued that the king was sovereign over his territory. "The sovereign prince is accountable only to God," Bodin wrote in his famous *Six Books of the Republic*—and by God he did not mean the Catholic Church.

In the following century, the English philosopher Thomas Hobbes (1588–1679) put realist ideas together in a different way. Hobbes was the first scholar to translate Thucydides's ancient masterpiece on realism into English from the original Greek. He did not stop there. Hobbes built an entire political theory in his own masterpiece *Leviathan* (1651), in which he said that all individual men (we can substitute "persons") in their natural state are afraid of one another—they need an all-powerful state to protect them. Life in this "state of nature," Hobbes wrote, was "solitary, poor, nasty, brutish, and short." The situation, he said, is analogous to that of sovereign states facing one another in the international system. These states must perpetually eye one another and prepare for war.

Still later, the Scottish philosopher David Hume (1711–1776) argued that it was natural for states to balance one another's power, and that states that did not do so would find themselves conquered by their more powerful neighbors. Hume wrote that the ancient Greek city-states described by Thucydides were rational in taking steps to block the rise of Athenian power. By contrast, those states that bandwagoned with (i.e., joined with) ancient Rome a few centuries later made a grievous mistake, because they enabled the rise of an empire that ended up swallowing them.

Hume's French contemporary Jean-Jacques Rousseau (1712–1778) developed realism still further. When Rousseau was a young adult, a well-known priest, the Abbot of St. Pierre, had written a plan for perpetual peace. After the abbot died, his relatives asked Rousseau to publicize his plan. In 1761 Rousseau published what became a famous essay on the abbot's plan in which he explained and seemed to praise it but then dismantled the argument piece by piece. Plans for perpetual peace, Rousseau argued, cannot work. The rulers of great powers—monarchs and their ministers—will never give up their right to consolidate power at home and expand it abroad. Princes are naturally competitive, always comparing themselves to one another. Their appetite for power is boundless. Each cares about his own good, not the general good. Rousseau argued that it would take a massive use of force to coerce the states of Europe into a peaceful federation. For Rousseau, as for all realists, the human race was stuck in a bleak world, and trying to escape would only make things worse.

To be sure, these centuries produced writings in the opposite direction—writings more like that of Dante. Thinkers such as Erasmus, Émeric Crucé, and the Duc de Sully deplored the anarchical international system and wrote plans for overcoming it. But the plans of these men had relatively little influence.

Why did realism flourish as a theory during these centuries? Why was it virtually unknown in Europe before Machiavelli?

History shapes theory (and vice versa). Roughly between the years 1500 and 1650, modern states formed in Europe. From 1650 until around 1780, those states acted fairly consistently with the expectations of realism. Afterward, the American and French revolutions (1776–1783 and 1789–1795, respectively) changed the international system so much that realism's explanatory power was reduced. But between 1500 and 1780—and especially in the latter half of that period—realism was the best theory explaining world politics. The great powers competed intensely with one another, fighting many wars and building large empires to shut one another out. They traded relatively little with one another.

What happened after 1500 in Europe was that a complex medieval political system, analyzed later, gave way to a system of sovereign states, or discrete pieces of territory, each with its own government, most recognizing the sovereignty of the others. These sovereign states formed a system because they interacted in various ways—culturally, religiously, and particularly politically by diplomacy and occasionally war. Early modern sovereign states were driven by external fear and competition, and by internal forces as well, to expand their power outward and extract resources from poorly defended territories and societies. Thus the most powerful states of early modern Europe—called the great powers—both attacked smaller powers and one another and conquered, colonized, and exploited lands in the Americas, Africa, and Asia. Indeed, by 1700 there was a near-global system penetrated by, but larger than, the European international system.

Today's global political system is one of legally sovereign states, territorial units with defined borders that recognize no authority above themselves. This system emerged in Europe 500 years ago and spread all over the world through European imperialism and the anti-imperialist and nationalist reactions it generated. Alternative systems have existed in certain times and places, and empires have been especially common. For centuries China had a "soft" empire or suzerainty, in which lesser kings in lands such as Korea and Vietnam paid tribute to the Chinese emperor. The ancient Mediterranean was dominated by a hard empire (the Roman), as was medieval West Africa (the Malian). In recent decades the European Union has been attempting a still different kind of system, one in which states voluntarily "pool" some aspects of sovereignty but retain others.

The Medieval European System

Let us go back even earlier than Dante, to the year 1154. A map of France in that year (Figure 2.1) illustrates the point. There was a Kingdom of France (encompassed by the dark border). But the king only ruled the region around Paris and a small area around Bourges. The other areas were duchies (ruled by dukes), counties (ruled by counts), or other territories ruled by nobles. All were loyal to the king of France in a formal sense, but many had more actual power than he.

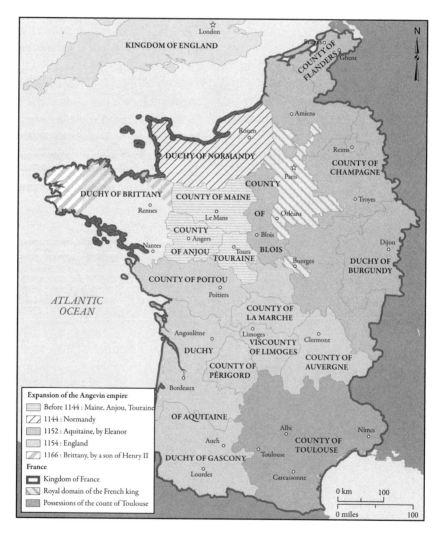

FIGURE 2.1 Expansion of Angevin empire in modern-day France.

Of course, kings and kingdoms fought wars in medieval Europe. The most consequential was probably the Hundred Years' War between England and France (1337–1453). When we say "England" and "France," however, we do not mean the separate states that you might have in mind. The two countries were heavily mingled politically. The kings of England—from the Plantagenet dynasty—had originally come from Anjou in France. They were dukes of several territories in France, which gave them still more wealth yet also made them vassals of the kings of France from the Valois dynasty. In the 1320s Edward III of England claimed the French throne, but the French nobility and bishops rejected the claim. Within a decade, England and France were at war, and the war went on, in fits and starts, for more than a century. Early on the English won victories, including the famous lopsided one at Agincourt, immortalized by Shakespeare in *Henry V*. Later the French rebounded and drove the English out of France. The main thing to keep in mind is that it was not really "England" and "France," in the modern sense, that were fighting. It was rather kings who were fighting, one of whom (the English) owned territory in the other's kingdom (France) and who had subjects of the other (the king of France) fighting on his side. And this was not at all unusual at the time.

Dante's theory of universal monarchy makes more sense in light of the Hundred Years' War and similar complex conflicts of that age. Political units and loyalties overlapped, and it was reasonable to argue for a single universal ruler.

Figure 2.2 Battle of Agincourt, 1415.

The Great Transformation

That complex and (to us) strange medieval system of overlapping rule and uncertain and shifting political borders is long gone. Traces of it exist today in the European Union, where states have pooled some elements of their sovereignty and created a kind of supranational state. And scholars such as Margaret Keck and Kathryn Sikkink have likened the role of NGOs (non-governmental organizations) and other transnational groups in today's world politics to that of the medieval church.[4] In a more sinister vein, the so-called Islamic State (ISIS) has a medieval-like view of world politics, in which the caliphate it is trying to re-establish is not tied to discrete pieces of territory but exists wherever Muslims pledge loyalty to it.

But these partial exceptions do not touch the main point: the European medieval system gave way many centuries ago to a system of sovereign states. Around the year 1500 a slow-motion political earthquake began, and the continent reassembled itself politically into a set of competing kingdoms, each much more centralized internally, each with more certain borders. Under the new system, a king's domain was a state, and he was sovereign over it. As political scientist Hendrik Spruyt puts the matter, states had a hierarchical authority structure, with the king or prince at the top. Aristocrats and the church (and, later, merchants) retained some power, to be sure, but they acted more in service to the king than before. And kings eyed one another with suspicion, knowing that each might want to seize some or all of another's territory.

Material Changes

Scholars differ over how and why the medieval political system fragmented into a set of sovereign and competing states ruled by powerful kings. Some scholars look to technological changes. Some of these changes were in weaponry. Charles Tilly links the growing centralization to the greater capacity of rulers to extract resources from their territories and to use those resources to make war. "War made the state," Tilly has written, "and the state made war." Barry Posen agrees, arguing for a kind of Darwinian evolution in which the fittest rulers and political units survived. Competition among princes produced improvements in military firepower, which further exacerbated competition in which only the fittest—strong states—survived.[5] The introduction of gunpowder (invented in China) into Europe led to more powerful weapons—the handheld arquebus in the sixteenth

4. Margaret Keck and Kathryn Sikkink, *Activists Beyond Borders* (Ithaca, NY: Cornell University Press, 1998).

5. Barry R. Posen, "Nationalism, the Mass Army, and Military Power," *International security* 18, no. 2 (1993): 80–124.

FIGURE 2.3 Dutch musketeers, ca. 1580.

century, followed by the musket and artillery pieces such as the cannon—that in turn rendered castles newly vulnerable and increasingly obsolete (Figure 2.3). Firearms and artillery thus helped give an advantage to the offensive and made it easier to conquer larger amounts of territory. Thus one king (or sometimes an upper aristocrat who became a king) found it easier to conquer other aristocrats. That would help explain both how kings came to subdue the aristocracy and why small counties and duchies gave way to larger states.

Hendrik Spruyt agrees that the modern international system evolved in Darwinian fashion, but argues for an economic rather than a military driver. Transportation technology improved, which made it easier to move goods and people around Europe. The resulting increase in trade and migration in turn led to the rise of merchants and the cities that they founded. Cities and the burghers (merchants) who ran them clashed with landholding aristocrats, and they became rivals for power. Kings saw an opportunity and made deals with burghers against aristocrats, and the resulting bargains weakened the aristocracy and empowered kings. In other words, money mattered as well as guns. Both of these mechanisms of change—military and economic—were self-reinforcing: change begat more change.

Changes in Ideas

A second type of change that helped produce the modern states system was change in ideas and beliefs. The changes are summed up in the two famous "R" words: Renaissance and Reformation. Both of these movements had their origins in the Latin slogan *ad fontes*, or "to the source." The "source" was the ancient world of learning and culture upon which medieval society was built. Medieval learning held up ancient sources—the Bible in religion, Greek and Roman sources in philosophy and science—as authoritative. But scholars had to rely on inadequate copies of corrupt translations of these sources. For example, many of the works of the ancient Greek philosopher Aristotle were translated into Latin from Arabic (and Arab scholars earlier had translated them from the original Greek). And over the centuries scholars had added many interpretations onto these texts, so that few actually had ever read the originals.

Returning "to the source" meant finding the original sources—Plato, Aristotle, the Hebrew Bible, the Greek New Testament, and so on—and learning the original languages. The Renaissance, usually seen as beginning in the fourteenth century in Florence, was the expression of this "to the source" movement in science and art. The Reformation, which began in the early sixteenth century in Germany, was its reflection in religion.

How did all of this relate to politics and the emergence of the modern international system? The essential story is that the Renaissance challenged traditional authorities—especially the Catholic Church. Even though clergy and devout Catholic laymen were some of the leading figures in both movements, and these men did not intend to undermine religion, the practical effect was just that. Scholars came to see that the original sources did not always say what they had thought they said. Over time, the undermining of the medieval worldview led to new ways of thinking about science. The old idea, taken from Aristotle, that matter moved because of "final causes" or internal purposes was replaced by a new idea that matter moved because of external mechanical forces such as gravity. Galileo, Francis Bacon, Rene Descartes, Isaac Newton, and others ushered in the scientific revolution. Eventually thinkers applied these new, mechanistic ideas to human society, which helped give rise to modern realism, as we discuss later.

In the realm of religion, a similar broad change took place. In northern Europe, more and more churchmen began to claim that the practices of the Catholic Church were not consistent with the original doctrines of the early church. Martin Luther (Figure 2.4), Ulrich Zwingli, John Calvin, and other scholars broke away from the Catholic Church and founded various Protestant denominations. In preceding centuries clergy would occasionally protest against some teachings or practices of the church, but all of these would-be reformers eventually failed and sometimes met with a violent death.

Luther and the other reformers, however, succeeded. One reason was the new technology of the printing press (invented by Johannes Gutenberg ca. 1440). Another was that Luther gained political protection. Various German nobles—dukes, counts, and so on—had long chafed at the authority of bishops. Only in the early sixteenth century was the prestige of the church damaged enough to allow them to do something about it. So, several nobles protected Luther and his followers and allowed them to continue translating the Bible and propagating their faith. Many of these rulers were sincere in their embrace of Protestantism, but it probably did not hurt that doing so meant that they could seize the

FIGURE 2.4 Martin Luther by Lucas Cranach the Elder.

FIGURE 2.5 Henry VIII of England.
Source: World History Archive/Alamy Stock Photo.

extensive lands held by the Church and reap resources from them. Most notorious in this regard was Henry VIII of England (1491–1547; Figure 2.5), who closed churches and seized church lands. Even rulers who remained Catholic, such as Francis I of France and the dukes of Bavaria, were able to negotiate new arrangements under which monasteries and cathedrals would hand over to them a fixed percentage of their revenues.

So, in the fifteenth and sixteenth centuries kings began to concentrate power in their own hands by taking it from nobles and the Catholic Church. In centralizing power, they gradually formed sovereign states. Kings were able to do this because of new developments in military and transportation technology and new ideas that challenged the authority of the Church. There were still regions of Europe where nobles hung on to power, but ironically it was in one of those—what is now Germany—that a long and devastating war was fought that cemented state sovereignty.

The Thirty Years' War and State Sovereignty

The steady seizure of power by kings and the decay of the Catholic Church's authority that played out in the Renaissance and Reformation came to a head in the Thirty Years' War (1618–1648), a conflict that involved most of Europe but was fought mainly in Germany. The Habsburg Emperor-Elect Ferdinand made it clear that he intended to destroy Protestantism. In 1618 Protestants in Bohemia (now part of the Czech Republic) revolted against the Habsburgs, triggering intervention by outside Protestant and Catholic powers. Victories by Catholic Habsburg forces drew a series of interventions over the ensuing years—first by the Danish king, then by the king of Sweden. When these Protestant interventions failed, Louis XIII, the king of France—himself a Catholic—began to fear that the Habsburgs would become too powerful in Europe. In 1635 France joined the war and eventually subdued the Habsburgs. In the Peace of Westphalia of 1648, all warring parties agreed that religious differences should no longer be a cause of war. Each prince—king, duke, count—could decide for himself what would be the religion in his own territory. In Latin the principle was *cuius regio, eius religio* ("whose the realm, his the religion").

That little Latin formula was of monumental importance, for it meant that finally European rulers recognized one another's sovereignty over precise pieces of territory. Catholic and Protestant rulers recognized that they had no right to try to change the religion of one another's domains. By 1648 not only had monarchs successfully grabbed more and more power from their nobles and the church, but each had agreed to give up the old medieval norm of divided sovereignty (see Figure 2.1).

That is not to say that all the early modern European great powers that rose from the ashes of the Thirty Years' War remained the same. The Netherlands, one of the most successful states, was a republic, not a monarchy. And the Netherlands pioneered a different route to success that departed in significant ways from what realist theory would expect. Indeed, as you will read in Chapters 3 and 4, nobles and later merchants began to push back against monarchs in Great Britain and other states in the eighteenth century, leading to yet another slow but fundamental transformation that produced a new kind of state and, eventually, a new kind of international system.

The System of Sovereign States

But we are getting ahead of the story. By 1648 Europe was a continent dominated by sovereign states—a very different place than it had been in 1200 or 1500. Now kings were the dominant actors, and each set about subduing other power-holders on his territory. Louis XIV of France set the pace. The Sun King kept his nobles and the Catholic Church in France subdued; he taxed his subjects relentlessly and went to war time and again. Other monarchs in Austria, Russia, Prussia, and England imitated his example and continued to centralize more and more power. What are now Germany and Italy did not go through this process; they remained divided and weak, playthings of the great powers. (Italy and Germany were both finally to unite into great powers in the late nineteenth century.)

The kings of Europe were less worried than their forebears about threats to their power from their own subjects, but that is not at all to say that they were secure. Far from it: Europe's crowned heads eyed one another with jealousy and fear. Each worried about how much power the others had, and thus about power trends—who was gaining and who was losing power at any given time. The root causes of this jealousy and fear are complex. No doubt the kinds of people who want power are prone by nature to compare themselves to their peers and to want to be better than they are. This is one theme of Machiavelli's *Prince*, discussed earlier in this chapter. But two other causes interacted to produce this system of fear and suspicion.

The first cause was described well by Hobbes in 1651: the absence of a world- or Europe-wide government to judge disputes among kings and to punish aggression. In other words, the European international system was anarchical; each sovereign was independent of all others. Hobbes argued that individual men in this "state of nature" will constantly fear violent death. He wrote that if you want to see what the state of nature is like, observe how Europe's monarchs stand in relation to one another:

> [I]n all times, Kings, and Persons of Soveraigne Authority, because of their Independency, are in continuall jealousies, and in the state and posture of Gladiators; having their weapons pointing, and the eyes fixed on one another; that is, their Forts, Garrisons, and Guns upon the frontiers of their Kingdomes; and continuall Spyes upon their neighbours, which is a posture of War.

Today, realists note that the international system still lacks a world government, and they insist that, at the end of the day, Hobbes's world is our world. Nothing really has changed.

But a second cause was present in the seventeenth and eighteenth centuries that is less common today, at least in many parts of the world: the belief that all the components of power, including wealth, were in fixed amounts. The assumption about wealth was especially important. Wealth derived, it was thought, from natural resources only. Farmland, fishing grounds, gold and silver mines—these were what made a king powerful, and there were only so many of these to go around. The result: kings and their ministers believed that states were necessarily in perpetual competition over scarce resources. To use a familiar analogy, there was only one pie. It was not possible to expand the pie or to bake more. The only question was how many pieces of the pie each king would get. In that kind of situation, it would be surprising if sovereigns were not preoccupied with how much power they had relative to their peers.

Thus Europe's monarchs competed in two chief ways, both involving violence: imperialism and war.

Islam and the Ottoman Empire

It is important to recognize that one of Europe's great powers during these centuries was a semi-outsider, in terms of geography, culture, and history.The Ottoman Empire, centered in what is now Istanbul, Turkey, was for many centuries a major player in the Mediterranean Sea and southeastern Europe.It was the caliphate or Islamic empire that had its origins centuries before, in the emergence of Islam.

Arabs had routinely followed an annual pilgrimage to Mecca even before the Prophet Mohammed was born in 570. At the time the Quraysh tribe ruled Mecca and Mohammed descended from this Hashemite tribe. He was initially consigned to Bedouin guardians. In the Muslim account, the clanging of bells awakened Mohammed from a cave in 610. There he received the message from the archangel Gabriel telling him that he, Mohammed, was God's long-awaited Messenger to the World. Ultimately Mohammed came to believe in himself and his message. But he was an illiterate forty-year-old camel merchant chosen as God's Prophet, and his task would be arduous to say the least. Following his death, Muslims compiled God's instructions (Allah's revelations and teachings) in written form, the Quran. The Sunna, comprising records of Mohammed's words and deeds, gives instructions on everything—laws of inheritance, punishment for crimes, and the proper positions in sexual intercourse. The Quran regards the Hebrew and Christian scriptures as corrupted texts. It accepts Jesus Christ as a prophet, though not as divine. It contains both harsh and admiring statements about the Jewish people.

Initially, citizens of Mecca resisted Mohammed. The caravans he led were questioned. But Mohammed accepted killings even during Ramadan and reacted accordingly against resistance by so-called infidels. Mohammed died in 632. Abu Bakr al-Siddiq succeeded him as caliph. This resulted in a growing movement against Western control. Within a decade Muslim armies captured Roman territories in the East (Palestine, Egypt, Syria, Northern Libya, and Cyrenaica.) Thus began centuries of collision and war with the Eastern Roman (Byzantine) Empire, whose capital, Constantinople (now Istanbul), finally fell to the Ottoman Turks in 1453.

European Imperialism, 1488–1715

The Ottomans were great sailors, but they confined their empire mostly to the Mediterranean, southeastern Europe, and Middle East. The European kings, however, even while amassing power at home were gathering resources from further abroad, using new technologies of transportation and warfare to push outward and extract resources from lands near and far. When in 1492 the king and queen of Spain authorized Christopher Columbus to find a westward route to India, they were not simply enabling a romantic explorer to follow his dream. Columbus and his men sought riches, and Ferdinand and Isabella would rule whatever territory Columbus could conquer. Years before Columbus discovered the Americas for Spain, Portuguese explorers had begun exploring the African coast and trading for gold and slaves. In 1498 Vasco da Gama reached India. Soon French, English, and Dutch explorers joined the competition, sailing the Atlantic and Pacific in search trading opportunities. The Europeans conquered these areas because of their superior military technology and the fact that, unknown to them, they brought with them diseases to which the natives had no immunity.

These private traders are a group we shall return to in subsequent chapters because they eventually undermined the centralization of state power and realist theory. In these early centuries, however, they ended up as tools of the monarchs and kingdoms they represented. The rulers commissioned them and offered them protection and, in return, demanded sovereignty over the areas they conquered and a share of their profits they extracted. The kings of Portugal, Spain, France, and England and the leaders of the Dutch Republic all sought to monopolize trade in the areas they discovered—that is, each exploration company was determined to be the only Europeans buying and selling with the Africans, Asians, and native peoples they encountered. If a French explorer claimed a stretch of coastline, it belonged to the king of France, and the French would fight to repel explorers and colonists from other European powers.

It was not only the Atlantic European states that expanded outward via the seas. The Eastern European great powers expanded overland. Under various Habsburg emperors, Austria swelled eastward and southward, encompassing all or much of what are now Hungary, the Czech Republic, Slovakia, Poland, and the Balkan states. Under Ivan III (the Great), Ivan IV (the Terrible), and other tsars, Russia moved eastward into Asia and eventually through Siberia all the way to the Pacific.

All of this expansion was driven by many factors, one of which was the rulers' insatiable desire and need for still more resources, a need itself driven by fear of falling behind other European rulers. Today economists speak of a "zero-sum game": a set of interactions, like a game, in which a gain for one party is a corresponding and equal loss for the other party. The states of Europe were in such a highly competitive game.

Wealth was believed to come chiefly from precious metals, preeminently from gold. The economic theory called mercantilism was widely held and practiced. A state should trade, the theory said, but should import only raw materials such as farm products and minerals; it should manufacture its own goods and consume and export them. A state should accumulate gold and silver and never use them to pay for imports. The state should be as economically self-sufficient as possible. And the point of commerce was to build up the power of the state—not to improve the lot of private citizens.

Political scientist Robert Gilpin has called mercantilism the economic face of realism, and it is not hard to see why.[6] If each state should only trade under conditions so favorable to itself, it really only could trade with lands that it could coerce—in contrast to today's world (or the Middle Ages, for that matter). States were reluctant to trade with others because they all wanted to sell manufactured goods, not buy them, and they all wanted to import gold and silver and raw materials, not sell them. So they traded with their colonies and strove to keep the costs of extracting wealth in those colonies low—hence the practice of chattel slavery, in which Africans were forced to travel across the Atlantic in horrendous conditions and were sold to property owners to do the labor—mining gold or silver, and cultivating sugar.

Under mercantilism, it was vitally important to have many colonies, so states competed for them and fought wars over them. (See Chapter 9 where we explore neo-mercantilist theory, which has become popular in some parts of the world in recent decades. Neo-mercantilists do not worry about accumulating gold and silver, but they do emphasize that a state should have a trade surplus and specialize in manufacturing and exporting industrial and high-technology goods.)

By 1763, the Americas looked like the portrayal shown in Figure 2.6. Note the Europeans' domination of both North and South America. To understand developments outside of Europe, we need to understand the rise of the modern state and realism in Europe.

War and Statecraft in Europe, 1650–1715

Within Europe itself, the young states fought wars frequently. Some of the wars were over colonies; these are sometimes called wars of trade. Britain and the Netherlands fought three such wars in the late seventeenth century, and Britain gained New Amsterdam, which it renamed New York. Other wars were over direct control of territory in Europe, as in the Great Northern War between Russia and Sweden (1700–1721). A third type of war was one peculiar to monarchies: wars of monarchical succession.

Political scientist Charles Lipson has noted that one of the central problems in all of politics is succession of rule, which has historically been one of the leading causes of destructive wars. Every king wanted to have at least one son ready to succeed him when he died (in some countries, such as England, the law permitted a daughter to succeed as queen). But sometimes a king died without a lawful heir. In such cases, various claimants to the vacant throne would jockey for position, backed by local and foreign patrons. Widespread intermarriage among European

---

6. Robert Gilpin, *The Political Economy of International Relations* (Princeton, NJ: Princeton University Press, 1987).

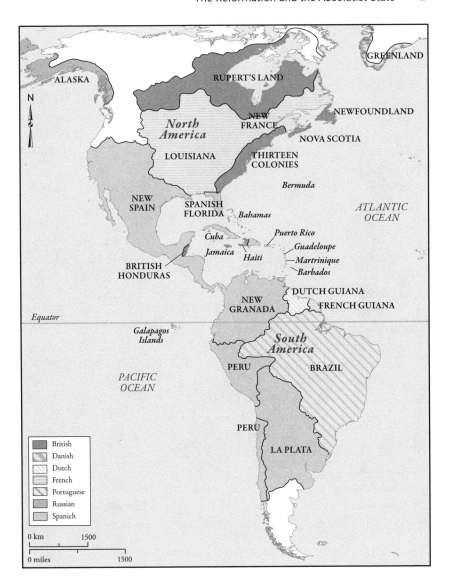

FIGURE 2.6 Colonial holdings in the Americas in 1763.

royal houses meant that there was often genuine ambiguity as to who ought to take the throne. Because all great powers except the Dutch and Venetian republics were monarchies (and many royal families were related by blood or marriage), great powers were interested in one another's monarchical succession—that is, in who would succeed a given king or queen. Who took the throne in state A meant a very real gain or loss in power for the king of states, B, C, D, and so on.

The War of Spanish Succession (1701–1714; Figure 2.7) is an example of how monarchical succession could lead to horrific international war. Charles II of Spain (1661–1700) was sickly and had no heir. The courts of Europe knew this and monitored his condition closely. As he lay on his deathbed, the jockeying intensified. Charles was a Habsburg, and his Habsburg cousins ruled Austria, so you might think Charles's successor would come from Austria. But Louis XIV of France was married to Charles's sister, and so his son or grandson had a plausible claim as well. Louis badly wanted to have a close relative on the Spanish throne, because he and his dynasty, the Bourbons, were long-time adversaries of the Habsburgs, and France was surrounded by Habsburgs (to the south in Spain and parts of Italy, to the east in Austria, and to the north in the Spanish Netherlands).

There was even a third claimant. The Duke of Bavaria—a small German state—was the great-grandson of Charles's father, and so he declared himself rightful king of Spain. This three-way contest between the Austrians, the French, and the Bavarians led them to compromise by agreeing to divide Spain into three parts—each to be ruled by one of the claimants. But then Charles himself, although dying, became infuriated at the idea that his kingdom would be partitioned. As he lay there, Charles declared Louis's grandson Philip his sole heir.

Louis knew that if he rejected the offer, Charles would just offer the same deal to the Austrians, but that if he accepted the offer, war might follow. Louis agreed, and the Spanish crowned Philip V Spain's first Bourbon king. The Austrian Habsburgs could not accept the loss of all of Spain to another family, and other European great powers were already afraid that Louis's France was becoming too powerful. So, a grand anti-French coalition formed: Austria, England, the Dutch Republic, Prussia, and several smaller German states banded together and attacked France.

The war lasted thirteen years and killed an estimated 400,000 people. The peace treaties allowed Philip V to rule Spain and its American colonies but prohibited him from ever ruling France. Austria gained the Spanish Netherlands.

Conclusion

Thucydides, the ancient Greek realist, wrote that "the strong do what they will, and the weak suffer what they must." That certainly was the case in the War of Spanish Succession, in which Spain itself lost some of its holdings. More generally, in the decades surrounding that war, that was politics as normal. States were identified with the kings who ruled them. Those kings consolidated more and more power at home and expanded their power outwardly as far as they could. They feared one another. Following the theory of mercantilism, they nearly stopped trading with one another, as kingdoms had done in the Middle Ages, and instead seized colonies in the Americas, Africa,

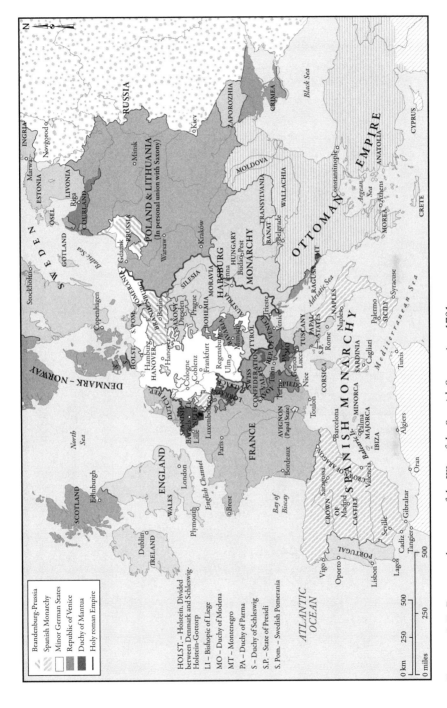

FIGURE 2.7 Europe at the outset of the War of the Spanish Succession, 1701.

and Asia in order to trade with them. States formed and broke alliances and fought wars frequently.

This was the high era of realism in Europe, and Europeans carried their competition via imperialism to much of the rest of the world—to the Americas, Africa, and Asia. States continue to exist to this day; some of their leaders believe that they exist in a zero-sum world, and wars still happen. But much has changed since the classic era of realism in early modern Europe. A new type of state appeared in the late seventeenth century—a trading republic in which power was dispersed and international cooperation was encouraged—and began slowly to transform the international system. Trading republic 1.0 was the Netherlands. Version 2.0 was England. We turn to these states and their development in Chapter 3.

FURTHER READING

Doyle, Michael W. *Ways of War and Peace: Realism, Liberalism, Socialism.* New York: Norton, 1997.

Hobbes, Thomas. *Leviathan.*

Hume, David. "Of the Balance of Power," in David Hume, *Essays Moral, Political, and Literary.*

Keck, Margaret, and Kathryn Sikkink. *Activists Beyond Borders.* Ithaca, NY: Cornell University Press, 1998.

Lipson, Charles. *Reliable Partners: How Democracies Have Made a Separate Peace.* Princeton, NJ: Princeton University Press, 2005.

Machiavelli, Niccolò. *The Prince,* 1532.

Nexon, Daniel H. *The Struggle for Power in Early Modern Europe.* Princeton, NJ: Princeton University Press, 2009.

Owen, John. *The Clash of Ideas in World Politics.* Princeton, NJ: Princeton University Press, 2010.

Pade, Marianne. "The Renaissance: Scholarship, Criticism and Education," in Christine Lee, ed., *Handbook to the Reception of Thucydides.* Wiley-Blackwell, 2014

Rosecrance, Richard. *Rise of the Trading State.* New York: Basic Books, 1986.

Rousseau, Jean-Jacques. *The State of War.*

Spruyt, Hendrik. *The Sovereign State and Its Competitors.* Princeton, NJ: Princeton University Press, 1996.

Tilly, Charles. *Coercion, Capital, and European States, AD 990–1992.* Oxford, UK: Blackwell, 1992.

3 TRADING VOCATIONS AND DOMESTIC LIBERTIES

Introduction

When the international system of Europe was dominated by absolute monarchies adhering to mercantilist ideas, states aimed at conquering territory and engaged in "warre" to do so, as prescribed by Niccoló Machiavelli and Thomas Hobbes. Just like Josef Stalin in the twentieth century, they believed the more territory they could acquire or seize the better. They did not worry about the sentiments of the inhabitants of the countries or provinces they were subduing. But the centralized monarchical states, with their mercantilist empires and emphasis on conquest of territory, never completely dominated Europe. In the Netherlands and then in England (which combined with Scotland in 1707 to form Great Britain), merchants—people whose livelihood depended on production and commerce—had more leverage than elsewhere. Their increasing wealth gave these trading classes growing leverage over their governments. The Dutch and British aristocracy made common cause with the merchants to force the government to protect property rights and to allow free commerce. Those two countries thus took a distinctive path and became the first two modern liberal trading states. By contrast, in Spain, France, Austria, Russia, and rising Prussia, kings continued to amass power and regulate commerce heavily. The eighteenth century, then, shows us two types of great power: absolute monarchies and liberal commercial states.

Still, in the seventeenth and for most of the eighteenth century, territory was the main focus of attention and conquered lands switched hands rapidly during the Thirty Years' War. With Sweden, Russia, Austria, and France seeking new conquests and converts, this was a classical realist period. Antagonists cared only about advancing their own cause, not about opinion in other states.

Louis XIV's Reign: The Peak of the Monarchical State

Let us return to the kind of state that was prominent in Europe in the seventeenth century and the kind of international system it participated in. It was called an "absolute" monarchy because the king was the sovereign—the supreme power with the final say over taxes, treaties, wars, and so on. Monarchy as a political form peaked under Louis XIV. This did not mean that the French king had more actual power than, for example, absolute dictators who came later, such as Hitler, Stalin, or even the emperor Napoleon. Those latter three could get what they wanted without interference: thus, Stalin slaughtered the kulaks and Hitler the Jews. Using the *levée en masse* to support him, Napoleon could send armies across marshy fields and find them intact on the other side; rates of desertion were remarkably low, and this was not merely because men feared their officers. French nationalism forged a collective will to carry the revolution to neighboring countries and resist counterattacks.

Yet Louis XIV—in a pre-nationalist age—squeezed all the power available under the monarchical form of government. He emasculated France's nobility—big landowners who in the Middle Ages had been very powerful—by moving them to Versailles, his new and ornate palace outside Paris, thereby depriving them of local roots and supporters. He insisted they attend all court functions from his awakening and toilette to nightly ablutions culminating in withdrawal to his bedchamber. In so doing Louis helped to sever the already tenuous connection between noble and peasant and made the latter ever more dependent on the king. The king and the peasantry were natural allies in any case. Louis needed cavalry and foot soldiers, and the middle class would not generally serve unless they were paid. Peasants provided much of the manpower. The king needed support in all parts of the country.

For their part, the peasants had to worry about brigands taking their crops at the end of the growing season. The king could mobilize mounted troops to chase those brigands off. The peasants naturally linked themselves with the king's cavalry and facilitated royal rule of agricultural areas, broadening the king's control and further undercutting the nobility. This also enhanced Louis's military capability, for that sway could be projected into neighboring duchies and countries. Louis also took command of taxes through his installation of regional Intendants (tax collectors and administrators) to funnel monies to the king. Thus the only question after

1660 (when Louis assumed the reins of power) was whom the French monarch would attack first—the Dutch or the Habsburgs. Generally speaking, he wished to move as close to the Rhine as possible, gobbling up the territory in between.

Roving Versus Stationary Bandits

This centralization of power and the aims that it reflected followed a long historical evolution. Understanding that evolution requires understanding the complex relationship between political rulers and economic producers, between politics and economics, between power and wealth. Kings and other rulers wanted power and needed wealth to get and sustain it. Producers—farmers, merchants, manufacturers, and bankers—wanted wealth and needed protection from thieves and one another. Rulers and producers, then, usually struck some kind of bargain in which rulers protected producers in their country and producers paid taxes to rulers. The terms of these bargains varied widely; sometimes rulers granted monopolies to particular producers, and sometimes rulers sapped producers' incentives to produce by taxing them too heavily. Rulers and producers always had different interests, and each invariably tried to exploit the other even as they cooperated. The tension between rulers and producers, including merchants and financiers involved in trade, was crucial to the story of how states and ultimately the international system changed over time.

We begin with the most basic kind of economic production: farming. In the age of hunter-gatherer societies, settled agriculture was impossible. Farmers needed the protection of a reliable chief or prince. Moving from place to place along the Silk Road in the thirteenth century, the Great Khan and his relatives and heirs could not provide this kind of steady protection, nor did they wish to do so. Khan was a "roving bandit," in economist Mancur Olson's telling description. Settled agriculture required dependable rulership, which in turn required that the "bandit" or ruler be stationary—permanently set in one place so that the farmers could count on him. Sedentary rule not only helped the farmers, it also made the bandit's (ruler's) revenues steadier, if lower per unit of depredation.

The Rise of Merchant Adventurers

Stationary rule was well and good, but while tillers of the soil may have benefited, economic production and consumption always was more complicated than that. Across history, in all kinds of societies, people generally like to trade some of what they have for some of what someone else has. Economic theorists were to figure this out later, in the eighteenth century, but ordinary people knew it all along: once their property and lives are secure, everyone is better off in material terms if they specialize in producing a few things and barter for or buy in voluntary exchanges whatever else they need. In the typical village not everyone makes houses, shoes for humans or horses, bricks, or glass; rather, some are carpenters, some cobblers, some blacksmiths, some masons, and some glaziers, and all of these buy from and sell to one another. In the same way, cities and regions are better off on the whole if they specialize and trade with other cities and regions.

But trade requires certain reliable, risk-taking people to conduct the transactions—to carry goods and money and, in more advanced systems, to guarantee delivery and payment and to extend credit and collect debts. So there developed in some places in Europe merchants and financiers who wanted to meet the demand for trade and indeed to draw exotic goods like spices, sugar, cotton, and textiles from all corners of the earth. Accordingly, a merchant class was formed around the cities. Although merchants needed princely protection from bandits and pirates, a crucial fact about this merchant class and the cities they dominated was that they enjoyed a measure of independence from kings and emperors. Merchants relied on riverine or oceanic trade routes which their king could not dominate. Private trade increased, further augmenting merchants' latitude. New products from Asia (spices and sandalwood) and Latin America (sugar and coffee) entered European markets. Much later (after 1780) these gains were crowned by the machine-produced textiles of the Industrial Revolution.

This merchant class emerged early and grew only gradually. Markets appeared in the medieval period from 1200–1400, but they were not free.[1] Guilds controlled who could become an artisan and regulated the prices and quality of goods. Trade spread, however, as commercial cities emerged offering exchanges of goods along trade routes defined by major river systems and the Mediterranean basin. The Champagne Fair in northeastern France, initially held annually, was a regular focus of exchange.

Cities and Kings: The Tug of War

Rulers sought to use this trade to broaden their contacts abroad. Venice prospered by buying food from the shores of the Black Sea and selling glass (with cobalt-blue colors), textiles, and decorative objects to neighbors along the Dalmatian coast or farther away. Genoa competed with Venice for primacy in the Mediterranean, seeking greater access to Eastern markets, but later both Italian cities found that distant Portugal had outmaneuvered them in getting spices from around the Cape of Good Hope. The drive for more trade and the Renaissance rediscovery of ancient learning (noted in Chapter 2) helped spur innovation in transportation, and when the Portuguese explorer Vasco da Gama rounded the tip of southern Africa and continued to India (Figure 3.1), domination of the Adriatic or even

---

1. Fernand Braudel, *Civilization and Capitalism, 15th–18th Century*, Vol. 1: *The Structures of Everyday Life* (Berkeley: University of California Press, 1992).

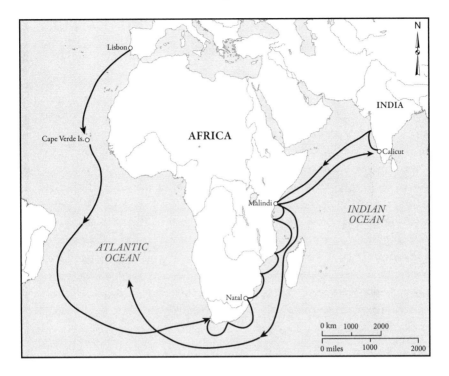

FIGURE 3.1 Vasco da Gama's route to India, 1497–1499.

the Mediterranean lost importance, and Atlantic cities like Lisbon, Seville, Antwerp, and Amsterdam could become centers of trade with the East.

Geography, then, made a difference. Water was the cheapest means of transportation. Within Europe, port cities, rivers, and canals facilitated trade between them and across nearby seas.[2] (Human ingenuity and enterprise also played a role, as engineers dug canals to ease boat travel within their countries.) Merchants, even without royal sponsorship, could proceed on their own to exploit these networks. Given England's interlacing of rivers and canals, for example, along the River Thames, only a few places in that country were more than ten miles from a waterway which ran to the sea. Port cities like Bordeaux, Nantes, Newcastle, Liverpool, London, Bremen, Hamburg, Amsterdam, and Rotterdam fashioned a quasi-independent existence. They did not need revenues from the state (and Hamburg did not formally join the united German Empire until 1899); they earned returns through private trade. By the seventeenth century a loop of trade extended from the Baltic Sea along the North Sea and Atlantic coast into the Mediterranean. Notwithstanding the slaughter of the Thirty Years' War

---

2. This interpenetration of waterways, facilitating trade, was lacking in both China and Russia.

(1618–1648; see Chapter 2), some parts of Europe, such as the Netherlands and England, grew richer and more prosperous.

Finance further strengthened the trading and international role of cities. Antwerp, the sixteenth-century financial center, was ultimately blockaded by Spain, but the money simply moved north, to where the Spanish Armada of ships could not reach, paving the way for the rise of Amsterdam. With huge coffers of riches and an abundant merchant marine and navy, the Dutch could dominate others' markets, determining price and cost in the process. They monopolized spices for sale in Europe and others had to meet Dutch demands if they wanted cinnamon, cloves, sugar, and later tea and china tableware in the manner of the rapidly enriching Dutch bourgeoisie.[3]

Some of these great cities were ensconced in powerful states that protected their commerce. The cities, of course, wanted to trade within their own states, and most monarchs were happy to facilitate that because it enriched their own coffers. And as Fernand Braudel tells us,[4] integrated national markets paved the way for success in foreign trade. Virtually no European state was large or resilient enough to provide for its needs wholly through internal trade.

Cities Versus Kings: Comparing France and England

Economists Douglass North and Robert Paul Thomas have written about the tension between commercial cities and political elites during these centuries. In some cases, such as Spain and France, the rulers gained the upper hand, amassing great power but stifling economic growth. Earlier in this chapter we discussed France as an absolute monarchy under Louis XIV. Louis was not unique. From the time of Charles VII (1403–1461), kings of France had weakened the French aristocracy more and more. French kings raised revenues for their expensive wars by taxing the peasants heavily, selling offices to aristocrats, and granting monopolies to guilds.

The centralization of power in France meant that French kings were relatively unconstrained domestically and could make war against other states at will. (And as noted in Chapter 2, absolute monarchs in Europe had many wars.) But in the long run absolute monarchy led to national decline. Trade was restricted within France, and no national market developed. The French populace lacked many incentives to innovate and become more productive. A country with a relatively large population, powerful army and navy, and massive amounts of fertile farmland, France entered a slow decline in the seventeenth and eighteenth centuries.

---

3. Simon Schama, *The Embarrassment of Riches: An Interpretation of Dutch Culture in the Golden Age* (New York: Vintage, 1997).

4. Fernand Braudel, *Civilization and Capitalism, 15th to 18th Century,* Vol. 3, *The Perspective of the World* (New York: Harper & Row, 1984).

The story in Spain, another absolute monarchy with fabulous wealth and a formidable army and navy, was similar.

The situation was quite different in England. It had kings and wealth producers as well, each needing to cooperate with the other but also wanting to exploit the other. In England, however, producers had a stronger hand, and they played it well. The Tudor monarchs who ruled from 1485 to 1603 tried to do as the French monarchs had and seize power from the nobility, but never quite succeeded; they always had to ask Parliament for permission to tax, and the House of Commons was dominated by merchants who were reluctant to finance endless wars. The Stuart monarchs who followed continued to try to centralize power; reaction from the House of Commons triggered a civil war (1642–1651) and later a peaceful revolution (1688) that brought a new king, William III, over from the Netherlands. England thereby became a constitutional monarchy in which the monarch was constrained by law, as made and interpreted by Parliament.

In practice, constitutional monarchy meant that English monarchs were much more limited than their French and Spanish counterparts in their ability to interfere with commerce. England developed a patent system that gave people incentives to innovate by letting them profit from their own inventions. The English also imported a number of practices from the Dutch. England was friendly to commerce and was a pioneer of joint stock companies, insurance, securities and commodities markets, deposit banking, and central banking to regulate money. In the seventeenth and eighteenth centuries, as France and Spain were declining, England and the Netherlands were growing.

Cities, Commerce, and Liberalism

This story about the competition between merchants and kings, or cities and states, is not just about money and power. It also is about ideas. Liberal political influences—valuing freedom of communities and individuals from state control—were particularly associated with free-flowing river-borne trade and estuaries that led to the sea. Merchants and financiers were more open to outside ideas and people. The more widely they traded, the more tolerant they had to be of unfamiliar ways of doing things. They knew that business would be better if those ideas and people were protected by law, not by the whim of a king. Thus, cities tended to be more tolerant than the countryside of religious dissenters. Those countries in which cities and merchants had more power—the Netherlands and England—also pioneered religious toleration.

Looking ahead, China in the twenty-first century exhibits the same tension between wealth producers and political rulers. Trading cities along China's coast such as Shanghai, Guangzhou (Canton), Shenzhen, and Hong Kong have grown rich and prominent through manufacturing and exporting. They are protected by the Chinese state but show, in varying degrees, a measure of independence from the ruling Chinese Communist Party. These commercial cities are likely to be the leaders of liberal reform in China. In contrast, landlocked political areas like Xinjiang, Jilin, and Mongolia lie along land-bound transport routes and, being more dependent on the Chinese state, are unlikely to stimulate domestic change in their neighborhoods.

Political loyalty and the very meaning of the state also differed in early modern Europe. France's Louis XIV is still famous for saying "L'état, c'est moi" ("I am the State"). He was the sovereign, just the sort of ruler Thomas Hobbes wanted. No one could truthfully say "I am the State" in a constitutional monarchy such as England. Sovereignty in England resided in "the King in Parliament." It was not completely clear what that meant, and that was the point: power was distributed and balanced in England.

Even Louis XIV, however, was not really all-powerful. In the Eastern despotisms such as traditional China, Egypt, or Turkey, loyalty was only to emperor or a single chief of state. There was no parliament to dilute that authority. But in the West, there had always been a legislative alternative (estates-general or parliament) to mitigate such powers. The refusal of the kings of France to call the estates-general for nearly 200 years was illegitimate in the eyes of many of their subjects. Then there was the Church. In Eastern monarchies religion did not exist apart from the state. But in the West kings had to put up with a measure of independence and stubbornness from priests and religious establishments. The struggle between pope and prince, for example, was at the center of Western development with the acceptance of "Two Swords," settled largely in favor of independent states and separate religious affiliations in 1648.

Wars and International Relations

To say that we see two distinct types of state in European history is not to say that the absolutists were always more warlike and expansionist and the constitutional ones were always more peaceful. The Netherlands and England (Great Britain after it united with Scotland in 1707) were far from pacifistic. Both were involved in the great wars of the period, including the Thirty Years' War (1618–1648), the Nine Years' War against France (1688–1697), and the wars of the Spanish Succession (1701–1714) and of the Austrian Succession (1740–1748). Indeed, the Dutch and English fought three wars against each other (1652–1654, 1665–1667, and 1672–1674). Those wars were fought in part because the English insisted on monopolizing all trade with their colonies; the Dutch, with their superior merchant fleet, wanted free trade. More generally, in England particular kings and aristocrats retained much power; cities and merchants were not to become truly predominant for centuries. And of course absolutist states such as Spain and France continued to threaten the security of the constitutional states, forcing the latter to defend themselves. Realism, with its emphasis on states, international anarchy, and shifts in the distribution of power, remains the best theory at explaining the international relations of this era. But the seeds of a new kind of state and international system were already germinating in the cities, banks, and merchant ships of Europe's powers.

Indeed, even the most powerful kings in Europe, the absolute monarchs such as Louis XIV, could never fully suppress alternative seats of power, and those eventually came back to haunt them. As absolute monarchies began to decline and bankrupt their societies in the late eighteenth century, the subjugated land-owning aristocrats were to push back hard, weakening kings and opening the door to those merchants we have been discussing and their demands for more liberty.

The Coming of the Age of Revolution

"War made the state, and the state made war," the sociologist Charles Tilly has written of early modern Europe.[5] He might have added that in the late eighteenth century war was to begin unmaking the absolutist states that were so fond of it. Absolute monarchs and their supporters believed that their system was superior, because it made more sense to concentrate sovereignty in the hands of a single ruler. The eighteenth century is even called the era of Enlightened Absolutism. The Enlightenment was a philosophical and cultural movement that had begun in the seventeenth century. Enlightenment thinkers such as René Descartes and Voltaire in France, Thomas Hobbes and John Locke in England, David Hume in Scotland, and Immanuel Kant in Prussia urged people to cast aside the old science and old authorities and to "have courage to think for yourself," as Kant put it in his 1784 essay, "What Is Enlightenment?" Enlightenment ideas eventually helped liberalize states and the international system. But early on, kings such as Frederick the Great of Prussia, Catherine the Great of Russia, Maria Theresa of Austria, and Louis XVI of France harnessed the new scientific learning produced by the Enlightenment and put it to their own purposes. They used new engineering techniques, for example, to make rivers more navigable and to produce faster ships.

But absolute monarchies were set up to fail in the long term. Adhering to a mercantilist theory that said the world had only so much wealth and hence each king was in a zero-sum game with all others, they were driven to severe competition and war. At the same time, absolute monarchies were afflicted with inefficiencies that made it more and more difficult for them to pay for these wars. As North and Thomas write, they overregulated their economies and did too little to secure

---

5. Charles Tilly, *Coercion, Capital, and European States, A.D. 990–1992* (New York: Wiley-Blackwell, 1992), 67–95.

property rights, sapping initiative and short-circuiting innovation. In Chapter 4 we shall see how the system crashed in the late eighteenth century with what historian R. R. Palmer calls the Age of the Democratic Revolution. In those years the liberalizing tendencies of cities and merchants fought back and began to dominate certain states—first and foremost, the newborn United States of America, an exemplary liberal republic. The tendency took a violent and tragic turn in France and then in Europe as a whole, as the forces stalemated and plunged the continent into decades of war. Although states were now on the scene that were more interested in trading than in conquest and were able to carve out areas of peace, the international system as a whole remained one of anarchy, fear, and war.

International Relations Theory: Emerging Liberalism

Our main argument in this book is that, when it comes to international relations, history makes theory. No single international relations (IR) theory is best across time and space. Instead, unfolding events and the emergence of new institutions affect which theory is most fruitful. We saw in Chapter 2 that the early modern period, which destroyed the medieval system of mingled and overlapping powers (and put in its place centralized discrete states ruled by powerful monarchs), was dominated by realist thought. Machiavelli, Hobbes, and other thinkers were right to stress the importance of coercive power, international anarchy, fear, and military prowess. The adequacy of realism persisted into the eighteenth century. Enlightenment thinkers such as David Hume and Jean-Jacques Rousseau emphasized the risks of international anarchy and the need for states to balance against one another's power. Rousseau was different from Machiavelli in that he did not celebrate war or warriors, but he ended up being quite pessimistic about the possibility of a transformation of the international system of his time. Breakout could only be brought about by a great war, he thought, which "would perhaps do more harm in a moment than it would guard against for ages."[6]

Even as realism continued as the dominant discourse in IR theory, however, the urban commercial culture whose dynamics we have analyzed began challenging this pessimism by producing a growing counterliterature. This was the liberal side of the Enlightenment, which said that if people can reform national society on more rational principles, they can do the same in international relations. Essential to their plans was a global extension of voluntary exchange of goods—the free trade that some cities and even states (the Dutch) already practiced.

---

6. Jean-Jacques Rousseau, "Abstract and Judgment of Saint-Pierre's Project for Perpetual Peace" (1756), in Stanley Hoffmann and David Fidler, eds., *Rousseau on War and Peace* (Oxford: Clarendon Press, 1991), 100.

Adam Smith, a brilliant Scottish writer, made powerful arguments against mercantilism that remain influential today. In his book *The Wealth of Nations* (1776), Smith argued that states should stop interfering in commerce, for when they favored some producers over others, they skewed production and trade in unnatural ways and made a national economy less efficient. Mainstream political leaders believed that empires made a nation strong, but Smith argued that they were a net drain on society. He posited an "invisible hand" uniting producer and consumer: what consumers did greatly influenced producers in terms of particular products, styles, and price. Producers, in turn, could create demand by offering new products. Without directly consulting one another, both producer and consumer benefited and *created wealth*. In other words, the mercantilists were wrong: the amount of wealth in the world was not fixed but could be expanded if only monarchs and the states they ran understood how the world really works.

These trading links, wrote Smith, could be extended among countries. Smith saw that countries would trade with one another on the basis of "advantage" in particular lines of goods. Those having advantage in cloth would trade that product for wine from another country. Englishman David Ricardo carried the analysis further with his theory of comparative advantage. One nation did not have to have an advantage across the board to trade with a partner. Indeed, trade was justified if each party had different national efficiencies for the production of the two goods at home: even if one state had an absolute advantage in both cloth and wine, it should specialize in the good in which its advantage was greater and trade for the good in which its advantage was lower.

The analyses of Smith and Ricardo made a powerful case against traditional imperialism and war and in favor of free trade and peace. Following such principles, Immanuel Kant concluded that the spirit of commerce might help do away with war. He also argued for the "categorical imperative" in ethical relationships. One should not do any action if the maxim (general rule) of the action, if universalized (applied to everyone), would be immoral or self-defeating. Is suicide ever justified? Not according to Kant, because if the maxim governing killing oneself (namely, that one can withdraw from all moral obligation) were universalized, moral obligation would disappear and death would be justified. For Kant, suicide was thus immoral. In the relation among nations, the same kind of reasoning held. An individual country's resolution to make war on another could not be universalized without placing the world in constant self-defeating warfare. Also, could one country be imperialist, seizing colonies? No, because all countries could not do that successfully. (A few might succeed, but most would fail). On the other hand, though Kant did not make this point directly, could one country become liberal or democratic? Yes, it could, because it would not prevent other countries doing the same (and might even encourage them). The "categorical imperative" was, in a sense, like the economist's insistence on avoidance of "congestion" in the principles followed among nations. One country might benefit from raising tariffs, but all (canceling each other) could not do so. Congestion occurred if everyone put on higher duties, for then no one would benefit.

It is important to note that many of these writers agreed with Rousseau that the international system that existed at the time was deeply flawed and presented states with perverse incentives. Kant in particular was a kind of contingent realist: he acknowledged that international anarchy was dangerous and that it could be necessary (if not moral) to fight a war against an aggressive enemy. The difference was that Kant believed that it was possible to transform the international system and make it less dangerous. Another Enlightenment thinker, Baron de Montesquieu (1689–1755), wrote that the problem was monarchy itself: monarchies were predisposed to fight. Republican government *within* states would pacify relations *among* states. As we shall see in Chapter 4, Kant, Thomas Paine, and others developed further their thinking about republicanism and international relations. Republics, unlike despotisms, were governed by law and would represent the true interests of the nation as a whole—meaning that they would prefer trading to raiding. Republics also would find it easier to trust one another.

But for any given country, the transition from despotism to republic could be difficult. As monarchical countries traded, and their merchants and cities became more powerful, they would feel pressure to liberalize and democratize. The monarchs and their supporters could resist, however, sometimes brutally. Unanticipated events such as economic depressions, coups d'état, or assassinations also sometimes threw countries and regions off of a liberalizing path. This was true in the eighteenth century and has been ever since. Yet other factors prevent some countries from following them. In a sense, today we are seeing a similar drama play out in real time in places such as China, Russia, and the Middle East. In Chapter 4 we shall see how these dynamics played out more than 200 years ago in a few republics, including the young United States and France, and in the international system as a whole. Wars certainly did not end, and commercial republics continued to fight them. But these states nonetheless began a slow transformation of the international system that is still unfolding today. Although many rulers manage to thrive as despots and successfully conquer and incorporate foreign territory, the national advantages of political and economic freedom are real, and the international system favors liberal democracy more than it did in the time of Rousseau and Kant.

Conclusion: The Present Equilibrium

There are two forms of modern state (and quite a number which have not yet modernized): one is democratic capitalist and the second might be called mercantilist (authoritarian) capitalist. Each has been successful over a range of its developmental curve: The United States combined emerging democracy with economic growth and capitalism; China since 1978 has grown rapidly without democracy and relied on mercantilist exclusion to support its industry. Both have depended on the world market to sell their wares, and their growth has relied on that market.

As we will discuss at more length in Chapter 9, it does not follow that China must follow a realist or non-cooperative course. Its economic dependence fosters at least a minimal cooperation with other nations, regardless of Beijing's domestic institutions. Liberalizing coalitions, as Etel Solingen has shown, can bring cooperation even where domestic politics remain authoritarian overall. But China is a country at odds with itself. Elements in the ruling Communist Party, particularly in the People's Liberation Army, see the world in realist terms. It is they who are pressing for outright territorial control of the East and South China seas. The powerful business and banking communities push in a different direction, toward peaceful commerce. They believe East Asians (and others) can grow rich together. It remains to be seen whether one side in this tug of war will prevail and, if so, which one.

More surely, liberalism brings cooperation when both sides are democratic, as the Nordic countries (Scandinavia) as well as the European Union show. The opposite combination of withdrawal from the world economy and authoritarianism has particularly malign impacts. Countries cut off from each other have generally bad (if any) relations. However, in practice such withdrawal will be difficult because most countries today do not have within their borders all the technology, resources, manpower, and markets they need to be self-sufficient. They are at least partially dependent on outsiders and economic flows from abroad. Even formerly introverted nations like Cambodia and Burma have accepted at least minimal economic cooperation with other nations. The one holdout today is North Korea, a self-impoverishing extortionist state.

In Chapter 4 the story continues of how British-style institutions, which empowered commercial actors and their ideas about liberty, spread into France and other countries. The story is not a simple one of the spread of peace, rationality, and commerce. It is rather one of clashing ideas, in which classes of people and the state contend for influence. In this refractory admixture, liberal trading states had to act in accordance with realism even as they worked slowly to undermine the realist international system.

FURTHER READING

Braudel, Fernand. *Civilization and Capitalism, 15th–18th Century,* Vol. 1: *The Structures of Everyday Life*. University of California Press, 1992.

Braudel, Fernand. *Civilization and Capitalism 15th–18th Century,* Vol. 3: *The Perspective of the World*. New York: Harper & Row, 1984.

Israel, Jonathan. *The Dutch Republic: Its Rise, Greatness, and Fall 1477–1806*. Oxford, UK: Clarendon Press, 1998.

Kant, Immanuel. *Perpetual Peace and Other Essays*. Translated by Ted Humphrey. Indianapolis: Hackett Press, 1983.

Levi, Anthony. *Louis XIV*. New York: Da Capo, 2004.

Rosecrance, Richard. *The Rise of the Trading State*. New York: Basic Books, 1986.

Solingen, Etel. *Regional Orders at Century's Dawn: Global and Domestic Influences on Grand Strategy*. Princeton, NJ: Princeton University Press, 1998.

Schama, Simon. *The Embarrassment of Riches: An Interpretation of Dutch Culture in the Golden Age*. New York: Vintage, 1997.

4 LIBERALIZATION, REVOLUTION, AND REACTION

The Seeds of a Liberal International Subsystem

In the preceding two chapters we showed that the early modern international system was dominated by centralized absolute monarchies. These states, exemplified by the France of Louis XIV, were mercantilist: they believed that the world's wealth existed in a fixed amount and hence that states would always be in a zero-sum competition for that wealth. Thus Europe's great powers frequently fought wars, sometimes catastrophic ones, over territory in Europe and in the areas they colonized in the Americas, Africa, and Asia. It is no surprise, then, that realist IR theory predominated. States acted in the ways that realism predicted: they were perpetually suspicious of one another and wary of becoming economically interdependent.

But we noted that the seeds of a new kind of state already were germinating—a state with different ideas and different domestic interests that eventually would construct a different kind international subsystem within the larger realist system. In the Netherlands (a republic, not a monarchy) and then in Great Britain (a constitutional monarchy), cities and the merchants and bankers who lived in them were allowed more political influence than their counterparts in Austria, Russia, Spain, Prussia, or France. The Dutch and British states were more liberal internally, allowing more political dissent and religious pluralism, and their foreign policies were geared to favor trade. The king of England and the Dutch stadtholder could not raise taxes at will, but had to ask a national legislature—the British Parliament and the Dutch States General, respectively—for permission.

In this chapter we shall see how the British liberal model outperformed the French realist model and how, as a result, many French—particularly the rising middle classes—wanted to make France more like Britain. They failed, as France's rulers pushed back and a revolution broke out in 1789 that spiraled downward into violence, authoritarianism under Napoleon, and decades of war, including with Britain itself. Realism, then, was far from finished. Rulers who benefited from the old mercantilism-conquest model and believed that it was best held on to power, and liberals and republicans who would have preferred commerce found that they had to play the realist game of balance of power.

To be sure, the Dutch and British had powerful navies and empires and were far from pacifist. They competed with other great powers, including each other, for territory, and so they were fully paid-up members of the realist international system of the time. Britain in particular was in many ways a traditional monarchical state that sought monopolies and was determined to sustain and expand its empire. Had Britain been a perfectly liberal trading state, after all, there would have been no need for Adam Smith to write his *Wealth of Nations* (see Chapter 3) to correct Britain's institutions and policies. In 1756 Britain's government declared that during wartime it would use its powerful navy to prevent neutral states from trading with its enemies—a blatant move to control commerce on the high seas. (International law was primitive at this point; a century and a half later, when Britain did the same thing during World War I, it was a clear violation of international law.) Within the country, political representation and competition were severely limited. The vast majority of British subjects could not vote for their representatives in the House of Commons, and many House members represented "rotten boroughs" in which few people lived anymore (such as Old Sarum, nearly a ghost town with a grand total of seven voters) and a wealthy patron controlled the outcome. Other House members represented "pocket boroughs," where a wealthy patron owned many houses and could populate them with docile tenants who would vote his way.

Despite all of this, Britain, unlike most European states at the time, did have mechanisms for reform. Its (unwritten) constitution also prevented the king from raising taxes without the permission of Parliament. This constitutional constraint on monarchical power gave tax increases more legitimacy with the king's subjects and the government more flexibility. In sum, Britain's institutions gave it more adaptiveness and equipped it well for international competition. Meanwhile, eighteenth-century France lacked even Britain's constraints on monarchical power. More than a dozen regional *parlements* existed, but no nation-wide legislative session (called the Estates General) had been convened since the reign of Louis XIII in 1614. France did engage in a great deal of trade and had a merchant class and commercial cities such as Nantes, Bordeaux, and Marseille. But the commercial classes were effectively shut out of power, taxed without representation. The clergy and aristocracy, meanwhile, enjoyed centuries-old rights and privileges that effectively exempted them from taxes. Over the decades, as the traders grew in number and wealth, their frustrations at the unfairness of their situation grew as well. In France the political hierarchy did not correspond to the economic base. Like a majority of European monarchies at the time—Austria, Russia, Prussia, Sweden, Denmark, Spain, and Portugal (but not Britain)—France had an "absolute monarchy". An absolute monarch was not accountable to his subjects; he ruled by divine right, making him accountable only to God. But other European absolute monarchs had adopted the scientific principles of the Enlightenment, including a fair tax code, a measure of religious toleration, and modern principles of financial accounting. French kings lagged behind the other absolute monarchs.

To see the difference between Britain and France during this period, consider parallel economic crises that occurred at roughly the same time: the Mississippi Bubble in France and the South Sea Bubble in Britain. The buildup to the crises came during the War of the Spanish Succession (1702–1713; see chapter 2), which left both governments heavily indebted. The Scottish economist John Law offered a plan for the French Crown to repay its debts. The plan involved the formation of a central bank that would swap French debt for equity (shares) in the Mississippi Company (later renamed the Company of the West and then the Company of the Indies), financed by printing more money. The Mississippi Company monopolized development in what is now the American Midwest and Deep South, then ruled by France. Investors in France, the Netherlands, and elsewhere bought shares in great quantity, driving share prices ever higher. The English central bank did essentially the same thing, swapping debt for equity in the South Sea Company, which had investments in South America. Share prices in that company skyrocketed as well.

As always happens, these speculative bubbles burst. In 1720, first in Paris and then in London, panicked investors pulled their money out and lost fortunes as share prices plummeted. What is important for our purposes is the different ways in which France and Britain reacted to the crisis. The French made John Law the scapegoat (not that he did not deserve it) but otherwise did little to reassure investors that they could put their money in France and its colonies in the future. France's central bank collapsed and its stock market shriveled, as French peasants and landlords kept their assets at home and foreign investors such as the Dutch put their money elsewhere. The British central bank, by contrast, continued allowing depositors to remove funds, making it what economic historian Charles Kindleberger calls the lender of last resort—a reliable financer for investors. Investors continued to finance British debt over the next decades. England's stock market flourished. This Anglo-French difference in response to a financial trauma was to have large consequences during the eighteenth century. As Kindleberger writes, France lagged behind Britain "in developing paper currency, banks, a central bank, a clearing house, insurance companies, and security markets (except for *rentes*) by about a century." The French were still debating the use of bank notes as late as 1867.[1]

With its superior financial machinery, and institutions that gave people incentives to invent more efficient ways of producing things, Britain also pioneered what became known as the Industrial Revolution, which greatly raised national wealth. Machine production of textiles began around 1780. Productivity rose when standard units flew along an assembly line, undermining the previous advantages France and India enjoyed in handcrafted production. Britain initially dominated trade in industrial products, for no one could compete with British machine-produced wares.

The Rivalry of France with Britain

Historian P. G. M. Dickson has written that Britain's financial advantage helped it defeat France in several eighteenth-century wars.[2] That brings us to the fact that Britain and France were serious rivals during this period, particularly over their colonies in North America. These two countries were, of course, far from being the only consequential European states in the world in this period. Other states continued to jostle and compete. And of course Europe itself was not the only important geopolitical space in the world. But most other major power centers in the world were weakening. The once-mighty Ottoman or Turkish Empire had suffered a series of defeats at the hands of Russia and entered its final slow but steady decline. The Mughal Empire in India was well into a deep decline of its own, to the point that the British East India Company (backed politically by the British government) became its official protector in 1771. In the Persian Empire, the Zandiyeh Dynasty was collapsing. Only the Chinese Empire, under the Qing dynasty, held its own. China's economy was the world's biggest, and when the British East India Company approached the Chinese emperor about a trade treaty, the emperor was little interested, saying that China already had all that it needed.

But the Anglo-French rivalry of the eighteenth century was to drive political change in North America and France, which changes ultimately propelled the emergence of the liberal international subsystem in the next century. In the

---

1. Charles Kindleberger, *World Economic Primacy: 1500–1990* (New York: Oxford University Press, 1996), 111.

2. Quoted in Eric S. Schubert, "Innovations, Debts, and Bubbles: International Integration of Financial Markets in Western Europe, 1688–1720," *Journal of Economic History* 48, no. 2 (June 1988): 305.

nineteenth century and indeed up to the present day, that liberal subsystem was to penetrate the rest of the world, including China, as we shall see in Chapter 6. Dynamics between Britain and France in the 1700s also illustrate the difficult path the liberal international subsystem has in spreading across countries—the reaction, pushback, and international war that liberalism provokes in the short run even as it works to pacify and enrich states in the long run.

The border between Britain's east coast colonies and New France, which stretched through what are now the U.S. Midwest and Deep South, was ambiguous (see Figure 4.1), and settlers from both countries were putting pressure on that border. In the 1750s French troops began building forts in the Ohio Valley, alarming British settlers who wanted to move west. The French and the Native Americans had a working relationship, and the British colonists feared that they would be hemmed in. Virginia militia led by a young officer named George Washington attacked Fort Duquesne in 1754.

In 1756 the Seven Years' War began, with France and Britain the main antagonists. One of the theaters of war was that Anglo-French border in North America, and that is why Americans call it the French and Indian War. But the Seven Years' War extended into Europe and even Asia. France threatened the homeland of Britain's King George II, the German territory of Hanover. Britain entered an alliance

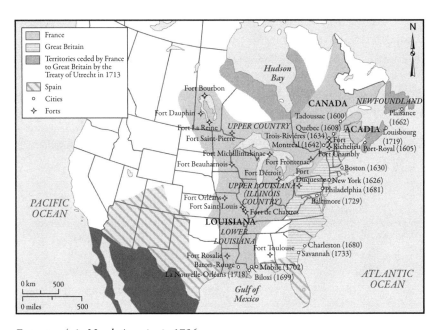

FIGURE 4.1 North America in 1756.

with Prussia to protect Hanover, and France formed an alliance with its longtime rival Austria. The Seven Years War eventually involved Spain, Sweden, Russia, several German states, and the Mughal Empire in South Asia. The war ended in 1763 with the Treaty of Paris, which ratified net gains for Britain and corresponding losses for France—the main change being that Britain took over all French possessions east of the Mississippi River (apart from some tiny islands off of the Newfoundland coast). The Treaty of Paris confirmed England's primacy economically and imperially within Europe. New markets opened. Commerce had been made "to prosper through war," as William Gladstone was to put the matter a century later.

It was not surprising, therefore, that a few years later, when the American colonists revolted against British rule, France helped the colonists (or Patriots, as they called themselves). The British government made a strategic error: it raised taxes on the American colonies to pay down the debt from the Seven Years' War. The problem was that the colonies all had charters with the king that said they only could be taxed by their own colonial assemblies, which they had elected. Believing in the English principle that they should not be taxed by a parliament in which they had no representation, the colonists revolted, and the rest is history. The final battle at Yorktown in 1781 could not have been won without French naval and military help. Admiral de Grasse cut off a seaward retreat for Cornwallis's forces and the same George Washington, with the aid of French soldiers under the Marquis de Lafayette, defeated them on land.

But France then confronted its traditional plight: victories could not be translated into new territory, nor into greater political support at home or in the rest of Europe. The war ended with another Treaty of Paris, this one in 1783. France got no new land, nor were there monies to pay for French exertions. Foreign Minister Vergennes's diplomacy was successful in humbling England in the New World, but there were few gains to win plaudits at home. The French believed that the young United States of America would be a staunch ally against Britain, but even that was not to happen, as the Americans were uninterested in allying with any European power.

The French Revolution was an earthquake in international politics, and it was extremely complicated. Motivated by a desire to have constitutional institutions like Britain and the young United States, France's liberals faced severe pushback from Crown and aristocracy. Many liberals became radicalized and violent, and relations with Austria and Prussia, and then with Britain, spiraled into war. In the United States Thomas Jefferson, John Adams, Alexander Hamilton, and other founders disagreed about relations with the French Republic, which eventually deteriorated into Napoleon's despotic rule. The lesson? It can be hard to move from absolutism to constitutional and liberal rule, and sometimes severe polarization and catastrophe result!

France in Crisis, Revolution, and War

Ironically, even though Great Britain lost most of its North American holdings in 1783, it still bested France over the course of the eighteenth century. This was the case even though France had three times Britain's population. Britain remained solvent, while France's model of centralized government, a heavily regulated economy, a mercantilist empire, a lack of financial innovation, and conquest and rivalry with other great powers had finally accumulated so many failures that the country entered a crisis. Bankruptcy loomed. An even greater irony, one of history's greatest, followed: in attempting to imitate Britain's institutions so as to dig their country out of its hole, France's reformers brought on not only a revolution but another long, destructive war with Britain.

In the 1770s France looked like it was going the way of the Netherlands, Britain, and the young United States—toward liberalism, or the dispersal of political power and an openness to reform. Thomas Jefferson wrote to James Monroe in 1788, "I think it probable [France] will within two or three years be in enjoiment of a tolerably free constitution, and that without it's having cost them a drop of blood." Jefferson was not irrational to think that France would become like the United States. French thinkers, some of whom were his friends, were among the most prominent in the so-called Enlightenment, the vast outpouring of writing and opinion in literature, politics, philosophy, and economics in the seventeenth and eighteenth centuries, which aimed to run society on rational principles. Denis Diderot, the Marquis de Condorcet, the Physiocrats (Turgot, Quesnay, and others), and above all Jean-Jacques Rousseau saw supposedly free Frenchmen wasting away in chains. Society had to break these shackles for them to become free. How could this be done? France was to have its radicals, Babeuf and the "sans-culottes" (the lower orders who wore trousers rather than knickers), who wanted to seize wealth and redistribute it to the poor. But Condorcet reasoned that change would come voluntarily because it was in everyone's interest. He and other French Enlightenment thinkers agreed with the Scottish economist Adam Smith that, left without government coercion, rational self-interested people would enter voluntary exchange under the guidance of an "invisible hand." Buyer and seller need not consult each other, and yet the actions of each would serve the interest of the other.

But in fact no invisible hand united the nobility with the rest of society in France, and king and nobility were to resist the change that Enlightenment philosophers thought they should embrace. After 1783 a succession of financial officials made clear to King Louis XVI that he had to raise taxes on the clergy and aristocracy—the so-called First and Second Estates. In 1789 a desperate Louis convened the Estates General, the national assembly, for the first time in nearly two centuries to enact the new taxes. (Note that Britain, by contrast, had a Parliament that met regularly.) It was a calculated risk; the last meeting, in 1614, had made no financial changes. Influenced by the philosophical writings of Montesquieu and Rousseau, many delegates called for greater equality. The heavily taxed Third Estate—the commoners, consisting of both peasants and the commercial middle class or bourgeoisie—believed it deserved fairer treatment. But neither the First nor the Second Estate would give up its tax-free status. This blockage meant that a much more thoroughgoing transformation was required, one that would not be accepted voluntarily by all parties.

The Third Estate, inspired in part by the successful American colonists a few years earlier, inaugurated a revolution to force its will on clergy and nobility. Purporting to act on behalf of France as a whole—*la Nation*—the Third Estate abolished feudalism and established universal legal equality on the night of August 4, 1789. The national assembly also seized church lands, using this wealth to back a revolutionary currency (the *assignat*). Taxes were apportioned to all classes; the old privileges of the other estates disappeared. Legal equality also meant that all members of society could be conscripted to serve in the army. Many nobles left to find havens abroad. But the size of the French army more than doubled from 200,000 to 400,000.

Expropriation of church lands and the onset of taxes led many nobles and clergy to flee France, going to the nearby Austrian Netherlands (today's Belgium). The flight of the émigrés in turn became an international issue, and Frenchmen demanded the nobles either return or be expelled by the Austrian authorities. The rulers of Austria and Prussia, already concerned about revolution spreading to their realms, responded by declaring that they were considering invading France to overturn the revolution. This so-called Declaration of Pillnitz may have been a bluff, but it was precisely what one prominent faction of revolutionaries, the Girondins, had been expecting. Comprising lawyers and writers (including Thomas Paine, famous as publicist of the American Revolution) and representing the middle class, the Girondins argued that Austria and Prussia saw revolutionary France as a dire threat and were surely going to attack. France would be in a better position, they continued, if it attacked them. The Assembly agreed and prevailed upon the king, Louis XVI, to declare war.

The French revolutionaries believed that their armies, motivated by "liberty, equality, and fraternity," would fight harder than apostles of the old regime. This ultimately proved true, but France lost the opening battles. At the Battle of Valmy on September 20, 1792, the tide turned. The following day the Assembly abolished the monarchy and declared France a republic. Some Girondins joined with an even more radical faction, the Montagnards (Mountain), in declaring the dethroned Louis an enemy of the state who was plotting with other European monarchs to destroy the revolution. In January 1793 the government executed Louis and his wife, Queen Marie Antoinette. Monarchists throughout Europe, including England, were horrified. Concerned that Britain was going to join the war on the side of Austria and Prussia, in February 1793 France declared war on that country as well. As the British politician Edmund Burke was later to put it, France had become an "armed doctrine." Ironically, France's attempt to reform itself to become more like Britain ended up in violent revolution and war against Britain itself.

Within months the Montagnards, purporting to represent the poor (the *sans-culottes*), had destroyed the Girondins, expropriated the lands of the nobility, and launched the Reign of Terror. The Terror was first controlled by the Committee on Public Safety, headed by Maximilien Robespierre, but eventually spun out of his control as executions were done without restraint. By the Terror's end in July 1794, 30,000 had been killed, at least 10,000 by guillotine in Paris alone (one of the last being Robespierre himself). Meanwhile, with nobles swept away from the officer corps and military careers opened to talent regardless of social rank, such parvenus as the young Napoleon Bonaparte were able to make names for them-selves. At Lille, the Vosges, Mainz, and Jemappes, France's revolutionary armies enforced their will on continental opponents.

Napoleon, More War, and Economic Blockades

With matters spinning out of control within France, in 1795 a group of five, called the Directory, took over France's government. The Directory halted the revolu-tion at home but carried on the war abroad. As Bonaparte rose through the ranks, French military efficiency rose with him, culminating later in victories in Italy and in Egypt (1798). In 1799 Napoleon seized power in a coup d'état, naming himself First Consul. In 1804 he crowned himself "Emperor of the French." In making himself a monarch, Bonaparte disillusioned liberals and republicans all over Europe and the Americas. The German composer Ludwig van Beethoven, devoted to the principles of the revolution, had dedicated his path-breaking Third Symphony to Napoleon; upon hearing of the coronation, Beethoven ripped up the dedication page and excoriated him as just another "tyrant."

France under Napoleon was to carry on with its policy of war and conquest, subjugating most of central Europe, Italy, and Spain, and allying for a time with Austria, Prussia, and Russia (see Figure 4.2). As it was to do against Nazi Ger-many more than a century later, Britain stood alone against Napoleonic France for much of this time. The Anglo-French rivalry continued, and Britain contin-ued its tradition of using its navy, the world's biggest, to monopolize trade. In May 1806 the government blockaded ports all along the North Sea and Baltic coasts. Napoleon answered in November with the Berlin Decree, setting up his Continental System, prohibiting all economic exchange and even commu-nication between Europe and Great Britain. Britain retaliated a year later by banning all trade by neutral countries (including the United States) and the French Empire.

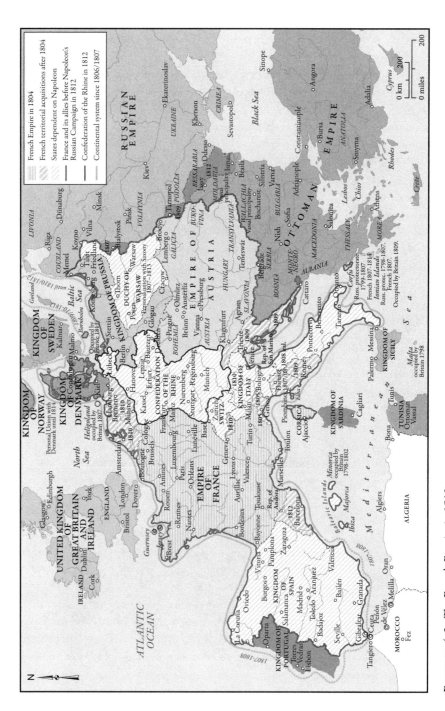

FIGURE 4.2 The French Empire in 1812.

These British Orders in Council clearly were in line with realist and mercantilist behavior. But it is important to note that within Britain itself, liberal and commercial interests continued to have a legal voice in Parliament and the press, and they spoke out against the Orders. They argued that the United States merchant marine, already large and prospering, had been subverting Napoleon's Continental System by smuggling British goods into Europe. "Up to the very date of your Orders in Council . . . every advantage flowed into your lap," the liberal Lord Erskine told Parliament in March 1808. "America . . . continued to smuggle your goods into France, for her own interest, and France contrived to buy them for hers. The people huzzaed their emperor in the Tuilleries [Palace] every day, but they broke his laws every night." The same month the merchants and manufacturers of London and Liverpool petitioned for a rescission of the Orders, which were producing "fatal consequences to the interest not only of the petitioners, but of the commerce and manufactures of the empire at large; and [are] likely to interrupt our peace with the United States of America, our intercourse with which, at all times valuable, is infinitely more so since we are excluded from the continent of Europe."[3]

The U.S. government showed that it could play the retaliatory game as well, and it placed a series of embargoes on trade with Britain. Finally, as English factory workers were thrown out of work by the thousands, Britain's government revoked the Orders in Council in 1812. But it was too late: fed up with disrespect for its merchant marine on the high seas, Congress declared war on Britain before word could reach Washington of the British policy change. Once again two liberal trading nations were at war.

Democratic Revolutions and the International System

For all the mercantilism and war of this period, it is no wonder that realists today continue to insist that liberalism and democracy did not and do not change international politics in any significant way. Realists acknowledge that liberals *believe* their countries to be distinctive—more peaceful, rational, and interdependent— but maintain that liberals are deceiving themselves. And the American and French revolutions did not banish war or mercantilism from the world. Indeed, in the short term they triggered more of these things.

To see why, we need to consult leading Enlightenment thinkers of the time. In *The Rights of Man*, his robust defense of the early French Revolution (1791), Thomas Paine explains the problem in this way:

---

3. Quoted in Tom Holmberg, "The Acts, Orders in Council, &c., of Great Britain [on Trade], 1793–1812," The Napoleon Series, http://www.napoleon-series.org/research/government/british/decrees/c_britdecrees1.html, accessed on September 11, 2015.

All the European governments (France now excepted) are constructed not on the principle of universal civilisation [republican government], but on the reverse of it. So far as those governments relate to each other, they are in the same condition as we conceive of savage uncivilised life; they put themselves beyond the law as well of GOD as of man, and are, with respect to principle and reciprocal conduct, like so many individuals in a state of nature.[4]

In other words, for Paine and other republicans, a republic could not avoid war and conquest as long as it had despotic neighbors—neighbors that were aggressive precisely because they were afraid of its institutions. A peace-loving state in a dangerous world must be ready for war. Paine saw no contradiction in his own advocacy of war against European monarchies; he even advised Napoleon on invading Britain (which Napoleon never did).

Immanuel Kant, the Prussian philosopher, agreed with Paine on the problem of republics facing hostile monarchies. In his 1795 essay "Toward Perpetual Peace," Kant argued that the state of nature among countries is brutal, just as Hobbes the realist had written more than a century earlier. Republics were different, and will form a league of peace. But between that league and outside powers, the Hobbesian state of nature continued, where states have the "right ... to make war upon one another (for example, in order to bring about a condition close to that governed by right)"—by which he meant "becoming more republican." When a republic defeated an authoritarian state in war, the defeated state may "be made to accept a new constitution that is unlikely to encourage their warlike inclinations."[5] In other words, for Kant, republics could not only fight non-republics but could coerce them into becoming republics. These ideas of Paine and Kant were commonly held and affected the way France's revolutionary leaders acted toward their neighbors.

A second problem for European liberals is that they faced serious resistance and reaction from absolute monarchists and advocates of the old regime. In the 1790s most European countries were highly polarized by events in France: liberals wanted to bring the revolution to their country, while conservatives were alarmed and wanted to overturn it in France. Both left and right, then, became quite radical, and it was difficult to find middle ground for compromise. Liberals and republicans were pulled into more violence against monarchists, and monarchists were pulled into more violence against republicans.

These problems of international and domestic polarization combined to make for decades of war and conquest. The French in particular saw that if they were going

---

4. Thomas Paine, *Rights of Man*, chapter 5.

5. Immanuel Kant, *The Metaphysics of Morals*, trans. Hans Reiss (New York: Cambridge University Press, 1970), 170.

to have republican allies, they had to make them by force of arms. This, of course, only aggravated the problem. The further east they moved, attacking absolute monarchies, the greater the opposition. Napoleon saw himself as a moderate who domesticated the revolution, but the same polarization continued in most of Europe.

Thomas Jefferson's prediction about France becoming a peaceful republic, then, was wrong. Instead, France became an object lesson in the perils of waiting too long for liberal reform. Still, notwithstanding all of the wars, the Age of the Democratic Revolution did have profound long-term effects on moving the international system away from realism and toward liberalism.

First, ideas about equality were shown to be consequential, and their appeal spread across countries. The rebellious American colonists demanded either representation in the British Parliament or, failing that, independence from British rule. In historic terms, the Patriots' victory meant that no imperialist could ultimately expect to succeed in permanently holding another country or colony.[6] As populations were urbanized and mobilized politically, the invaded colony would likely resist imperial rule, however subtly or brazenly the aggressor might treat it.

The French Revolution added another shift. Feudalism, which divided society divided into three estates (clergy, nobility, and commoners—the last estate covering everyone from business owners to peasants), each with its own rights and privileges, had lost its legitimacy. It gave no popular voice to Frenchmen as a whole. Repressive rule in Europe eventually was going to have to be lifted. Events in France in 1789 and after inspired people in Europe and the Americas. Many rose up in revolt against their rulers, starting in the French colony of Haiti in 1791.

Even the Napoleonic Empire, coercive as it was, pressed liberal ideas outward onto other societies. The French imperialists imposed their vision by force, but it was in some ways a liberal vision; the German philosopher Hegel called Napoleon "the world-spirit on horseback." Wherever they conquered, France's armies and bureaucracy overturned the old institutions of traditional monarchy and aristocracy and brought equality before the law and meritocracy within government. Partly in response to the ideas carried by the French into Spain and Portugal, the 1810s and 1820s saw waves of liberal revolution and independence all over Spanish and Portuguese colonies in Latin America and the inauguration of republics throughout the region. Over the ensuing decades these republics were to compile mixed records of liberalism, all lapsing into periods of authoritarianism over the next two centuries and all acting in an essentially realist manner for much of their history. In the very long term, however, most were to contribute to a Western Hemisphere with remarkably little international war and increasing amounts of trade and investment.

---

6. See Carl Kaysen, "Is War Obsolete? A Review Essay," *International Security* 14, no. 4 (Spring 1990): 42–64.

IR Theory in the Age of Revolution

We already have noted that this period, in which republican revolutions were happening, saw a flowering of non-realist theorizing. Enlightenment thinkers, seeing their plans for reordering society coming to fruition, were rejecting the claims of realism, particularly those about permanent competition among sovereign states for territory that could only be alleviated by a balance of power among states. Some of this theorizing appears hopelessly naïve today, such as Paine's belief that republics were inherently pacifistic. Jeremy Bentham, the English utilitarian philosopher, published a *Plan for a Universal and Perpetual Peace* in 1789. The *Plan* called for the establishment of an international court to settle disputes among nations. The court's authority would rest on the power of public opinion. Bentham believed that under such a system Britain and France would stop fighting over colonies, shrink their militaries, and forgo international alliances. Of course, a realist could easily retort that it was not clear why the British and French (and Austrian and Prussian and other) governments would assent to such a scheme.

More realistic, and more lasting, were the contributions of Kant. His essays in the 1780s and 1790s recognized that all of the schemes for eternal peace foundered on this problem: How to get the rulers of Europe to agree to permanent peace? Kant argued that in fact they would not, and that only republics—ruled by law and tending toward commerce over conquest—would practice peace among themselves. He argued also that history was moving in the direction of republican government. For one thing, war was getting more and more destructive and costly, bankrupting countries. In country after country, people would demand (as they had done in France in 1789) that they have more of a say in their government. Republics would multiply, in other words, not because people were becoming more reasonable or moral, but because despotic government was becoming so expensive. In recent years political scientist Michael Doyle has argued that Kant was essentially correct. The number of republics (or liberal democracies) has expanded, unsteadily but unmistakably, since the 1790s, and those liberal democracies tend to trade more with one another and to enter and remain in international organizations. While they continue to fight wars, they never fight them against one another.

This is what scholars today call the Democratic Peace or Liberal Peace. Realism, which says that domestic systems of government do not affect international relations in any systematic way, cannot account for the absence of war among liberal democracies. Kant predicted it at a time when the world had hardly any such states. Liberal countries still care about and exploit power and feel insecure when they have too little of it. But their patterns of behavior and interaction are distinctive. They compete in the economic and cultural realms. They are not interested in conquering more territory, because they are better off trading with and investing in other countries. Thus, in the twenty-first century it pays for observers to keep track of not just which countries have the most guns, ships, and troops, but which countries are democratic, which are not, and which appear poised to change from one form of government to the other.

Ever since the 1780s states have existed on a continuum of cooperation and conflict. At one end are conflictual and isolated states that see themselves as being in fatal competition with all other states. The extreme case today is North Korea; another state that has been at this end of the spectrum for several decades is Iran. Such states have sought to avoid dependence on the resources of the outside world. Extremely autocratic, they find few bases of cooperation with other nations. As a country liberalizes internally, however, its foreign policy tends to do so as well, producing a greater accommodation with other nations. South Korea democratized in the late 1980s, abandoned its isolation, and has had much better relations with its neighbors Japan and China. As the number of democracies comes to exceed the current number of about ninety states, cooperation is likely to increase in the system as a whole. On the other hand, sometimes countries backslide from democracy, as Germany did in 1933 and Russia has since the late 1990s. Backsliding states act more in conformity with realism.

At the far extreme of authoritarianism—in which an all-intrusive government controls every element of society, including thought—cooperation among nations declines to the vanishing point, as it did with countries like Hitler's Germany. Stalin's Russia modified its isolation by briefly siding with Europe and the West against Hitler, but that cooperation disappeared shortly after Nazi Germany did. In general, extreme authoritarians have few willing allies, only coerced servitors. In between—the middle of the continuum—cooperation can go either way, and economics will be particularly important to diminish the use of force if contending parties have solid trading relationships and markets creating interdependence with one another.

Postlude: After Napoleon, Liberal-Conservative Tension

Looked at one way, the Age of the Democratic Revolution failed. It brought decades of war, the authoritarian Napoleonic regime, and, in 1815, a restoration of the old order in Europe. Realists felt vindicated, and realists ever since have looked upon Europe after 1815 as a model of rational international politics. As we discuss at the end of this chapter, however, that view is simplistic.

Here is how it happened. In 1814 an allied coalition of Britain, Prussia, Austria, Russia, and other states combined to defeat Napoleon's armies and exile the general to the Mediterranean island of Elba. Leaders of the victorious allies gathered for a long conference in Vienna to decide how to restore order throughout war-torn Europe. During this Congress of Vienna, Bonaparte escaped from Elba, returned to France, and gathered his army for one last attempt. Without doubt one of history's great generals, Bonaparte nearly succeeded. But in June 1815 the allies, led by Britain's Wellington and Prussia's Blücher, vanquished his armies at Waterloo in Belgium and this time exiled Napoleon to St. Helena, in the South Atlantic, where he died in 1821.

Relieved at this final victory, the Congress of Vienna resumed and the French nobility rushed back to France from exile, hoping to resume their titles and lands. In one sense, the Congress re-established the old regime—"legitimate" or hereditary monarchies—in France and all of the countries that their allies had pried from the French Empire.[7] But the institutions were not quite as they had been before. With Britain taking the lead in reconstructing France's regime, the new king, Louis XVIII, ruled as a British-style constitutional monarch. Equality before the law remained in place; there was no return to the old system of three unequal estates. France's nobles did not get back all their lands. Their demands would be judged by an elected legislature (on restricted suffrage). Their Departments were ruled from Paris, as they had been under Napoleon. The same was true of many of the liberated lands: hereditary monarchy returned, but with somewhat more liberal institutions.

As to the international system, the Congress set up what may be a historically unique system called the Concert of Europe. Guided by Prince Metternich, the foreign minister of Austria, the great powers formed a Quadruple Alliance and agreed that they must coordinate and consult frequently about changes in the balance of power among them. Metternich's reasoning was realist: it was shifts in the balance of power, such as increases in French power in the 1790s, that caused big wars and jeopardized international order. Thus, if one of the major states gained or lost territory, leaders from all of them would meet periodically and agree on measures to restore the balance by reassigning territory. Recognizing that France retained the greatest military potential on land, the powers allowed it to join the Concert in 1818. For the first time since 1713 (the Peace of Utrecht), the great powers were in accord.

The Concert of Europe often is regarded as realism's golden age, when wise statesmen in a multipolar international system understood the principles of the balance of power and cooperated to ensure peace. No great power fought any other directly until the Crimean War of 1853–1856, and there was no Europe-wide war until 1914—a century after Napoleon left the scene. The Concert of Europe did not abolish international anarchy and the problems it brings; rather, savvy leaders managed those problems. This is the claim of Henry Kissinger, a realist scholar and statesman who was U.S. secretary of state under presidents Nixon and Ford. There is much to this claim, and Nixon and Kissinger self-consciously re-enacted this kind of realism during the Cold War in the 1970s, when they brought America into a period of détente (relaxation) with the Soviet Union.

---

7. See Arno Mayer, *The Persistence of the Old Regime: Europe to the Great War* (New York: Pantheon, 1981).

But in fact it was not only fear of imbalances of power that held together the Concert. It also was mutual fear of liberalism—the ascendancy of the middle classes and their demands for institutions friendly to commerce and liberty. Metternich called this the spread of British institutions to the Continent of Europe, and he did not like it. He, Tsar Alexander I of Russia, and other elites knew that the end of Napoleon did not mean the end of the ideas that brought on the Age of the Democratic Revolution or of the classes of people who hated the old monarchies and nobility of Europe. The spirit of 1789 remained, embodied in underground networks, Masonic lodges, and universities, coiled and ready to spring forth in rebellion and revolution at any time in nearly any place. Metternich himself employed secret police throughout the Austrian Empire and monitored closely what republicans and constitutionalists were doing. The historian Frederick Artz has written that "the mere introduction of democratic or nationalist ideas anywhere in Europe could easily stir up disruptive movements. . . . Hence, revolutionary ideas in speeches, books, or newspapers frightened Metternich, even if they appeared as far away as Spain, Sweden, or Sicily."[8]

Many of the periodic meetings of the great powers were provoked by liberal uprisings in various places in Europe. The impressive cooperation that the powers displayed was often intended to suppress these uprisings. For example, in 1820 a wave of rebellion started in Spain and spread to Portugal, Naples and Piedmont (Italy was not yet a united country), and Greece, forcing absolute monarchs to assent to a liberal constitution. (News of the Spanish rebellion reached Latin America, triggering a similar wave in Colombia, Venezuela, Argentina, Uruguay, Peru, and Mexico.) In January 1821 the rulers of Austria, Prussia, and Russia agreed that Austrian troops would put down the rebellions in Italy. The following year absolutists pushed back in Spain, and Russia called on the other great powers to join in invading Spain to overturn the revolution there. At the same time, alarmed at the liberal uprisings in their neighbors, voters gave the absolutist party an electoral victory in France. In April 1823 France sent 100,000 troops over the Pyrenees into Spain to restore the absolute monarchy there. Similar uprisings and coordinated suppressions took place in the early 1830s and in 1849.

It is significant that the one great power that consistently stood apart from these coordinated great power suppressions of liberalism was Great Britain, still a constitutional monarchy. Indeed, the British sometimes quietly intervened to help liberals in smaller states. Britain did so because, being an increasingly liberal trading state itself, it was encouraged rather than threatened by the spread of its own values. In 1830 France went through another revolution when liberals there had had enough of the absolutist aggrandizement of King Charles X and his group of aristocrats.

8. John M. Owen, *The Clash of Ideas in World Politics: Transnational Networks, States, and Regime Change 1510-2010* (Princeton, NJ: Princeton University Press, 2010), 146.

France became a constitutional monarchy under Louis-Philippe and joined England as a kind of Western liberal league. In 1832 Britain itself became more democratic with the Great Reform Act, which doubled the number of people who could vote. A divide emerged between those two Western powers and the Eastern absolute monarchies of Austria, Prussia, and Russia. In the West, liberal-commercial forces continued to strengthen. In 1846 Britain abolished its Corn Laws, opening itself to imports of grain and its imperial holdings to trade with other countries. In Eastern Europe, meanwhile, absolutist forces continued to strengthen, determined more than ever to keep liberalism from spreading into Germany and Italy.

Although ties between Western Europe and the United States were relatively weak, and indeed America and Britain were to come close to war a few more times in the nineteenth century, a rudimentary Western cooperation emerged as well. Following France's 1823 invasion of Spain to suppress liberal revolution, U.S. President James Monroe issued his famous Doctrine warning Europe to keep its hands off of Latin America and the Caribbean. The U.S. Navy lacked the ability to enforce the Monroe Doctrine, so the British Royal Navy did, thereby safeguarding young Latin American republics from monarchical rollback. The United States itself, meanwhile, spread westward in fits and starts—granted, often in a most illiberal way—bringing its institutions and commercial culture with it as it spread over North America.

All the while, in the United States and Western Europe, technological progress in production continued, bringing efficiency gains and economic growth. Great Britain began to champion free trade, leading to a virtuous cycle of economic growth, technological progress, and a reinforcement of the institutions that brought those things about. Figure 4.3 depicts the difference in growth rates across the world's regions from 1830 to 1890. Notice that the steepest rise is that of Britain.

In the Realm of Theory

Even as the major powers of Europe continued to diverge in their internal makeup and their external behavior and to exist in an uneasy tension, theorists of international relations came in two corresponding types. Realist thought was prominent in German lands. *On War (Vom Kriege)*, the masterpiece from Prussian military theorist Carl von Clausewitz, was published in 1833. In it Clausewitz famously states that "war is a continuation of politics by other means." His fellow Prussian Leopold von Ranke, often called the father of the modern discipline of history, wrote about the balance of power in glowing terms, as a kind of mystical phenomenon in which God achieves his purposes in history. The Prussian economist Friedrich List argued that free trade, pushed by liberal economists ever since Adam Smith (see Chapter 4), was actually a ploy that would produce an international hierarchy, with more advanced nations (namely Britain) on top. List recast

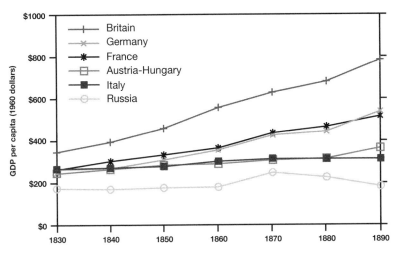

FIGURE 4.3 Increases in economic growth in Europe, 1830–1890.
Source: After Bairoch, 1976.

mercantilism in nationalistic terms, resulting in what is called neo-mercantilism. These and other German writers held up the centralized sovereign state as the primary actor in world politics, acting according to a logic of its own as outlined centuries earlier by Machiavelli (see Chapter 2).

At the same time, Western societies were producing more liberal writing on world politics. Following the defeat of Napoleon, liberal businessmen in Britain and France founded the Peace Movement. Arguing that war destroyed commerce and was becoming increasingly obsolete as productive classes of people became more predominant, these businessmen allied with Quakers, who had a religious objection to war. In Britain and the United States, Quaker Peace Societies took up Jeremy Bentham's project of international dialogue and law. Richard Cobden and John Bright (the latter himself a Quaker) helped bring together the Peace and Free Trade movements. Their writings and speeches from the middle of the nineteenth century inveigh against the balance of power and British intervention in the power struggles of Europe.

Conclusion: Birth Pangs of International Liberal Order

This chapter has shown that although centralized (absolutist) states continued to be powerful in the eighteenth and nineteenth centuries and realism remained the best theory of international relations, the liberal international subsystem continued to emerge in the laboratory of Great Britain. Liberal ideas about government and the national interest affected that country and spread to its neighbors and its colonies. A constitutional monarchy, Britain became the world's leading power because of its institutions, which allowed the commercial classes a say over taxes, all persons were equal under the law. In Britain's chief rival, absolutist France, by contrast, the nobility and clergy had special rights and privileges and the king could raise taxes at will. Absolutists at the time believed that France's system was superior, but over the course of the eighteenth century France nearly bankrupted itself with its system of mercantilism and war. Britain was able to succeed, only running into trouble, ironically, when it violated its own principles and tried to tax its North American colonists without allowing them representation. The young United States that came out of that struggle had institutions much like those of its mother country, only, as a federal republic, it was still more decentralized.

In France and other societies on the Continent of Europe, pressure from the urban commercial classes continued to build, but rulers continued to suppress them, causing the explosive revolutions of the 1780s and 1790s. The French Revolution spiraled into horrific violence, war, and the authoritarianism and imperialism of Napoleon. France entered the nineteenth century as a deformed and aggressive would-be liberal state, and its regime was ultimately vanquished by a coalition of Britain and Europe's absolutist states. The victorious allies restored the old monarchies in France and the lands the French armies had conquered.

If constitutional states such as the Netherlands and England were set up to prefer trading to conquest, why did they fight wars and build empires? First, as Adam Smith knew, they still had domestic actors strongly interested in state protection so they could enjoy trading monopolies. Second, as Immanuel Kant knew, they existed alongside powerful absolutist states and had to defend themselves and their interests. As we will see in later chapters, it took more big wars and the emergence of the United States as liberal hegemon in the twentieth century to foster conditions under which constitutional states could consistently follow a liberal foreign policy.

Realism tells the superficial story well enough. All of the great powers, including constitutional Britain, formed and broke alliances, tried to expand their empires, and waged war. Yet deeper forces were at work that were slowly undermining realist logic and statecraft. First, it already was becoming evident that the old absolutist, mercantilist model of conquering territory and monopolizing its resources was an inferior mode of statecraft. Military acquisition of land was fraught with uncertainty and risk. Sweden grew larger but could not keep her conquests when challenged by Russia as well as German states. France added one third of its size as a result of Napoleon's victories, but had to give most of it back in 1815. Russia's 3 million square miles were tripled as she moved territorially through Siberia toward the Pacific Ocean. But these were vast undeveloped and Arctic settlements that added little to Russia's power.

As we have discussed, liberal states—Britain and the Netherlands, and then later the United States—engaged in conquest as well. The British more than doubled the size of their empire, added Canada and India during this period. They did so in part because, in the eighteenth and nineteenth centuries, conquest outside of Europe was much easier than within it. Overseas territories lacked the technology and political mobilization to resist. They needed investment, and indirect rule (through local nabobs) was applied to them, thereby limiting direct imperial involvement. During the Napoleonic Wars, Britain also tried to control all foreign trade (as did France). This, too, it did in part because it was easy: its Royal Navy was the world's mightiest.

But commercial actors and their intellectual allies continued to argue against this system of territorial conquest, empire, and monopoly. Followers of Adam Smith tirelessly pointed out that Britain impoverished itself with these policies. In the 1840s, with the abolition of the Corn Laws, these arguments finally won the day. The British Navy and banking system began to underwrite a global trading system, and the maintenance of a territorial empire became more difficult to defend. As we shall see in Chapter 6, by the late nineteenth century Europe had conquered 85 percent of the world. Territory was no longer easy to take. The old imperial model at that point could only suggest that each European state try to take colonies from the others or try to conquer one another's home territory.

Yet those old ideas persisted in Germany, Austria-Hungary, and Russia, as monarchs and nobles clung to their privileges and allowed only very limited institutional reform. The story ended badly, with the twentieth century's two catastrophic world wars. It is to that story that we now turn in the next two chapters.

FURTHER READING

Broers, Michael. *Europe After Napoleon.* Manchester, UK: Manchester University Press, 1996.

Broers, Michael. *Europe Under Napoleon.* London: Tauris, 2014.

Bukovansky, Mlada. *Legitimacy and Power Politics: The American and French Revolutions in International Political Culture.* Princeton, NJ: Princeton University Press, 2010.

Dickson, P. G. M. *The Financial Revolution in England.* London: Macmillan, 1967.

Doyle, Michael W. *Ways of War and Peace: Realism, Liberalism, Socialism.* New York: Norton, 1997.

Hinsley, F. H. *Power and the Pursuit of Peace.* New York: Cambridge University Press, 1967.

Howard, Michael. *War and the Liberal Conscience.* New Brunswick, NJ: Rutgers University Press, 1978.

Kindleberger, Charles. *World Economic Primacy 1500–1990.* New York: Oxford University Press, 1996.

Kissinger, Henry. *A World Restored: Metternich, Castlereagh, and the Problems of Peace.* New York: Houghton-Mifflin, 1957.

Owen, John M., IV. *Liberal Peace, Liberal War: American Politics and International Security.* Ithaca, NY: Cornell University Press, 1997.

Owen, John M., IV. "The Canon and the Cannon: A Review Essay," *International Security* 23, no. 3 (Winter 1998/99): 147–178.

5 LIBERALIZATION, BACKLASH, AND THE WORLD CRISIS

Introduction

Today, liberal democracies form a system within a system—a club of states that never intend to fight one another, that trade with one another extensively, and that invest in one another's economies. They also deliberately entangle themselves with other states in a tight web of international rules and institutions.

But it took centuries for this liberal club to emerge. The story is one of merchants, or the middle classes, within countries gaining power and influence in certain states, especially Great Britain and the United States. They did so by developing new ideas about economics and statecraft which the new middle classes used to steer their countries toward more trade and less war. This did not mean uniform or steady liberal progress. The early decades after the fall of Napoleon in 1815 saw some successes as global trade grew under British leadership, but an economic depression that began in 1873 weakened the merchants and pulled the great powers away from trade and toward land grabs in Europe and indeed in Africa and Asia. An era of "New Imperialism" took place between 1880 and 1914. Although Europe's economies remained interdependent on many measures, fear and suspicion skewed international relations and renewed zero-sum competition. World politics spiraled into a crisis that culminated in the horrific Great War of 1914–1918, also known as the First World War. The full flowering of the liberal international system would have to wait several more decades.

History and Theory

"The grandeur of history lies in the perpetual conflict of nations, and it is simply foolish to desire the suppression of their rivalry. Mankind has ever found it to be so," wrote German historian Heinrich von Treitschke in 1898. Treitschke, a leading academic of his time, added that a state that defied this rule would either dissolve into anarchy or fall prey to a foreign enemy. You will recognize, by now, that Treitschke was a realist: he focused on states (or nations) as the only important units in world politics and became convinced that none of these could ever escape from the struggle for territory, wealth, and power.

Treitschke was far from alone in his time. His contemporary Friedrich von Bernhardi wrote in *Germany and the Next War* (1911) that conflict among states was a positive good. "War is a biological necessity of the first importance, a regulative element in the life of mankind which cannot be dispensed with, since without it an unhealthy development will follow which excludes every advancement of the race, and therefore all real civilization."[1] Nor were Germans the only people who thought this way. U.S. Navy Admiral Alfred Thayer Mahan argued in *The Influence of Sea Power upon History* (1890) that nations were in a struggle for power and that the most successful—the Dutch in the seventeenth century, the English more recently—did so by having the world's best navy. Britain's Halford Mackinder disagreed because he focused on land power but concurred that nations were in a perpetual competition. In "The Geographical Pivot of History," Mackinder contended that whoever gained the Heartland—a key area in Western Russia—would dominate the World Island (of Eurasia), and whoever dominated the World Island would in turn dominate the World.

Realism, then, was alive and well in the late nineteenth and early twentieth centuries. But so was liberalism, particularly the British version that began with Adam Smith in the eighteenth century and ran through Richard Cobden and John Bright in the nineteenth century. The Englishman Walter Bagehot, editor of *The Economist*, wrote in *Physics and Politics* (1872) that social evolution was evident in history, in which people moved from despotic war-like states to law-governed, democratic ones—precisely because the latter were more advantageous. The result, he thought, would be more peace: "Since war has ceased to be the moving force in the world," wrote Bagehot, "men have become more tender

---

1. Quotes are from John M. Hobson, *The Eurocentric Conception of World Politics: Western International Theory 1760–2010* (New York: Cambridge University Press, 2012), 154–155.

to one another."[2] A few decades later Norman Angell, another Englishman, wrote that the nations of Europe were so economically interdependent that war was too expensive and made no sense. Angell titled his famous 1910 book *The Great Illusion*—the illusion being that war still paid.

These realists and liberals differed from their predecessors and from counterparts of today. One difference is that, in keeping with the social thought of the time, some realists and liberals were racist, and overtly so. Their analyses were infected with an assumption that humanity was divided into higher and lower "races." Some realists were Social Darwinists, believing that the nations or races of the world were in a struggle to survive. Mahan and Mackinder worried that the "white race" would be overwhelmed by the "yellow race" unless Europeans and Americans cooperated in building military or naval capability. Some liberals were imperialists, believing in what the poet Rudyard Kipling called the "white man's burden" to lift up the "new-caught, sullen peoples, half devil and half child."[3]

The racism resulted from increasing interaction between Europeans and the Asian and African peoples they colonized in the nineteenth century. The white peoples constructed a theory to support the policies of domination they were carrying out. History, in other words, shaped international relations theory during this era as in all others. But beneath the racist views there remained our two fundamentally different takes on world politics: realists saw it as a perpetual realm of power struggle, whereas liberals saw it as a realm of possibility for more peace, democracy, and prosperity.

We shall see in this chapter that theory shaped history as well. Liberal ideas about free trade and self-government affected the foreign policies of Great Britain, and because Britain was the global economic hegemon, those ideas increasingly affected the entire world. Realism (*Realpolitik*) was practiced by Otto von Bismarck, the German chancellor, as he brought about the unification of Germany by expenditure of blood and iron in the 1860s and 1870s. (He did so by defeating Austria and then France.) The emergence of a united Germany, along with a severe economic downturn in the 1870s, pushed European states, including Britain, France, and Germany, the United States, and Japan into a "New Imperialism," in which they essentially divided up most of Africa and Asia among themselves. Territory was becoming a dominant instrument of power, and as the twentieth century dawned, realist ideas began to dominate the thinking of many leaders.

---

2. Walter Bagehot, *Physics and Politics* (London: Henry King, 1872; reprinted, Kitchener, Ontario, Canada: Batoche, 2001), 47. Bagehot's claim was premature to say the very least, but it did indicate how those who engaged in trade felt toward one another.

3. Rudyard Kipling, "The White Man's Burden" (1899), in *The Collected Poems of Rudyard Kipling* (London: Wordsworth Editions, 2001), 334-35.

The Nineteenth Century: Prime Time for Realism?

Realist theory always points us to the "great powers," their conflicts, and the shifts in the distribution of power among them. *Great powers* are those states that are most able to get their way in the international system—to bring about war or peace, trade or autarky, justice or injustice. During the Cold War (see Chapter 8), the United States and the Soviet Union were really the only two great powers and in fact were called the "superpowers." After 1990 the United States briefly enjoyed being the "unipolar hegemon." At some point in your lifetime (between now and 2050 or so), China may become America's equal or even surpass it, and leaders and experts around the world now regard the Sino-American relationship as the most important in the world.

The century between the defeat of Napoleon in 1815 and the outbreak of the First World War in 1914 is often considered an exemplary realist era. That is because the five great powers—Britain, France, Austria, Russia, and Prussia (which became a united Germany in 1871)—ran European and, to a large extent, world politics. The British ruled India; the Ottoman Empire became increasingly hollowed out, as we shall see in this chapter. China, once the world's greatest power, decayed and was slowly picked apart by the Europeans.

The European powers conducted their affairs wisely at times and brutally at times, but they usually cooperated with one another. They avoided big wars despite having conflicts of interest, changes in the balance of power, and competition over colonies. The wars they conducted—the Crimean War of 1853–1856 and the wars of Italian (1859–1871) and German (1866–1871) unification—were limited. Only when prudence was forgotten, particularly by Germany, after 1890 did international relations become dangerous to all powers again. That is the story that realist scholars have told. Henry Kissinger, the famous American Cold War statesman, published a book in the 1950s laying out this story, though reserving for himself a more Kantian perspective.

The realist account has much truth to it, and it is especially helpful in explaining the late nineteenth century and the origins of the First World War. It misses, however, some crucial underlying trends that continued to work slowly to transform world politics. The liberal international subsystem discussed in Chapter 5 continued to develop within the larger realist international system during the nineteenth century. Here again, Britain was key to this system because of its ideas, its powerful commercial class, its vast wealth, and its possession of the world's largest navy. Other countries wanted to emulate Britain. During these decades British elites outlawed the transatlantic slave trade and gradually became more democratic; merchants oriented toward free trade triumphed in Britain in the 1840s, shifting the world's greatest empire from mercantilist to liberal (in economic terms). Democratic institutions also deepened in the United States and elsewhere in the Americas as well as in France. Democracy also gnawed away at the foundations of monarchy elsewhere in Europe but in most places was suppressed for many decades. The Concert of Europe (the members of the Quadruple Alliance plus France) met periodically to control threats to the peace in Spain, Belgium, and Egypt.

The liberal international subsystem that emerged in the nineteenth century was immature and flawed. It continued to exist within the larger realist system and the traditional states that upheld it. The idea that conquest always paid, that raiding was better than trading, continued to hold sway as the European powers went on a new binge of imperialism in the 1880s in Africa and Asia. And even trading states such as Britain and the United States used coercion to pry open foreign territories to commerce. They did this in part out of fear that other states would try to lock them out of access to raw materials and colonial markets. The contest for power and wealth, fueled by the Industrial Revolution and fears that the losers would be destroyed, intensified as the nineteenth century drew to a close, setting up Europe for its greatest catastrophes, the world wars of the twentieth century.

The Napoleonic Wars, the Industrial Revolution, and International Trade

Big wars have complicated effects on states and international relations. On the one hand, they depress international trade. The wars of the French Revolution and Napoleon certainly had this effect in Europe. In Chapter 4 we discussed Napoleon's Berlin and Milan decrees, which sought to give the French Empire sole control over transatlantic and European trade. Economic historians have traced how Napoleon's Continental System raised prices of the protected goods in most countries, enriched producers of those goods, and gave them more political clout, which in turn enabled them to extend their tariff protection after the war ended. For example, British grain farmers succeeded in getting Parliament to pass the Corn Laws in 1815, which kept foreign grain out of the country. Similar dynamics were at work in France and in the United States (which fought the War of 1812 against Britain and wanted to protect its New England manufacturers).

Big wars also can push states away from democracy by enabling the executive branch (king, president, prime minister, chancellor) to grab power from congresses and parliaments, the press, the courts, and other institutions. Mobilizing a society's resources for a major war requires reducing the "veto points" in a government, that is, the number of actors and institutions who can block or delay the chief executive. In the case of the Napoleonic Wars, this effect was amplified by the discrediting of democracy among elites in Europe. Democracy in France had produced the violent excesses of the Revolution in the 1790s and ultimately Bonaparte's aggressive authoritarian empire in the decade following. Victors in a total war—in which the defeated powers surrender without conditions—get to dictate terms, and the enemies of Napoleon were determined to restore the old Bourbon monarchy in France. In the aftermath of the war, then, the grandson of the executed Louis XVI was established on France's throne as Louis XVIII. It was ambiguous whether the new king was a constitutional or an absolute monarch, but he and his successors moved France toward the absolutism of Austria, Prussia, and Russia. Indeed, as discussed in Chapter 4, at the Congress of Vienna (1814–1815) the winning powers restored vestiges of the old monarchical houses over those European states that Napoleon had conquered.

By 1820, then, it appeared that the liberal league of states within the broader realist international system that Thomas Jefferson, Immanuel Kant, Condorcet, Benjamin Constant, and so many other Enlightenment thinkers had hoped for was finished. Appearance is not always reality, however, and in this case liberal actors continued to work to reform national and international politics in their preferred direction.

First, liberal networks continued to thread across Europe and periodically rose up in rebellion. The absolute monarchists tried to destroy these movements but found that they could not. In 1830, a liberal revolution broke out in France, overthrowing the absolute monarchy and establishing Louis Philippe as a bourgeois monarch explicitly imitating the system of Great Britain. The French Revolution of 1830 triggered liberal uprisings in several other European states. In 1848 an even larger liberal revolutionary wave began in France and rolled over most of the Continent.

Second, the Napoleonic Wars that ended in 1815 actually laid the groundwork for significant growth in international trade. As Findlay and O'Rourke point out, when Napoleon invaded Spain and Portugal in 1808, the news soon reached those countries' New World colonies, triggering a chain of rebellions and eventually the independence of a number of new republics, from Mexico and the Caribbean in the north to Argentina and Brazil in the south. With these lands now freed from colonialism and economic monopoly, they were open to trade with other countries. Their economic interactions with Great Britain and the United States rose sharply. Argentina became a British preserve, though not a colony.

Third, the Industrial Revolution that had begun decades earlier in Britain continued there and spread to other parts of Europe and to the United States. Especially important were innovations in transportation, communication, and manufacturing. The invention of the steam engine by the Scotsman James Watt in 1781 led to the steam locomotive in 1804 and the oceangoing steamship in 1813. These innovations were to reduce transportation costs dramatically and increase international trade.

Before, when sea transport was relatively slow, it only made sense to trade goods overseas that had a high value relative to their weight. With the dramatic lowering of shipping costs, it made more sense to export and import many more types of goods. Refrigeration also made meat and foodstuffs into export items.

The dissolution of the Spanish and Portuguese empires and the new transportation technology combined to end the mercantilist era in the nineteenth century. After that, great powers ceased trading only with their colonies and extended their commerce to other states. The abandonment of classical mercantilism, however, did not mean the automatic triumph of Smithian free trade or the emergence of universal peace and cooperation. As Findlay and O'Rourke write:

> Before 1815 . . . international trade had been seen by governments as a means of extracting rents, by driving a wedge between the prices paid to producers in one location and those paid by consumers in another. The question then was who was going to get these rents, and as we have seen the result was international competition between overseas trading companies, and frequent warfare in the age of mercantilism. Trade-related conflict was thus inherently *inter*national in nature. Cheaper transportation and intercontinental trade in competing goods implied that the politics of trade would now also involve *intra*national conflict, between those groups in society who gained as a result of intercontinental trade and those who lost.[4]

So the world did not move directly from mercantilist colonialism to free trade, because there were producers in each country that resisted. As noted in previous chapters, in each country free trade hurts some producers—those whose products do not enjoy a comparative advantage in world markets—and those producers typically use their political clout to seek governmental protection from foreign competition. These less competitive producers are opposed by producers of goods that do enjoy a comparative advantage globally. As we shall see later in this chapter, sometimes the free traders win, sometimes the protectionists win, and sometimes there is a mixed outcome.

Most economists agree that, by and large, states grow richer when they eliminate barriers to international trade such as tariffs. Under free trade, states specialize in whatever they enjoy a comparative advantage in and sell it to foreigners so they can buy the other things they need. In past centuries, states did not trade freely because they feared doing so would render them vulnerable to foreign blackmail. Today they resist free trade when those sectors of their economy that would lose from it prevail in the political realm.

---

4. Ronald Findlay and Kevin H. O'Rourke, *Power and Plenty: Trade, War, and the World Economy in the Second Millennium* (Princeton, NJ: Princeton University Press, 2009), 387.

Great Britain Liberalizes Itself and the World

Even so, the nineteenth century saw the liberal international subsystem broaden and deepen. Crucial to its continued development was the ongoing liberalization and empowerment of Great Britain and the propagation of British ideas and policies. We previously discussed how Britain's superior institutions of constitutional monarchy, taxation, and finance enabled that country to industrialize early and outperform its rivals, especially France, in the eighteenth century. Britain continued to outpace the competition after 1815 and also continued to become still more democratic. As merchants gained wealth over the landed aristocracy, they continued to demand commensurate political power and greater religious toleration. In the 1820s official discrimination against non-Anglican Christians was ended, and in the coming years discrimination against Jews likewise became illegal. In 1832 the Great Reform Act almost doubled the number of people who could vote. It eliminated the rotten and pocket boroughs that were sources of political corruption and guaranteed that henceforth a government fell only when parliament lost confidence in it. Never again would the Crown dismiss a government on a whim.[5]

When Britain resumed trading on a major scale in 1815, it had high tariffs. The optimum tariff could be high because no other country had machine-produced goods to sell. Europeans bought British-manufactured goods because the Industrial Revolution had not yet begun to spread from West to East over the Continent.[6] After the continentals acquired machines, British manufacturers understood that other countries would only buy more of their products if those countries could sell more grain to British consumers. The British manufacturers targeted their country's Corn Laws,[7] which placed tariffs (taxes) on imported grain. Like all tariffs, the Corn Laws were favored by producers of goods that were not competitive on world markets—in this case, English farmers who grew grain. British governments also liked tariffs as an easy source of revenue. But the Corn Laws were unpopular among many of the factory workers and rural poor because they artificially inflated food prices.

In 1846 a now more democratic parliament repealed the Corn Laws, and Britain finally began to put into practice Adam Smith's ideas about free trade.

---

5. John M. Owen IV, *Liberal Peace, Liberal War: American Politics and International Security* (Ithaca, NY: Cornell University Press, 1997), 103.

6. Sidney Pollard, *Peaceful Conquest: The Industrialization of Europe, 1760–1970* (New York: Oxford University Press, 1981).

7. In Britain "corn" refers to what Americans call "grain"—including corn, wheat, barley, rice, and so on.

Soon all but a fifth of Britain's food came from overseas. Over the next decades cheaper foreign food reduced prices for the British and Irish populations. Because Britain did not enjoy a comparative advantage in grain production, the repeal also undercut the country's grain producers and weakened British landlords, including the great aristocracy. Power further shifted toward the urban merchant classes.

Repeal of the Corn Laws led to a liberal period in British trade. Over the next decade and a half, thanks to the continuing efforts of politicians such as Prime Minister William Gladstone, nearly all other British tariffs were removed.[8] Now the British empire shifted from being a simply the world's biggest exclusive economic zone, in which British merchants and ships monopolized all trade with the colonies (with exceptions such as the port of Singapore), to being a globe-spanning free trade zone—ruled from London, but open to commerce with anyone. Free trade diminished tariff revenue, and in theory it might mean less military spending and less war and conquest. Britain would use its economic leverage as a virtuous example to promote national success via commerce rather than conquest. Another milestone came in 1860 with the Cobden-Chevalier Treaty, a trade agreement between Britain and France (named for two free-trade liberals, Richard Cobden of England and Michel Chevalier of France). As a result, two of the world's greatest powers had greatly reduced their trade barriers for the sake of peace and mutual prosperity. Through Most Favored Nation clauses, they also extended their concessions to other countries.[9]

The nineteenth century often is called the era of *Pax Britannica* (British Peace) or of British hegemony. Political scientist Stephen Krasner has argued that British leadership was largely responsible for the expansion of global trade in the nineteenth and early twentieth centuries. With the world's biggest economy, deepest financial markets, greatest empire, and most powerful navy, Britain both removed some of the risk from free trade and used its leverage to get other countries to lower trade barriers as it had done. British ships patrolled the high seas, suppressing piracy and keeping crucial straits such as Gibraltar, Suez, and Malacca (in Southeast Asia) open. In the New World, Britain effectively enforced the Monroe Doctrine, the 1823 U.S. declaration that European great powers must not try to roll back the republican revolutions that began in

---

8. Peter Cain, "British Free Trade, 1850–1914: Economics and Policy," *Refresh* 29 (Autumn 1999): 1.

9. Arthur A. Stein, "The Hegemon's Dilemma: Great Britain, the United States, and the International Economic Order," *International Organization* 38, no. 2 (1984): 355–386.

the 1810s. The United States actually did not have anything like the power to enforce President Monroe's famous doctrine, but Britain did so, guaranteeing the continued political independence of the young republics of Latin America. The British did not do this out of altruism, and certainly not to help the United States. They did it out of self-interest: the British wanted to trade with Latin America, and if Spain and Portugal took their old colonies back such trade would be closed off.

That Britain was acting out of self-interest brings us to two important related points. First, when we say that the country was becoming more democratic and liberal in the nineteenth century, we do not mean that its leaders or citizens were necessarily acting out of moral motives. Some, such as religious reformers, doubtless believed they were doing the right thing. Yet, as we have stressed in previous chapters, it is the self-interest of merchants and traders that leads them to favor more liberal policies and institutions. Adam Smith wrote that it is out of selfish motives that general wealth increases, provided that countries have the institutions to channel that selfishness properly. Second, Britain during these decades continued to expand its empire and could act quite coercively and even brutally. One shameful chapter in British history will illustrate. By the nineteenth century the famous British appetite for Chinese tea was so great that Britain was running a large trade deficit with China—a country that had little demand for imports. To improve its balance of trade, British merchants increased the smuggling of opium from India—ruled by the British—to China. When the Chinese government tried to halt the import of opium, the British fought and defeated China in the First Opium War (1839–1842) and claimed a number of benefits, including Hong Kong. A Second Opium War (1856–1860) resulted in still more Chinese economic concessions, including dozens of open (free-trading) ports. Ironically, free trade sometimes had to be coerced. More generally, as we will show in subsequent chapters, the spread and durability of the liberal international subsystem is aided by the power of a liberal hegemon. In the middle of the twentieth century, the United States replaced Britain in this role.

The Burgeoning of International Trade

Because of this cycle of developments—the rise of middle classes and of liberal democracy, industrialization and economic development, the lowering of transportation and communication costs, and British hegemony—global trade across Europe and the Atlantic rose sharply in nineteenth-century Europe. Following the repeal of the Corn Laws in 1846, Britain was hungry for agricultural imports; it entered bilateral trade treaties and imported grain from the United States and Russia (which then ruled Ukraine, the most advantaged grain-producing region in Europe). Britain remained the world's most industrialized country, and its currency, the pound sterling, was the most widely accepted in the world. It was the world's biggest importer, exporter, and foreign investor, with the biggest merchant fleet.[10]

> In recent years, international relations scholars have become increasingly interested in how states learn from and imitate one another. Like businesses, states have certain goals—security, prosperity, independence—and they watch each other to see what works and what does not. In the eighteenth century, most European states imitated France's absolute monarchy. More recently, the growth of the liberal international system has been driven to some extent by countries' imitation of Great Britain's liberal constitutionalism in the nineteenth century and the United States' democratic capitalism in the twentieth. Each of these states in its heyday enjoyed great international success and spawned many imitators. An important question for the future is whether China's model of "market-Leninism" will inspire other countries to imitate it.

Industrial economies depend heavily on energy, and during this period energy was derived from coal and later petroleum, some of which had to be imported. England's exports went to the New World and the Empire, whose demand for textiles, railways and machinery increased; the colonies provided wool, grain, cotton, and minerals in return. Germany could not subsist on limited supplies of East Elbian grain and needed access to stocks from Russia via Odessa (Ukraine). Textiles and fashions of all kinds were traded between Paris, Milan, London, and New York. Medicines and medical equipment stemmed from Germany, whose chemicals were also in high demand for fertilizer. In a time of peace, international trade, at least partly financed by bankers in London, cascaded across national boundaries. For a while the gold standard was rigidly adhered to by all comers, and gold supplies were sufficient to support trade without a rise in inflation.[11] In short, the nation-state—however large—was not big enough to provide all national needs through its own resources and production. International trade offered the remainder of needed goods and bulwarked the edifice of peace or helped keep conflicts limited. This was characteristic of the late nineteenth and early twentieth centuries. The Rothschilds—legendary bankers—for example, did not believe that World War I could go on for more than a few weeks given the restraints of the world economy. (In this conclusion Nathan Rothschild was

---

10. WTO, *World Trade Report 2007*, https://www.wto.org/english/res_e/booksp_e/anrep_e/ wtr07-2b_e.pdf.

11. Gold discoveries in California, Australia, and the Yukon guaranteed that precious minerals would not be in short supply. They also contributed to world inflation.

premature, as the credit system expanded during the war to provide for the borrowing needs of the military opponents.)

British thinkers and politicians reformulated the ideas of Adam Smith (see Chapter 4) and propagated them at home and abroad. The Manchester School—so called because Manchester, England, was a center of manufacturing—was represented by politicians Richard Cobden and John Bright, who played crucial roles in abolishing the Corn Laws. Cobden told his fellow members of Parliament, "In a word, our national existence is involved in the well-doing of our manufactures. . . . To what are we indebted for this commerce? . . . The *cheapness* alone of our manufactures." In other words, not a large military, as the old mercantilists believed, but efficient production. Cobden continued, "The more any nation trafficks abroad upon free and honest principles, the less it will be in danger of wars. . . . I defy you to show me how any Government or people on the Continent can strengthen themselves, even if they chose to carry on a war of conquest."[12] Cobden and Bright were opposed by representatives of the landed aristocracy, but in the middle of the nineteenth century their ideas generally won the day.

During this period, markets wove largely peaceful networks. As we know, however, wars did not cease. Economically mercantilist and authoritarian states waged chronic conflict with one another. Imperialism led more than one country to seek large territories elsewhere. At the time Britain and Russia were playing the Great Game in Afghanistan and were aiming to acquire vast stretches of territory in the East. The British already had the seas of the world (three-fifths of the global area). The British Empire encompassed India and was encroaching on China. But according to Count Sergei Witte, political leader under Tsar Nicholas II, Russian merchants would acquire the trade of the area through new railroads constructed between Moscow, Vladivostok (on the Pacific), and Port Arthur (on the Yellow Sea, now part of China). Britain could not be ejected from India, but it could be outflanked by Russian mastery of the Eastern trade (in which railways were faster means of communication and transportation than ships).[13] Ultimately—so it was theorized—Moscow could use what Halford Mackinder later dubbed the "Heartland," a region in west-central Russia, to move further afield (east and south). The holder of the Heartland was thought to be able to expand (through railways) to the whole "World Island" (of Asia and Europe together). Communication across this vast area could be monopolized, so it was said, from one source.[14]

---

12. "Richard Cobden," in Arnold Wolfers and Laurence Martin, eds., *The Anglo-American Tradition in Foreign Affairs* (New Haven, CT: Yale University Press, 1956), 193–195.

13. Peter Hopkirk, *The Great Game: The Struggle for Empire in Central Asia* (New York: Kondansha International, 1992), 502.

14. Halford Mackinder, "The Geographical Pivot of History," *Geographic Journal*, Vol. 170, No. 4 (December 1904), pp. 298-321.

The Russians, however, were never able to execute this vision in concrete terms. Not only Britain but also Germany (in World War I) stood in the way of Russian expansion. Though the imperial rivals did not grasp the point, colonial rule could not go on forever. External control of a conquered province ultimately depended on the population's acceptance, initially by force of arms and then via persuasion. When firearms became available to colonial inhabitants in the later nineteenth century, they could revolt against imperialism. For most of that century, colonies remained quiescent, enduring foreign rule and having few means of resistance. The rise of the so-called "Mahdi" in the Sudan in the 1880s, however, sparked colonial opposition and led to the attack on Charles George "Chinese" Gordon, the British general who had been installed in Khartoum and entrusted with the task of putting down native revolts. The forces of the Mahdi, a self-proclaimed religious leader whose real name was Muhammad Ahmad, had obtained modern arms from the surrender of General Hicks in 1883.

The British government under the Liberal William Gladstone sent Gordon to recapture Khartoum, but it directed him to evacuate the Sudan and remove British citizens there. Gordon refused, entrenching himself and waiting for battle with the ever-advancing Mahdi forces. In January 1885, the Mahdi besieged Gordon, killed him, and ended British-Egyptian control of the Sudan. Gladstone stood idly by while Britain was humbled. Queen Victoria made her disapproval public, but it was not until 1898 and the entrance of a new Conservative government into power that a much larger army under George Kitchener—backed strongly by British public opinion—could regain control of Sudan.

The legitimacy of British imperialism was also challenged in India, beginning with the Sepoy revolt in 1857. Under the stern ministrations of the East India Company, Britain had not taken Indian feelings fully into account. But the new Enfield rifle proved to be the last straw. Enfield rifles had to be greased with pork and beef fat to load quickly. This process was much faster than that of the muzzle loaders previously in use. But handling pork fat contravened the religious teachings of the indigenous Muslim troops, and touching beef fat violated the beliefs of indigenous Hindu troops. These soldiers refused to unload Enfields from their packing cases. The British imprisoned the recalcitrant Sepoys or subalterns. In May 1857, however, the Sepoys seized the prisons, freeing their brothers. This led to two years of slaughter of the rebels by their imperial masters.

The violence of the reaction spelled the end of the East India Company's governance of India and resulted in a transfer of India to the British Crown. Under direct government rule, a new policy of religious tolerance of Indian subgroups was adopted. An Indian Civil Service of pro-British natives, Muslims and Hindus alike, was set up to ensure that sects could observe their own rituals. The Indians were temporarily pacified and fought on the British side in World War I. As we shall see in chapter 7, however, they sought and gained independence after World War II.

Notwithstanding its imperial struggles and wars, Great Britain, until 1890, was the most efficient industrial country in Europe. But it was hurt by the depression of 1873–1896. European states raised tariffs all around. Britain could sell to its empire, but not to Europe and particularly not to European colonies overseas (which imposed their patron's levies). Thus, as Lord Rosebery recognized, Britain had to peg out new claims to colonies to have a continuing market for its goods. And it did so, vying with France and Germany to gain the greatest empire.

Subversive Liberal Democracy

In earlier chapters we showed how rulers, intellectuals, and other elites typically observe the successes and failures of other countries to try to learn what makes for a prosperous and powerful country. The English learned about the virtues of trade and religious toleration from the Dutch in the seventeenth century; the French learned the virtues of limited monarchy from the English in the eighteenth century and the advantages of republicanism from the successful American struggle for independence. In the same way, nineteenth-century Britain's successful example of a liberal powerhouse deeply impressed other Europeans. Traditionally, leaders of most states, following the teachings of realism and mercantilism, believed that free trade would render a country vulnerable to exploitation by foreigners. But in the 1840s Britain demonstrated that opening your national economy could make your country rich and powerful. Furthermore, the British were especially adept at inventing technologies that improved economic efficiency. Britain was the leader both in international trade and in empire; others copied the British example and sought colonies as well. But no other country did as well as Britain. By 1897 it ruled one sixth of the world's territory and one quarter of the world's population. Queen Victoria was very proud of her extended domains.

An even more radical example of a successful liberal democratizing country was the United States. As a republic, America's political institutions were different from Britain's in crucial ways: Americans elected their head of state and had no hereditary aristocracy that enjoyed special rights and privileges. In the 1820s most American states granted full adult male suffrage and stopped supporting any particular Christian denomination. The 1828 election of Andrew Jackson, a backwoodsman who had risen as an army colonel to national prominence in Indian wars, showed that men from humble origins could grow up to be president. The standard European view had been that only small states, such as Venice or Switzerland, could survive as democratic republics.[15] When a great power became a republic, they believed, it would inevitably spiral into civil war

---

15. Jean-Jacques Rousseau argued this in his famous book *On the Social Contract* (1762), book 3, Chapter 3.

and chaos, as England had done in the 1650s and France in the 1790s. The North American republic, then, was a genuine experiment—and, for Europeans, a dangerous if seductive one.

All the more impressive were the survival and success of the United States in the nineteenth century. Not only did the country maintain its independence from the predations of France and Britain in the early years of the century, its republican institutions became entrenched. The United States was secure and its population and economy grew rapidly, thanks in part to continuing immigration from Europe. With its patent system and relatively free economy, the United States was producing an impressive amount of technological innovation, some of which—the combine harvester, the steam shovel, vulcanized rubber, the grain elevator, the pistol made from replaceable parts—improved economic efficiency, and some of which—the repeating rifle and the machine gun—increased military potential. Samuel Morse invented a viable telegraph in 1838 (at roughly the same time, English inventors came up with their own telegraph.) The United States expanded westward at relatively little cost to itself and appeared poised to swallow up all of North America. The United States was achieving all of these successes without a standing army, alliances, or the traditional instruments of European diplomacy. The enemies the United States confronted—a weakened Mexico, a few Spanish colonies, and the British fleet—could not stand in its way.

Of course, the United States then was not as liberal or democratic as it was to become later. Most obviously, a large portion of the country was neither capitalist nor fully democratic: women could not vote and the great majority of black Americans were slaves; whites coerced their labor. Slavery was the economic foundation of southern states, and indeed prosperity in parts of the North depended on cheap cotton exports derived from slave labor. Much of the country's westward expansion came through warfare against Mexico or Native Indian tribes. Like other market-oriented countries, the United States did not swear off conquest; it only carried it out when it was relatively cheap and easy. Finally, unlike Britain, nineteenth-century America did not practice free trade. Tariffs were its main source of federal revenue, and the individual income tax was not introduced until the 1920s. (Ironically, the southern slaveholding planters favored free trade because their cotton was internationally competitive; it was the northern manufacturers who favored the tariff.)

It also is important to note that, although the United States and Great Britain never fought a war after 1815, the two did not get along smoothly during these decades. Americans resented British wealth and power, and many feared a loss of autonomy should the two countries become too close politically or economically. The British tended to look down upon the United States as an upstart and upon Americans as coarse, loud-mouthed bumpkins. The long border with Canada (a British colony until 1867 and a British dominion thereafter), British colonies in the Caribbean, and British economic influence in Latin America provided many flashpoints for relations with the United States. Relations between the two liberal powers thus were vexed during the nineteenth century: the two countries had war scares in 1845, 1861, and 1895. Still, relations gradually became more pacific and productive. The "special relationship" between Britain and the United States began to emerge in the early twentieth century, as the two countries became more democratic and learned to trust one another.

Britain and the United States were distinctive in important ways and they practiced a different kind of foreign policy—one that looked to grow rich through trade. Through the successes and attractiveness of their political and economic institutions and policies, the two countries were helping the liberal international subsystem evolve. In 1831 the young French nobleman Alexis de Tocqueville visited America to study its prisons. He ended up writing *Democracy in America*, a masterful study of how self-government worked in the United States that is still widely studied and quoted. Tocqueville was convinced that democracy was the wave of the future for Europe, and Europeans had better understand what was coming their way. *Democracy in America* was (and remains) a candid look at the strengths and weaknesses of the United States, but its overall portrait is sympathetic, and it convinced many Europeans that they could learn from the American example.

At the same time, the British model of a liberal constitutional monarchy appealed to innumerable Europeans living under absolutist regimes. We previously discussed how from the 1820s until 1848 Europe was rocked periodically by waves of liberal revolt and revolution. Each time this occurred, the conservative great powers of Austria, Russia, and Prussia pushed back with their armies and police forces. Then the liberal movements went back underground, biding their time for another opportunity. The 1848 revolutions were the most serious, and for a time it looked like this "Springtime of Nations" would yield a Europe of thoroughly liberal-democratic, non-imperialistic nation-states. Liberals in Europe and the Americas thrilled to the news of revolutions in the German and Italian states and the toppling of governments in the great powers of France, Prussia, and Austria.

However, the following year, 1849, brought the counterrevolutionary backlash. Monarchs in Vienna and Berlin were shaken but did not fall. Together with the Russian tsar, they organized one more massive rollback of democracy, the biggest of all, marching tens of thousands of troops into the fledgling republics in central and southern Europe and setting monarchs back on their thrones. France became a republic once again in 1848, but within a few years the new president—Louis Napoleon, nephew of his more famous namesake—imitated his uncle and declared himself Emperor Napoleon III. Revolutionaries all over Europe were driven underground. Britain, it seemed, was now the only liberal great power, and the notion of a transformed international system of liberal trading states seemed to lie in ruins.

Appearances were deceiving, however. The democratic spirit released in 1848 did not disappear. Instead, it worked into these countries and their external relations, in two ways. First, nationalism came to the fore. Italians chafed under

Austrian domination of north Italy. Today we tend to think of nationalism as an exclusionary ideology that can be carried to extremes. Certainly the hypernationalisms of Nazi Germany, Fascist Italy, and Imperial Japan in the 1930s and 1940s were like this. But in the nineteenth century nationalism was seen, as historian E. J. Hobsbawm has written, as a liberator of peoples living under oppressive colonial regimes and empires.[16] People who spoke Italian or German in Europe were distributed over a large number of small states, each under the hegemony of one or another great power. The Austrian Empire ruled much of the Italian peninsula and controlled most of the rest indirectly. Austria and Prussia competed for hegemony over the multiple German states. Figure 5.1 shows Europe just before Italian and Germany unification; Figure 5.2, just after.

FIGURE 5.1 Europe in 1850.
Source: After Chase-Dunn and Lerro, 2008.

16. E. J. Hobsbawm, *Nations and Nationalism since 1780: Program, Myth, Reality* (New York: Cambridge University Press, 1990).

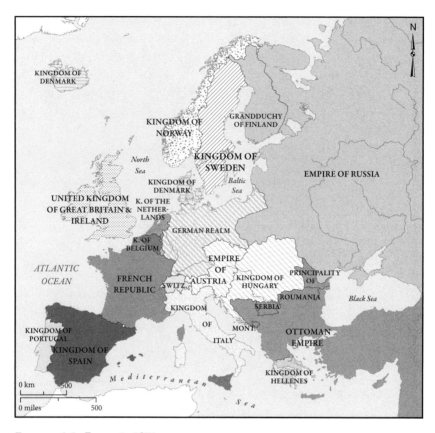

FIGURE 5.2 Europe in 1871.

In the 1860s both Italy and Germany were gradually united—not through a voluntary democratic process, but by powerful states making war. The Kingdom of Piedmont, led by liberal statesmen such as Count Cavour and Giuseppe Garibaldi, united Italy. The Kingdom of Prussia, led by the conservative Prince Otto von Bismarck, united Germany. Italian and German unification were nonetheless popular with most people in the absorbed smaller states because nationalism had become a widespread movement.

Second, the middle classes of Europe—the businesspeople, those who made their money and earned status from commerce rather than inherited titles and land—abandoned radicalism but did not give up the idea of reform. In the 1860s and 1870s they struck new bargains with the old ruling classes in much of Europe, based on a common acceptance of nationalism. In Italy and Germany, as well as in Austria, elected parliaments gained more power and opposition parties began to flourish. France under Napoleon III constituted a monarchy, but one more responsive to public sentiment than the old Napoleonic France had been. The government that emerged in Europe during this time was a "liberal-conservative" hybrid. The hybrid regime—linking right and left—rose above the 1848 revolutions. It supporters noted that the one European great power to escape serious turmoil in 1848 was Great Britain, the most liberal and democratic of their number. The British had a constitutional monarchy and a habit of gradual reform to head off revolution—they had expanded the vote in 1832, for example (and later in 1867 and 1884). Britain also was the richest of the great powers and had the world's largest empire. After 1848, the smart money was on the British model.

The 1870s: Backsliding Begins

Such is not to say that the other powers, much less the United States, became exactly like England. The rulers of Germany were not prepared to go as far as the British. Bismarck, chancellor under the new emperor, built the power of Germany on a coalition of "iron and rye," or industry and wealthy aristocrats. German governments were accountable to the kaiser, not the people, and the government suppressed both Catholicism and socialism. And it is important to recognize that there was one literally massive exception to the liberalizing trend in Europe. Russia, ruled by the tsars, stubbornly remained an absolute monarchy. As we will see in subsequent chapters, it is because of this refusal to reform that Russia spawned the radical, revolutionary communism that finally detonated during World War I and set up the Soviet Union.

Indeed, the 1870s saw a reversal of momentum of liberalism within many great powers and a weakening of the liberal international subsystem. This reversal was to last for many decades and would culminate in the two horrific world wars of the twentieth century. Key changes produced this result.

First were shifts in the balance of power in Europe. German and Italian unification were welcomed by most liberals at first, but they set off fears of a greatpower war. The major problem was Germany. A glance back at the maps in Figures 5.1 and 5.2 illustrates the geopolitical problem. The set of small German states in the first map provided a buffer between the other great powers, reassuring Russia, Prussia, France, and Austria that each was safe from the other. The second map shows that the buffer was gone by 1871, replaced by modern Germany, which quickly became Europe's leading military power and soon surpassed Britain as its leading industrial power. To mollify fears, Bismarck engineered a complex set of alliances across Europe neutralizing opposition. Meanwhile, nationalism spread to eastern and southern Europe and to the Middle East, awakening desires for independent nationhood among peoples who had never known it. Nationalism of the repressed nationalities weakened two already creaky empires—the Austrian and the Ottoman. The crumbling of these empires was to have huge consequences for the international system.

Second was the fact that Germany, Austria-Hungary, and Russia did not fully embrace the liberal program of individual rights and trade. Instead, many political and military leaders and intellectuals embraced realist notions of power and conquest. At the outset of this chapter we quoted various writers of the period who saw international politics as a zero-sum game driven by great-power competition and war. The evolutionary theory of Charles Darwin, which argued for the survival of the fittest species, was imported into geopolitical thought, resulting in a toxic form of realism.

Third was the Panic of 1873, sometimes known as the first Great Depression. The causes of the Panic were many and complex, but the effect was an economic contraction across the industrial countries that lasted for many years until at least 1896. Financial markets crashed, vast amounts of wealth were lost, hundreds of firms went bankrupt, and unemployment rose sharply. States responded by curtailing international trade in agricultural and other goods. The more each state slowed its imports, the more other states believed they had to do the same. States began to fear that national survival might require securing access to natural resources through the acquisition of empire. Notice in Figure 5.3 how, after the 1870s and the onset of depression, world trade fell off sharply. High tariff barriers became a kind of self-fulfilling prophecy: each state could observe its neighbors curtailing trade, as if it was no longer interested in getting wealthy together. This drop-off in trade had serious consequences for world politics by raising stakes of international competition and making that competition more intense. Political scientist Dale Copeland argues that when states expect their trading partners to cut them off, major wars can result.

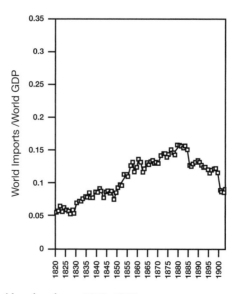

FIGURE 5.3 World trade volume, 1820–1900.

When great powers compete, they exploit one another's weaknesses, partly because each fears that if it does not, its rivals will. The mix of causes just listed—shifts in the European balance of power, backsliding from liberal reform, and the Panic of 1873—combined to cause "New Imperialism," a wave of European land grabs in Africa and Asia. The "Scramble for Africa" was triggered by weakness in the Ottoman Empire, which pulled Europeans into North Africa. At its height in the sixteenth century, the Ottoman had been one of the world's mightiest empires, dominating the eastern Mediterranean Sea, ruling southeastern Europe, North Africa, and much of today's Middle East. By the late nineteenth century it had lost many of its territories to Austria, Russia, and Britain, and Greece, Bulgaria, and other European lands had become independent states. In the early 1880s a nationalist Arab uprising in Ottoman-ruled Egypt and Sudan drew in the British, who, in the new international environment of scarcity and growing fear of competition, were worried about access to the jewel in the crown of their empire, India. At roughly the same time, to the south, Belgian explorers set up a colony in the Congo. A few years earlier, still further to the south, Britain had started to expand from the Cape of Good Hope—now a self-governing part of the British Empire—into lands held by Afrikaners of Dutch ancestry. As other Europeans saw the British expanding in Africa, they quickly concluded that they too needed colonies there and that they had better grab them quickly.

The Scramble was on. Italy, Portugal, France, Spain, and even Germany—whose chancellor, the masterful statesman Otto von Bismarck, had earlier declared colonization of Africa a waste of time and resources—began to conquer African territory (see Figure 5.4).

Under the New Imperialism, Europeans also drove deeply into Asia, as did the United States and Japan. Here again, the trigger was unrest in Asia itself. As recounted earlier in this chapter, the British East India Company had governed India until the rebellion (Sepoy Mutiny) of 1857. At that point the British Crown began to rule India directly. The British also moved into Southeast Asia, including Burma and Malaya. The French took Indochina (what are now Vietnam, Laos, and Cambodia). The Dutch took what is now Indonesia. In 1898, following its defeat of Spain, the United States took the Philippines. Following Britain's defeat of China in the Second Opium War (1858), China was effectively divided into economic zones by Britain, France, Germany, Russia, and the United States. In 1868, with the crowning of a new Japanese emperor (Meiji), Japanese aristocrats, seeing how their country's neighbors were being colonized and picked apart by Europeans, embarked on a strategy to make Japan more like a European great power. Eventually Japan itself joined the colonization of China and also annexed Korea. But its initial objective had been to prevent the partition of its own lands.

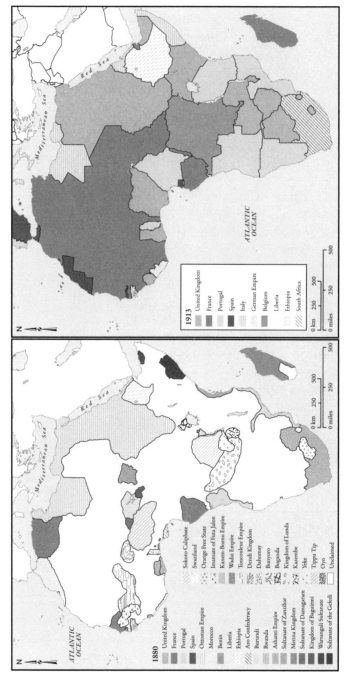

FIGURE 5.4 Africa before and after the Scramble.

The World Crisis

This renewal of realist-style great-power competition in the late nineteenth century continued and culminated, as we shall see, in the catastrophic world wars of the twentieth century. Global trade began to pick up again after 1900. But the patterns of intense international competition set after 1870 did not change. When all of the scrambling for colonies was over by around 1910, very little territory was left on the planet for the world's great powers to colonize. There was precious little cooperation among the great powers by this time; the liberal international subsystem that had been growing in midcentury was weak and shrinking. The old Concert of Europe system, under which the leading countries coordinated policy to make sure none gained so much as to jeopardize the delicate balance of power, had been weakened by the Crimean War of 1853–1856 (between Russia, on one side, and Britain and France, on the other) and German and Italian unification. Now the great powers began to practice old-fashioned competitive alliance building. In 1879 Germany and Austria-Hungary entered the Dual Alliance. In 1890 Germany ended its alliance with Russia, which responded by entering a Triple Entente with Britain and France. Under the influence of Social Darwinism, each state feared falling behind, and the two groupings of states began to tighten into blocs. The intensifying rivalry among the European great powers was a global problem precisely because the European powers controlled, politically and economically, so much of the world.

The main rising powers in 1900 were the United States, Japan, and the new Germany. (Italy aspired to this status but never established a strong enough presence outside of Europe.) The old established powers were Britain, France, Austria, and Russia. Each of the rising powers had won a war against a more established European state—Germany (Prussia) over Austria in 1868 and France in 1871, the United States over Spain in 1898, and Japan over Russia in 1905. Each had a rapidly growing economy (see Tables 5.1 and 5.2), and each was showing clear signs of converting its economic wealth into national power. Japan was starting from a lower base but was a potential threat to British and European interests in Asia because it was the one Asian country that was becoming a modern state capable of competing with the Europeans.

Table 5.1 Gross Domestic Product, Millions of 1990 Dollars*

	Britain	France	Germany	United States	Japan
1871	105,570	71,674	71,667	102,862	19,021
1910	207,098	122,238	210,513	460,471	64,559

*Currency is in 1990 International Geary-Khamis dollars, which uses as a baseline the purchasing power of a U.S. dollar in the year 1990.

Table 5.2 Gross Domestic Product Per Capita, 1990 Dollars*

	Britain	France	Germany	United States	Japan
1871	3,332	1,899	1,817	2,503	742
1910	4,611	2,965	3,348	4,964	1,304

*Currency is in 1990 International Geary-Khamis dollars, which uses as a baseline the purchasing power of a U.S. dollar in the year 1990.

As it began to lose leverage, Great Britain, the nineteenth century's global hegemon, eyed these three rising powers uneasily. In the 1890s and early 1900s, influenced by the ideas held by many of its leaders that international war was not inevitable and trade and long-term cooperation was possible among great powers, Britain considered conciliation with each of these rising powers. British leaders hoped that each of these other states could ease the impact of Britain's relative decline by sharing their goals for global politics and economics—by keeping countries and territories in the Americas, Asia, and Africa open to British commerce and by not picking apart the British Empire.

Britain ended up with cooperative relationships with Japan and the United States. In the Anglo-Japanese Treaty of 1902, each pledged to keep China open and not to join the other's enemy in case of war. Thus in 1904–1905, when Japan defeated Russia in a brief war over Korea, Britain did not interfere.

Britain entered no alliance with America—the United States did not believe in alliances at that point—but following disputes over influence in Latin America in the 1890s, the two liberal powers decided that their common interests were so strong that they should accommodate one another around the world. When the United States defeated Spain in what John Hay, the U.S. ambassador to Great Britain, called a "splendid little war" in 1898, Britain stood aside. Grateful Americans began to back Britain at international conferences, and both countries began to talk about their common "Anglo-Saxon" heritage. The often-discussed Anglo-American "special relationship" emerged in these years.

Germany was a different story. Resentful of British imperial and naval prestige, captivated by realist ideas about zero-sum international competition, Kaiser Wilhelm II (who inherited the crown in 1890) was bent on equaling or replacing Britain as global hegemon as soon as possible. Helped by his domestic coalition of "iron and rye" and influenced by Social Darwinist ideas prominent at the time, the kaiser set Germany upon a rapid naval buildup. A naval arms race with Britain ensued. In 1899–1902 Britain fought a war against white Afrikaners in southern

Africa—the Boer War—and Germany supplied the Boers with arms to undercut the British. Germany twice challenged French control of Morocco (1905–1906 and 1911), driving France and Britain more closely together. The stage was being set for the cataclysms of the next century.

Conclusion

At the close of the nineteenth century, then, the liberal international subsystem whose emergence we have described, led by powerful merchants in many of the great powers, was receding into the background. To be sure, many thinkers and statesmen continued to believe that trading was better than raiding, that conquest did not pay, and that trust was possible in international relations. Norman Angell's *The Great Illusion* was published in several editions after 1910. Had enough statesmen thought as Angell did, recognizing that for industrial trading states war was a game not worth the candle, perhaps no war would have occurred. In fact, many thinkers and statesmen continued to believe that conquest did pay, that all states were in a contest for supremacy, and that only the strongest would survive.[17] It would take two massive world wars and tens of millions of deaths in the first half of the twentieth century before enough minds could be changed and the liberal international system could fully emerge and become predominant.

FURTHER READING

Copeland, Dale C. *Economic Interdependence and War*. Princeton, NJ: Princeton University Press, 2014.

Darwin, John *The Empire Project: The Rise and Fall of the British World-System, 1830–1970*. New York: Cambridge University Press, 2011.

Ferguson, Niall. *Empire: The Rise and Decline of the British World Order and the Lessons for Global Power*. New York: Basic Books, 2003.

Findlay, Ronald, and Kevin H. O'Rourke. *Power and Plenty: Trade, War, and the World Economy in the Second Millennium*. Princeton, NJ: Princeton University Press, 2009.

Gilpin, Robert. *War and Change in World Politics*. New York: Cambridge University Press, 1981.

Krasner, Stephen. "State Power and the Structure of International Trade." *World Politics*, Vol. 28, No. 3 (1976), pp. 317–347.

---

17. See Richard Rosecrance and Steven Miller, eds., *The Next Great War?* (Cambridge, MA: MIT Press, 2014).

Owen, John M. *The Clash of Ideas in World Politics.* Princeton, NJ: Princeton University Press, 2010, ch. 5, "Crown, Nobility, and People, 1770-1870," pp. 122-160.

Rosecrance, Richard. *The Rise of the Trading State: Commerce and Conquest in the Modern World.* New York: Basic Books, 1986.

de Tocqueville, Alexis. *Democracy in America* (1835), trans. Harvey C. Mansfield Jr. and Delba Winthrop. Chicago: University of Chicago Press, 2002.

6 THE WORLD CRISIS CONTINUES

Introduction

This chapter surveys the fragility of even peaceable international relations where nations have few grievances against each other. Bellicose individual leaders, portents of decline, and alliance obligations may push nations into war when a more mature consideration would not do so. The consequences of war, however, are not salutary unless economic and political conditions are favorable and national objectives are at least partially achieved. World War I occurred for essentially trivial reasons, but its conclusion exacerbated the prior grievances and led directly to another war.

The world teetered between crisis and reform as it approached the summer of 1914. Nineteenth-century industrialization had opened a new vista of peaceful change to European states. England, Holland, and France—and to some degree even Germany—had progressed as a result of the open international economy, and the freedom of movement accorded factors of production like labor and capital. Industrial goods had brought economic growth to Germany as well as England, the United States, and Russia. War between European powers had been postponed after 1871 as capitalism mobilized resources across the globe for greater prosperity. Wheat production in Russia (the Ukraine) and the United States (the Midwest) had flown to world markets; German pharmaceuticals (such as aspirin) had captured much of the world.

Arnold Toynbee raised the possibility that the world had turned a corner with the growth of industrialism. Countries no longer had to fight; they could advance their positions in purely economic ways. Yet he also pointed out that the development of nationalism had undermined the integration of the continent.[1] Mercantilism, colonial acquisitions, and high tariffs had at least partly subverted peace. Countries thought that they might improve their position through territorial aggrandizement and acted accordingly. But by 1914 the supply of additional "colonizable" territory had run out, and potential imperialists were now hard up against each other for new lands to conquer. In international terms this returned a realist cast to relationships between previously friendly nations. The gains of Germany were said to impinge on England; the gains of Russia were said to be dangerous to Germany. In terms of Social Darwinism, countries believed that one either had to grow or be suffocated, to assert oneself or be tied to decline. Thus, the virtues of liberalism were not seized upon, and democratic tendencies were stanched by resurgent authoritarian states. Militaries and expansive proconsuls were given their head.

The failure of democratization lay at the heart of this deficiency. There have been three different bursts of democracy since the nineteenth century.[2] The French Revolution, somewhat surprisingly, did not produce the first wave, since after it the conservative nobility and traditional classes returned to power. Nor did the Revolutions of 1848 extend the purview of democracy. After a brief experiment, the liberally chosen Frankfurt parliament collapsed and autocracies resumed control. It took World War I to pave the way for change. It did so, with nineteen democracies emerging in its wake as the Russian, Turkish, German, and Austrian empires shattered and dissolved. This trend toward democracy, however, was canceled by the rise of fascism after 1922 when the numbers of democracies declined. After World War II, however, and the independence movements of colonial countries, the number of democracies swelled to a high of 36. They increased further with the breakup of the Soviet Union after 1991, only to be curtailed by new authoritarian tendencies in Egypt, Russia, and Turkey. Iran and China remained single-party states. Peace would not "break out" among such countries.

The autocratic character of states was marked in 1914. But the "Great War" still should not have occurred. The great powers were in relatively good shape economically, and war would not improve their position in any obvious or predictable way. It is true that except for France and Britain, the powers were authoritarian countries

1. Arnold Toynbee, *A Study of History* (London: Oxford University Press, 1939), vol. 4, 170, 175–176.

2. Samuel Huntington, *The Third Wave: Democratization in the Late Twentieth Century* (Norman: University of Oklahoma Press, 1991), 15–26.

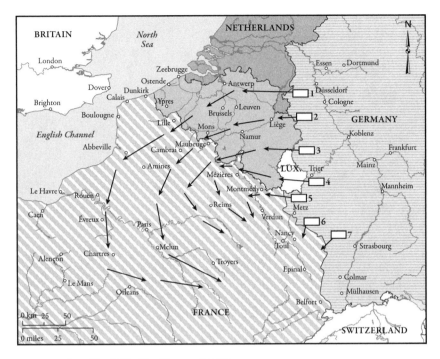

FIGURE 6.1 The Schlieffen Plan as of 1905.

in which executives and the military largely dictated outcomes, so they did not worry overmuch about popular opinion and perhaps could risk a challenge to other states. But further reform was in the air. The democratically elected German Reichstag would not inevitably go on doing the Kaiser's bidding given the shortage of money and the need for tax revenues. In 1912, because of financial limitations, Germany could not fund the expanded naval law and increases in army strength; new naval building had to be put off.[3]

Could an early military action succeed? Germany worried that Russia's railway construction would speed up her response to a German attack on France. By 1917, the Schlieffen Plan—which depended on Germany defeating France before taking on Russia—would become obsolete (Figure 6.1). From this standpoint, it was perhaps better to have a conflict earlier than later. But this conclusion depended on German success in the opening battles. Would Germany be able to sweep round the French left wing and penetrate behind Paris? Only if

---

3. Christopher Clark points out: "By 1916–17, German strategists believed, the striking power of Russia would be sufficient to nullify the calculations embodied in the Schlieffen Plan"; see Christopher Clark, *The Sleepwalkers: How Europe Went to War in 1918* (New York: Harper, 2013), 332.

Germany's ability to move within France was comparable to its ability to move within German frontiers—and it was not. The French controlled railways on their side, so the Germans would have to march on foot once they crossed the line, giving the French time to mount a defense, by taxis from Paris if need be. The Marne provided a barrier to stop or at least slow the German right wing.

The Triple Alliance was not superior to the Triple Entente in percentage of world industrial production, as shown in the following numbers (see also Table 6.1, page 118):

> Britain: 9.9%
> United States: 32.0%
> Germany: 14.8%
> France: 6.1%
> Russia: 8.2%
> Austria-Hungary: 4.4%
> Italy: 2.4%

This meant that in a long war in which all powers were fully mobilized, the Triple Entente was ahead of the Triple Alliance (whose Italian partner would not fight and joined the entente powers in 1916). The insufficiency, however, did not deter Germany from attacking, because it was hoping to win in a short war. As we have already seen, however, victory in a quick war depended on encircling the French forces, and this was very questionable.

Why then did the emperor give the green light to Austria on July 5 (in the notorious Blank Cheque, tendered at Potsdam to the Austrian emissary)? Here, more than rational factors played a role. Germany and even Britain had listened to the doctrines of Social Darwinism, which glorified vigorous, decisive action as a mark of superiority. How dissatisfied had Germany become? How eager was France to regain its strength? There were ideological currents roiling these issues. Did a country have to assert itself to avoid decline? Some Britons thought so. Sir Eyre Crowe declared that a policy of graceful concessions "must be definitively given up"[4] for good relations with Germany to be restored.

In 1914 the outbreak of war was not necessarily thought to be disastrous. Even if a great power lost the war, it might not be forever discredited and disarmed. The Austro-Prussian War (1866) and the Franco-Prussian War (1870–71) combined to show that a nation could recover from defeat and resume its place in the councils of nations. Austria became Germany's ally within three years, and France

---

4. Alan Alexandroff, "Before the War: Three Styles of Diplomacy," in *The Next Great War? The Roots of World War I and the Risk of U.S.–China Conflict*, ed. Richard N. Rosecrance and Steven E. Miller (Cambridge, MA: MIT Press, 2014), 9.

found a supporter in Russia. In each case the decisive battles had been fought within two to three weeks of the outset of hostilities. Thus, in 1914, great powers thought they could risk it. The war would not last long, and recovery from its effects would be rapid.

If one did not respond to challenge, moreover, what would allies think and how would they act? Germany could count Austria on her side in 1914, but how would Russia respond if it did not have France as an ally? After the signing of the Anglo-French Entente Cordiale in April 1904, Wilhelm II and Prince Bernhard von Bülow had set out to secure Nicholas II's support and had succeeded in convincing the rather simple-minded tsar to sign the secret Treaty of Björkö. Baron Lamsdorf was able to persuade Nicholas to annul the treaty, but the Franco-Russian alliance seemed weaker than ever.[5] Further, France had not supported Russia in the Bosnian crisis of 1908, nor had it strongly backed it during the Balkan Wars of 1912–1913. If France did not stand with Russia this time, Paris might wake up to find it no longer had a Russian ally. Thus the issue in 1914 was not merely whether material factors permitted war, it was also whether alliances would hold together in its absence. Technically, Russia and France might be better off fighting Germany in 1916 or 1917, but would the alliances survive the failure to act together in 1914?

German policy, in addition, had made agreement with England difficult. During Bismarck's tenure, Germany had religiously avoided naval construction and focused on ground forces to avoid challenging Britain. Under Caprivi and then von Bülow, however, Germany had embarked on an imperial policy (Weltpolitik) that, though begun late, would threaten the British position overseas and at home. The kaiser enthusiastically endorsed the naval doctrines of American Admiral Alfred Thayer Mahan, and Germany inaugurated the High Seas Fleet as early as 1898. This was popular with both public opinion and the industrialists who favored military spending and iron consumption. When the German naval minister, Admiral Alfred von Tirpitz, started building "Dreadnoughts," he soon came to recognize, however, that Germany could not afford even a 1-to-1.5 production ratio with England, to say nothing of equality.[6] Germany in effect conceded British continuing superiority in 1913. For Germany, of course, naval strength meant the balance overseas, whereas for England it entailed the protection of the British Isles against invasion. The Germans seem never to have fully understood how important naval superiority was for Britain.

---

5. Sidney B. Fay, "The Kaiser's Secret Negotiations with the Tsar, 1904–1905," *The American Historical Review* 24, no. 1 (1918): 48–72.

6. David D'Lugo and Ronald Rogowski, "The Anglo-German Naval Race and Comparative Constitutional 'Fitness,'" in *The Domestic Bases of Grand Strategy*, ed. Richard Rosecrance and Arthur A. Stein (Ithaca, NY: Cornell University Press, 1993), 65–95 (figures on production ratios appear on page 70).

Industrialization has complex effects on international relations. On the one hand, industrial countries care less about land than do agricultural or mining countries, because they do not need much land to generate wealth. On the other hand, they need access to raw materials and cheap food for factory workers, and those things come from certain types of territory. Severe economic downturns, such as occurred in 1873 and 1929, can trigger fears among industrial states about the international economy and lead them to be protectionist (to stop buying foreign goods) and imperialist (to secure raw materials from abroad). In such times industrial states can become dangerous to one another. This is one reason why world governments responded so swiftly and forcefully to the economic crisis of 2008: they wanted to avoid a replaying of the horrible 1930s.

There were other factors that predisposed the great powers to engage in conflict and war in 1914. During the nineteenth century the process of industrialization had spread over the European continent.[7] For a time it appeared that the machine age and the trade it engendered would bring an atmosphere of international peace.[8] From 1871 to 1914 national progress had been largely economic, with an exchange of industrial products and raw materials between

Table 6.1 Relative Shares of World Manufacturing Output, Percentages, 1860–1913

	1860	1880	1900	1913	1928	1938
Britain	19.9	22.9	18.5	13.6	9.9	10.7
France	7.9	7.8	6.8	6.1	6.0	4.4
Germany	4.9	8.5	13.2	14.8	11.6	12.7
Russia	7.0	7.6	8.8	8.2	5.3	9.0
Austria-Hungary	4.2	4.4	4.7	4.4	—	—
United States	7.2	14.7	23.6	32.0	39.3	31.4
Italy	2.5	2.5	2.5	2.4	2.7	2.8

Paul Kennedy, *The Rise and Fall of the Great Powers: Economic Change and Military Conflict from 1500 to 2000* (New York: Random House, 1987), 202.

7. Sidney Pollard, *Peaceful Conquest: The Industrialization of Europe 1760–1970* (New York: Oxford University Press, 1981).

8. A. J. Toynbee, *A Study of History*, Vol. 4 (New York: Oxford University Press, 1946).

east and west. Despite recessions (such as that between 1873 and 1896), growth had proceeded on both sides of the continent, and there was the prospect that further growth would lead to greater liberalization (and democracy) and that this would contribute to international peace.

At the same time, however, tariffs had risen, and trade was not fully free. Most of Europe had joined Britain and France in following a liberal trade policy in the 1850s and '60s; however, in the 1870s, motivated partly by the recession and partly by growing nationalist sentiment, European governments returned to protectionism and tariff wars broke out, stifling continental trade. When Caprivi tried to push back against the neo-mercantilist trend in 1891, it cost him the German chancellorship.[9] Nor did Eastern courts democratize; instead they instituted parliaments that did not enjoy full power to control executives. Mercantilist restrictions led to trade conflicts between Russia and Germany, Italy and Austria. Further, the spirit of imperialism infected many European powers, which sought greater amounts of territory overseas. Of the total global land area of 52.5 million square miles, Britain had appropriated about 12 million, or nearly 23 percent, and it had one-seventh of the world's population.[10]

Other states—France, Germany, Austria, and Russia—were left behind. It was not surprising, then, that Germany and France wanted to even up the spoils. This desire for territory was perhaps understandable as long as it was essentially free for the taking (from local pashas, sheiks, and tribal chieftains). But once there was no more "colonizable" territory left, a policy of imperialism meant war between European powers over already appropriated real estate and entailed much more serious conflicts. The challenge to Britain posed by French forces in Fashoda (at the headwaters of the Nile) in 1898 was an example. In a mercantilist age with rising tariffs, Europeans had greater difficulty selling to each other and found (their own) colonial markets much more congenial.[11]

Thus, the Industrial Revolution led to growth and economic interdependence, but because of high tariffs, it also produced international conflict over territory. Nationalism emerged to challenge internationalism. Openness rivaled empire for precedence.

Could success in one realm lead to success in the other—could one conquer enough territory to emancipate one's economy from the restraints of interdependence? Obviously, many in Germany and also Britain thought so. War might therefore be useful. But by 1914 no power could see a clear way to victory.

---

9. Pollard, *Peaceful Conquest*, 255–261.

10. *Encyclopædia Britannica*, 1911, vol. 4.

11. See the analysis in Eric Hobsbawm, *Industry and Empire* (New York: Pantheon Books, 1968), 105–107.

Domestic Change in Europe

The Great War should have changed all these convictions. The lessons of the Battle of the Somme in 1916 should have been decisive in themselves to cast war into the discard. In one day, July 1, 1916, it had put as many men out of action as the number of Americans killed in Vietnam from 1961 to 1975. Not only were there no real victors and huge costs, the losers—having suffered grievously—were willing within a few years to risk war again. How could this be? Who would repeat such slaughter?

> Realism does not explain states' misperceptions, particularly repeated and highly costly ones like the Axis made in World War II. The racial theory of the Nazis also led them to underestimate the Soviet Union: they believed that Slavic peoples were racially inferior to "Aryans." The militaristic ideology of Nazi Germany and Japan led them to underestimate the liberal democracies of the West: they believed that liberals only want to make money and lack the will to fight. It is true that liberal democracies do not like war because they usually can secure their interests more cheaply, but when pushed to the wall they do fight and typically have more resources to mobilize because they are wealthy. Studies show that democracies are more likely to win the wars they do fight.

Germany had lost the war and failed to win new territory and prestige. Japan had defeated both China (1894–1895) and Russia (1905) but felt discriminated against at the Paris Peace Conference when racial equality was not agreed to.[12] Germany had been forced to accept all the guilt for waging war, and the Versailles Treaty was a diktat imposed by the Allies to appease public sentiment at home. The wartime allies exacerbated opinion in the defeated or neglected states by insisting they pay their debts (or reparations) by transferring monies to Western nations. They could do so, however, only if they were allowed to export, and Western tariffs (the Smoot-Hawley Tariff) and U.S. and other devaluations made this difficult if not impossible.[13] Either debts or

---

12. As Antony Best writes, many Japanese believed that "the Great War had demonstrated that economic autarky was necessary in order to guarantee victory in any future conflict. For Japan, which was resource poor, this meant that if the country was to survive a clash with a Great Power or Powers, it required a larger empire that would provide it with a much greater measure of self-sufficiency"; quoted in Ronald Findlay and Kevin H. O'Rourke, *Power and Plenty: Trade, War, and the World Economy in the Second Millennium* (Princeton, NJ: Princeton University Press, 2008), 443.

13. See also John Maynard Keynes, *The Economic Consequences of the Peace* (New York: Harcourt, Brace, and Howe, 1920), 168–208.

Table 6.2 Unemployment Rates During the Great Depression*

	1929	1930	1931	1932	1933	1934	1935	1936
Britain	10.4	16.0	21.3	22.1	19.9	16.8	15.5	15.4
Germany			23.7	30.1	25.8	14.5	11.6	12.4
Austria	12.3	15.0	20.3	26.1	29.0	26.3	23.4	27.5
United States	8.2	14.5	19.1	23.8	24.3	20.9	18.5	16.7
Netherlands	7.1	9.7	18.1	29.5	31.0	32.1	36.3	40.5
Belgium	3.0	7.9	16.9	20.7	17.2	17.2	12.8	10.9
Canada	5.7	11.1	16.8	22.0	22.3	18.2	15.4	14.4

* In France and Italy, no figures for the size of the active work force exist, so it is impossible to calculate an unemployment rate. However, in France, applications for work increased from 9,710 per month in 1929 to 305,380 per month in 1932 and 522,634 in January 1936; in Italy, the number of recipients of social insurance increased from 300,786 in 1929 to 1,006,442 in 1932 (no figures are available for 1936, but there was a drop after a peak in 1933). The USSR did not release any labor statistics.

reparations had to be lessened or creditors would not be paid. Since creditors would never agree to the latter, debtors moved to policies of autarky (self-sufficiency). They would ration their purchases to those goods their exports would pay for and no more. This involved reducing their imports, impinging on the standard of living of their populations. To say this was unpopular was axiomatic, but in the context of the worldwide depression (1929–1939) it was a disaster (Table 6.2).

German numbers are based on a registry of unemployed workers (there are no figures for 1929 or 1930); U.S. and Canadian numbers are based on trade union returns; British, Belgian, Austrian, and Dutch numbers are based on unemployment insurance statistics.

It is a truism that fascist Germany and Japan opted for military expansion to find markets, raw materials, and substitutes (ersatz products) to meet their requirements. If other countries had high tariffs or controls on sales of vital materials, only domestically owned territories (colonies) could provide goods and markets. Japan resolved to create such dependent areas in East Asia, Manchuria and China, and Germany in East Europe, Poland, and the Soviet Union. War and military expansion was their means of doing so. A large-scale aid program for Germany and Japan might theoretically have substituted for war, but no Western government, beset by depression, would or could provide such aid. Figure 6.2 shows the average tariff level in each industrialized country from 1923 to 1939.

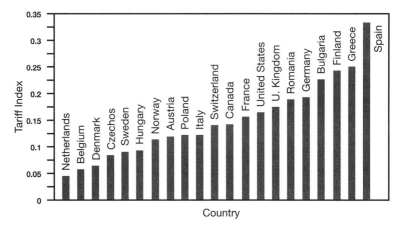

FIGURE 6.2 Western economic nationalism.
Source: After Simmons, 1994.

Thus, the collapse of the world economy in the depression cut the heart out of what had been general prosperity and turned one country against another. There were, of course, rabid nationalist and racist claims to justify these absurdities. Germany claimed to be the fount of a master race—the Aryan race. Japanese culture was proclaimed superior to China's. Nordic nations were to be admired, and Hitler revered Sibelius along with Beethoven. But the key to these attitudes was humming the myth of superiority in order to distract attention from Germany's decline in real terms. The German population consumed less as finance was diverted to rearmament. But as long as Germany made gain after gain—rearmament, the Rhineland, the Anschluss (union) with Austria, the seizure of Czechoslovakia—the German population could accept Adolf Hitler as their leader. These were all gains obtained without having to fight. Things changed, however, in 1939 because England and France ceased appeasing Germany.

Neither World War should have occurred—in cost-benefit terms, Germany and Japan could not defeat the United States and Russia, even if England was not involved. Yet they acted to bring them both into war. Strictly, this was not a realist outcome—it was violent, to be sure, but not dictated by strict power considerations. Germany never achieved more than one-third of America's war potential. England and France together matched German war production. How Germany could undertake to attack all three, the United States, France, and Britain (not even including Russia), was hard to understand. Only if America failed to mobilize was this enough. And as late as 1939 the United States was spending only 1.6 percent of its GDP on armaments. As Kennedy writes, "an increase in the defense-spending share of the American GNP to bring it close to the proportions devoted to armaments by the fascist states would automatically make the United States the most powerful military state in the world."[14] The U.S. margin over Japan was even greater. Tokyo's warship strength was 62 percent of America's in 1942, 50 percent in 1943, and a disastrous 30 percent in 1944.[15] Germany and Japan had an incentive to strike quickly if they were going to strike at all. But they never acquired the ability to defeat America even then. They should have hesitated and withdrawn their forces.

Post-War Crisis

At the end of World War I, France and England imposed a huge reparations bill on Germany, though the total (sometimes estimated at $50 billion) was never specified. The United States also expected war debts to be repaid by Britain and France. As J. M. Keynes pointed out, since no one had a remaining gold stock, this could be done only by allowing and encouraging the debtors to export to their creditors.[16] But Britain and France, to say nothing of the United States, would not allow this.

Public opinion would not permit the Allies to buy German goods in sufficiency. Germany could pay reparations only if someone lent them the money. This was arranged in the Dawes Plan of 1924, which gathered investors together to buy German bonds, thereby providing the funds with which to pay their debts (chiefly reparations). Seven percent interest was offered to attract investors, and there was a considerable demand for German bonds. This incentive sufficed until 1928, when the New York stock market began to soar. Some securities doubled in three or four years, reflecting a return of 18 percent. Who then would buy German bonds?

Equally, when the market tipped downward in 1929, German bonds were also affected and repayment in hard currency became questionable as Britain, Austria, and then Germany went off the gold standard. Finally, reparations payments had to be suspended and U.S. President Herbert Hoover called for a moratorium on all payments of war debts. The Hoover Moratorium ultimately became permanent.

When Hitler came to power on January 30, 1933, the wartime Allies were unsure whether his bluster was real or for effect. Perhaps in the end, they

---

14. Paul Kennedy, *The Rise and Fall of the Great Powers* (New York: Vintage Books, 1989), 443.

15. Kennedy, *Rise and Fall*, 333.

16. Keynes, *Economic Consequences of the Peace*.

thought, he could become an exponent of the status quo. The British believed that, given inducements, Germany "would agree to accept some form of revised Versailles armaments agreement that would not in practice leave Germany free to rearm."[17] The problem was that if they were wrong, Britain would need France as a strong ally. However, everything they did in the appeasement policy to draw Germany in would shove France away, until perhaps it was too late. It would have been ideal for Britain to have Washington on its side, but Roosevelt was so beset with domestic questions he could make no undertakings in foreign affairs. Accordingly, when Hitler violated the Versailles Treaty by sending German troops into Germany's Rhineland region on March 7, 1936, France and Britain did not quiver. This made defense of Czechoslovakia and Poland more difficult as Britain and France would now have to go through an even thicker swathe of German territory to assist them. Hitler told French philosopher Bertrand de Jouvenal that conflicts between Germany and France were ridiculous and should be put aside. Britain could believe that Hitler would not dare to risk a new war. Nor perhaps would he have to, as the British prime minister would return Austria, the Sudetenland (a majority-German region of Czechoslovakia), and the Polish Corridor to Germany on what was now a tarnished silver platter, thereby bowing to Woodrow Wilson's dictum of "national self-determination."

It is true that Chamberlain's appeasement policy would not give to Germany anything that was not "rightfully" theirs. The trouble was that if these concessions were not made peaceably, Hitler would take them by force. Thus, in the end Britain and France went to war over procedure, not substance—and the mode of German demands. Duff Cooper, the British naval minister, mobilized the fleet after the Godesberg meeting in August 1938, and it was only after this demonstration of resolve that Hitler agreed to the Munich settlement. A year later, it was not the Polish position that Britain and France were defending (where Hitler had the better of the irredentist argument), it was Hitler's methods of achieving the return of German territory. After Germany's attack on Poland on September 1, Chamberlain gave Hitler one day to withdraw his troops (which of course he did not do). Even after the Anglo-French declarations of war on September 3, the Allies did nothing. They waited for Hitler to attack them. At various postwar conferences, British military attachés said that the War Office had no plans to attack Germany. Failing Hitler's own initiative to start hostilities through an attack on France, the so-called "phony war" might have gone on for an indeterminate period.

---

17. Zara Steiner, *The Lights that Failed: European International History 1919–1933* (Oxford: Oxford University Press, 2005), 814.

As A. J. P. Taylor pointed out, the Allies presumably had enough troops to defend themselves in the West (a margin of one to one or even three to one), but they did not have enough to launch an offensive into Germany and across the *Westwall* or Siegfried Line (Germany's equivalent of the Maginot Line), where a favorable margin of three to one or five to one was essential.[18] It is thus easier to understand why Britain and France did not strike Germany directly when Poland folded in October 1939.

Of course, we know that such ratios did not deter Hitler or prevent the Manstein Plan, which involved a diversionary attack into Belgium as a prelude to the main thrust through the Ardennes forest and across the Meuse, allowing German forces to operate behind French and British lines as Allied troops mistakenly plunged into Belgium. If the French and British had stayed behind the lines in a defensive formation, they could have cut off the German Ardennes salient as it came through. But Allied commanders were reacting to counter another Schlieffen Plan, not a strike through Luxembourg, which they completely failed to anticipate. The French even denied their own Deuxième Bureau's intelligence that saw the Germans proceeding through Luxembourg.[19]

In the 1930s the progress of democracy was also stifled as tin pot autocracies mimicked Hitler and Mussolini. The depression brought autocrats to power in Eastern Europe, Spain, Germany, Hungary, Rumania, Poland, the Baltic countries, and Turkey—ostensibly to deal with the threat from the extreme left. In Eastern Europe, only one democracy (Czechoslovakia) remained. (Note in Figure 6.3 the sharp reduction in the number of democracies in the world in the 1930s.) Thus, when, after the defeat of France, Britain stood alone against Hitler in 1940, the democrats who might support her were in the Western Hemisphere or the Antipodes, and Roosevelt was hobbled by U.S. neutrality laws. German and Japanese victories were the order of the day through most of 1942, only mitigated at the end by Allied victories in North Africa and the Italian boot. Fortunately, at least in the short run, Hitler elected to attack Russia on June 22, 1941, thinking that the Soviet Union could be dispatched as the tsarist regime had been in March 1917. The Soviet people, however, stood steadfast in supporting their Russian masters, and Stalin received a great deal of Lend-Lease aid from the United States (trucks and food; SPAM, a mélange of pork, sustained many Soviet citizens week after week).

Hitler compounded his own problem by calling on the Reichstag to declare war on the United States on December 11, 1941. This had the great advantage of allowing the United States to fight in Europe and not be restricted to the Japanese

18. A. J. P. Taylor, *The Origins of the Second World War* (London: Hamish Hamilton, 1961), 115.

19. Ernest R. May, *Strange Victory: Hitler's Conquest of France* (New York: Hill and Wang, 2000), 357–360.

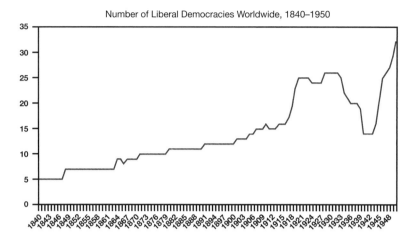

FIGURE 6.3 Number of liberal democracies worldwide, 1840–1950.
Source: After Doyle, 1983.

theater. By 1943 the issue was no longer in doubt as the productive apparatus of U.S. industry swung into gear. Churchill blessed the Pearl Harbor attack because he knew America's response would tell the tale against both Germany and Japan.

It was still hard to understand the Japanese calculations that led to the attack on Pearl Harbor. The key to understanding international relations is to realize that power alone does not control policy or decisions. The Japanese elite and Adolf Hitler had objectives they would pursue come what may. As the Japanese foreign minister Yosuke Matsuoka said, the Japanese believed they "could not obtain a tiger's cub without braving the tiger's den"— that they had to act decisively.[20] The Japanese military elite had suffered during the imperialist period of world politics, when European states took over much of the rest of the world. After 1920, they sought their own share of colonies. It was not sufficient to point out that nations like China and Thailand were already members of the League of Nations, recognized by all, and could not be partitioned or seized. Moreover, Japan's economic dependence (for iron ore and oil) was particularly on the United States. Did that entitle the Japanese to take over Texas and Minnesota? That Germany and Japan had relatively few colonies did not mean that they could simply demand their share and expect to be gratified. Perhaps Japan wanted economic security, but it could be achieved only by total concession or by war against the United States. As Paul Kennedy points out, "the United States had nearly twice the population

20. Robert J. C. Butow, *Tojo and the Coming of War* (Princeton, NJ: Princeton University Press, 1961), 308n.

of Japan and *seventeen* times the national income, produced five times as much steel and seven times as much coal, and made eighty times as many motor vehicles each year. . . . Even granted the high level of Japanese patriotic fervor and the memory of its staggering successes against far larger opponents in 1895 (China) and 1905 (Russia), what it was now planning bordered on the incredible"[21]—an attack on the United States. Such a strike would be rational only if the United States would sue for a compromise peace (after a few tenuous Japanese victories) in 1942. But this was to equate America's resolve with that of pre-revolutionary Russia in 1905. Anyone who believed that could be sold the Brooklyn Bridge on any Sunday in May—it was simply not credible. It was all very well for post-war Japanese scholars to claim that Japan's prospective "loss of face" did not permit it to back down in 1941, but countries back down all the time when suitably challenged, as did Soviet Russia in Cuba in 1962. There had always been an alternation in Western history of greater and lesser involvement in major power wars and greater or lesser toughness when challenged. Portugal had been a near-dominant power in the early sixteenth century but adopted a dependent stance after 1650. Sweden had been a near-dominant player during the Reformation but muted its policies after 1720. George Washington sought to reduce the fledgling U.S. involvement in French diplomacy in the 1790s. Denmark knew how to back down without suffering status anxiety. Switzerland's whole policy had been intermittent participation in Europe's wars. Italy havered in many instances. In a similar manner, Japan could have moderated its course in 1941 instead of attacking the United States.

Hitler's Germany had hoped that European states could be defeated one by one much like a fastidious eater plucks an artichoke, one leaf at a time. But this depended on separating enemies from each other. Hitler kept Russia from entering the war in 1939, but he could not divide France and Britain, who acted together.

Renaissance diplomacy had indicated that Hapsburg dominance had to be pursued gingerly, with occasional bones thrown to France and England. Hitler did not or could not do this and thus compounded the problem Napoleon faced of having too many states ranged against him and not knowing when and how to stop. Bismarck had solved this problem by isolating France while encouraging it to pursue a colonial vocation (he told the French that "the Tunisian pear is ripe—pluck it").[22] Hitler had no similar reassurance for Britain, for example, even though Hildebrand argues that an agreement with Britain was one

---

21. Kennedy, *Rise and Fall*, p. 303.

22. William Langer, *European Alliances and Alignments, 1871–1890*, 2d ed. (New York: Vintage Books, 1950), p. 221.

of Hitler's major objectives. (In 1941 Hitler's deputy Rudolf Hess flew a solo mission to Britain to try to negotiate a separate peace; the British threw him in prison.) Bismarck, serving for twenty-eight years, could wait to see his projects mature over time, but Hitler's timetable (spurred by fears for his health) was short—he thought he needed victories in the very near term, so Britain would have had to embrace Germany fervently and precipitately.[23] Even Neville Chamberlain could not and would not do this. He went to war with Hitler with no domestic ability to reach a compromise. After Churchill joined the cabinet, accommodating Germany became virtually unthinkable.

Nor should Chamberlain or Halifax have compromised. Hitler was the most execrable leader in German history. He aimed to rejuvenate Germany by conquering Europe and perhaps the world. He had no sense of limitation—either personal or national—no understanding of the restrictions upon German power. In moral terms his policy toward Jews and other minorities was to destroy them, even though Jewish citizens had been loyal supporters of their German nationality.

Conclusion

World War II, initiated in 1939 and expanded in 1941 (when Nazi Germany attacked Russia and declared war on the United States), brought the clash of autocracy with freedom to a temporary conclusion. There were then three separate worlds: the Western democratic world, the Soviet communist world, and the fascist world of Germany and Japan. World War II got rid of the third, and the Cold War got rid of the second, at least in its most vituperative version.

The question for the future remains: How vicious will the authoritarian world remain as it inexorably liberalizes? This question is tied to the type of unity the world can realistically expect before or after it moves toward peace. Broadly speaking, unity can be achieved by popular movements, or it can be negotiated by diplomats. The two have not always gone together in European or world history. Let us consider two examples. The first is the so-called Holy Roman Empire, or a broadened Germany, which was a loose amalgam of states that did not necessarily speak the same language and only served as an alternative to rule by the Catholic Church. It broke up in 1806 after invasion by Napoleon. But its unity was purely top-down—it was not supported by any amalgamation of the peoples involved. The second example is the unification of Germany in 1871, which excluded one of the major German states, Austria,

---

23. In a ludicrous extension this would have involved turning over British policy to the Cliveden Set and Oswald Mosley.

because at the time it ruled non-German (Czech, Hungarian and Balkan) realms. Of course, Kleindeutsch unification (without Austria) was to a degree popularly supported, but more in North German Protestant lands than in the Catholic South.

Nonetheless, German unity was fundamentally a diplomatic construction, negotiated by leaders of the constituent units or duchies themselves. Popular support depended upon economic and military action to bring dissidents on board. This strange mixture of support affected Germany's decision to start the Great War. As many historians have noted, the war was supposed to bring greater support for the unity of an otherwise partly disaggregated Germany. German war plans, as we have seen, were for a "quick war" that would not place undue strain on a tenuously united Germany. Whether this was a stimulus to war can be debated, but it was certainly a factor in the type of war that would be fought. The final implication is for European unity today and in the future. Even before publics had done so, European leaders had decided to bring European states together in a federative arrangement.[24] Thus European unity has always been "top-down," to be later supported by popular opinion and action. Popular support has usually been deficient because the rewards to constituent peoples have been so uncertain or lacking, as they are to this day. Backed by the United States, however, European unity has continued despite challenges from Russia and perhaps occasionally China. But economic upsurge has been a potent remedy to division, spreading the benefits to the population as a whole and winning support in return. Authoritarian states like Russia will gingerly support this outcome as long as they are not themselves undercut politically in doing so.

FURTHER READING

Butow, Robert J. C. *Tojo and the Coming of War.* Princeton, NJ: Princeton University Press, 1961.

Clark, Christopher. *The Sleepwalkers: How Europe Went to War in 1918.* New York: Harper, 2013.

Huntington, Samuel. *The Third Wave: Democratization in the Late Twentieth Century.* Norman: University of Oklahoma Press, 1991.

Kennedy, Paul. *The Rise and Fall of the Great Powers.* New York: Vintage Books, 1989.

Pollard, Sidney. *Peaceful Conquest: The Industrialization of Europe 1760–1970.* New York: Oxford University Press, 1981.

---

24. François Duchêne, "Europe's Breakthrough," in *Jean Monnet: The First Statesman of Interdependence* (New York: W. W. Norton & Company, 1994), 181–225.

Rosecrance, Richard N., and Steven E. Miller, eds. *The Next Great War? The Roots of World War I and the Risk of U.S.–China Conflict.* Cambridge, MA: MIT Press, 2014.

Steiner, Zara. *The Lights That Failed: European International History 1919–1933.* New York: Oxford University Press, 2005.

Taylor, A. J. P. *The Origins of the Second World War.* London: Hamish Hamilton, 1961.

7 THE COLD WAR: THE LIBERAL INTERNATIONAL SUBSYSTEM IS INSTITUTIONALIZED

Introduction

In this chapter and the next we shall show that during the Cold War both realism and liberalism captured central features of international relations. Because most coercive power in the world was held by two superpowers, the United States and the Soviet Union, and because these two states held radically different ideas about how to order national and international life, global politics was structured by a bipolar system. The superpowers did suspect one another at every turn and engaged in arms races and proxy wars in what was called the Third World. Within the U.S.-led Western bloc, however, countries were democratic, their economies became increasingly interdependent, and their relations became increasingly institutionalized or rule-governed. The liberal international subsystem finally came into its own, surrounded by a realist system. The members of the subsystem interacted extensively with states outside of it, and when they did so they generally followed realist tenets. But, like liberal Britain in preceding centuries, they slowly outperformed their non-democratic fellow states, essentially beating them at the realist game.

Max Roser of Oxford University has plotted international conflict since 1400.[1] He concludes that great power conflict has declined overall but that World War II represented a recent peak, akin to the Reformation and the Thirty Years' War. Civil wars have risen in violence, but international wars have declined. As journalist Eduardo Porter writes, "Zero growth gave us Genghis Khan and the Middle Ages, conquest and subjugation. It fostered an order in which the only mechanism to get ahead was to plunder one's neighbor. Economic growth opened up a much better alternative: trade . . . [War] was a real killer in the era of no growth. Up to half of all deaths among hunter-gatherers, horticulturalists, and other ancient cultures were caused by conflict. The bloody twentieth century—stage for two world wars, the Holocaust and other war-based genocides—still didn't even come close" to per capita levels attained in the seventeenth century.[2]

That is the world of fixed scarcity, in which anyone's gain is always someone else's loss. It is the world described by realism, a world of ruthless competition among states in perpetual fear of one another. And it often has been the preponderant system in world politics. In the years after World War II, realist theory enjoyed a revival, particularly in the United States. A cohort of scholars, some from Europe, took it upon themselves to educate Americans about the way the world really worked. Theologian Reinhold Niebuhr, journalist Walter Lippmann, diplomat George Kennan, and political scientists Hans Morgenthau and Henry Kissinger believed that Americans still clung to Woodrow Wilson's conviction that America could reform world politics and replace the old "might makes right" system with a lawful, peaceful world order. Generations of college undergraduates imbibed Morgenthau's six principles of political realism:

1. Politics is governed by timeless, objective laws that no country can overcome.
2. Interest, defined in terms of power and territory, is the best guide to international politics.
3. How states define power varies across history and geographical space.
4. Politics and morality are always in tension.
5. No country's particular moral principles are universally valid.
6. The political sphere has its own logic, distinct from the economic, legal, and moral spheres.[3]

For realists, it was inevitable that the United States and Soviet Union, allies during the Second World War, would fall into rivalry and even enmity after Nazi

---

1. Max Roser, "War and Peace Before 1945," accessed from OurWorldinData.org.

2. Eduardo Porter, "Imagining a World Without Growth," *New York Times*, December 2, 2015, B-9.

3. Hans J. Morgenthau, *Politics among Nations: The Struggle for Power and Peace*, 3rd ed. (New York: Knopf, 1963).

Germany and Imperial Japan were vanquished in 1945. Powerful countries that lacked a common enemy could not help but mistrust one another, because each knew the other was self-interested and defined its interests in terms of power. In the 1970s, Kenneth Waltz further refined realism into a structural theory, neorealism, which asserts that international anarchy and the balance of power among states (bipolar or multipolar) were the two most important facts about the international system.

All the while, however, liberal theorists toiled away and saw many features of world politics that pressed against realism. Among the liberal democracies of the world—in Western Europe, North America, and Japan—many of the ideas traceable back to Adam Smith and Immanuel Kant (see Chapter 4) came to fruition under the sponsorship of the United States. In the 1950s David Mitrany and Karl Deutsch theorized about integration and peaceful democratic communities. In the 1970s Robert Keohane and Joseph Nye analyzed interdependence among nations, and in the 1980s Keohane explicated how international institutions—mutually agreed rules—could lower the costs of cooperation among states even without a world government to enforce their agreements. Michael Doyle and others argued that Kant was right after all: republics or liberal democracies did not fight wars against one another—again, in spite of international anarchy.

World War II and the Institutionalization of the Liberal International Subsystem

In earlier chapters we saw how, even before there were any modern liberal democracies in Europe or anywhere else in the world, processes were in place that would later produce democracy and an emphasis on trade. Eventually, in the twentieth century, these factors produced an international subsystem of trade and self-government within the larger realist system of competition, empire, and war. From the twelfth through the sixteenth century, the Italian city-states of Venice, Florence, and Genoa were republics, ruled not by kings but by their elites, who became and stayed wealthy via trade. Venice, the most powerful, fought many wars over trading rights and routes. Unlike most monarchies of the time, Venice financed its wars with debt borrowed from its own citizens. Its republican form of government guaranteed that the citizens would be repaid, and thus the wars were more popular. Venice was not a modern liberal democracy, but it was more democratic than its opponents—controlled not by a single ruler but by assemblies of its wealthy male citizens—and also more successful in war than the Turks and other large territorial states and empires ruled by absolute monarchs.[4]

---

4. See David A. Lake, "Powerful Pacifists: Democratic States and War," *American Political Science Review* 86, no. 1 (1992): 24–37.

In the broad sweep of history, of course, not all nations have used democratization as a means of obtaining victory or influence in world politics. When non-democratic states have succeeded, the international system described by realism has predominated. As discussed in Chapter 6, in the 1930s, a time of dire economic distress, the Nazis threw off Germany's democracy and sought to build a vast territorial empire as a source of economic prosperity. They hoped to acquire in Eastern Europe and Russia a large swatch of ore-holding and oil-bearing territories (including Ploiești in Romania and Baku in Azerbaijan) that would make up for Germany's lack of such resources.

The Nazis were striving to follow their enemy Britain in taking imperial steps to colonize needed territories. There was a crucial difference, however: the British Empire had been built not by a rapacious central state seeking world domination but by private groups (non-state actors), such as the British East India Company and British East Africa Company, which sought monopolies overseas and the received protection from the British Navy and eventually the government. As the English historian John R. Seeley once wrote, "We seem, as it were, to have conquered and peopled half the world in a fit of absence of mind."[5] Of course, its empire did serve to make up for Britain's power deficiencies back home—to gain raw materials (oil and natural gas), markets, and food—and most Britons believed the empire served the national interest. That is what Germans wanted for Germany, too. But the Nazis were far from absent-minded about their acquisition of empire.

And the Nazis had in mind not colonies in Asia or Africa but an empire in Europe itself. Influenced by early twentieth-century realist writings on the Eurasian "heartland" as the key to world power, they were mesmerized by the natural and industrial resources of Western, Central, and Eastern Europe. Any country that could monopolize the industrial resources of their own country, Britain, the Low Countries, Germany, and Scandinavia, mating them with ores and petroleum in Eastern Europe and western Russia, would have an unmatched advantage in world politics.[6]

At the same time, in Asia, the Japanese were bedazzled by a vision of an empire including Korea, China, Indochina, Australia, and indeed most of the Pacific—an empire that would supply them with oil, tin, rubber, and other raw materials and provide a massive barrier to protect the Japanese home islands. An isolated United States could not expect to stand against such a combination of industrial, demographic, and raw material strength in the hands of aggressive authoritarian states.[7]

---

5. Sir John Robert Seeley, *The Expansion of England: Two Courses of Lectures* (Boston: Roberts Brothers, 1883).

6. This was basically Halford Mackinder's view of the region he called the "Heartland" in his essay on "The Pivot of History," The Royal Geographical Society, 1904.

7. Europe had more than twice the U.S. population (407 million people).

As we know, both Germany and Japan failed in their joint quest to subdue nations abundant in raw materials. Yet today, these are two of the world's most prosperous nations, with no thought of conquering their neighbors. How did this change come about? How could Germany and Japan succeed by failing?

The "Logic of the West"

Let us consider the German story. After their catastrophic defeat in 1945, mainstream Germans (in what was then democratic West Germany, not Soviet-dominated East Germany) embraced the ideas and policies of the liberal-democratic trading states. In effect, Germans accepted a bargain offered them by the United States and the rest of Western Europe: give up your ambitions of empire and your militarism, become a liberal democracy, rely on American military and economic protection, and get rich through foreign trade and investment. Under the Christian Democratic and later Social Democratic parties, West Germany became an exporting powerhouse and a member of both the North Atlantic Treaty Organization (NATO, the U.S.-led alliance) and what is now the European Union (EU). Germany is closely integrated economically and socially with Europe, the average German is better off than ever, and Germans' only thoughts of conquest pertain to the football pitch (soccer field).

American policymakers learned from the aftermath of World War I that an open economic order is best not only for prosperity but also for global peace and for U.S. interests. They also learned that a liberal great power must guarantee that open order and figured out that after World War II it had to be the United States. FDR, Secretary of State Cordell Hull, Britain's John Maynard Keynes, and others hatched plans for a set of international institutions, backed by the United States, that would reassure countries that when economic downturns happen, they need not seek autarchy—that is, not close their economies or start invading and seizing other countries' territory. This remains living history: most Western elites learn it and the lessons influenced response to economic meltdown of 2008 as well as EU's determination to deepen integration and not turn back.

Today's Germany is only the most dramatic case of a larger phenomenon—what we have been calling the liberal international subsystem. After World War II most countries in Western Europe, along with Japan, gave up their empires in return for American guarantees of security and prosperity through openness to foreign trade and investment. Those countries that were democracies remained so;

those that were not, became so. Economic growth through voluntary commerce replaced territorial expansion. Whereas in the eighteenth and nineteenth centuries only the beginnings of the liberal international system were evident (in the form of British-sponsored free trade and the example of American democracy), after 1945 the liberal subsystem became the most wealthy, powerful, and stable part of the broader international system. The subsystem consisted of an array of international institutions to guarantee the economic, political, and military security of America's friends, who remembered the upheaval, depression, and war of the 1930s vividly. The World Bank and International Monetary Fund (IMF) were created to handle balance-of-payment problems among countries so that they would remain open to trade. The General Agreement on Tariffs and Trade (GATT), forerunner of today's World Trade Organization (WTO), was constructed to lower barriers to international trade. In contrast to its economic closure in the 1930s, America now opened its economy to exports from Western Europe and Japan, giving these countries strong incentives to grow by exporting and making them less dependent on their now weakened empires. In the military realm, NATO, formed in 1949, was an American guarantee against a Soviet invasion.

The club of liberal democracies linked by an array of international institutions—what John Ikenberry has called the "logic of the West"—is one of the most remarkable success stories in international history.[8] As time has passed, each country has invested more in the system, making it less sensible to leave it. The system was jointly planned by Western statesmen, especially American and British, and underwritten by U.S. capital, military protection, and political will. Finally, after centuries of germination, the international system whose roots lie in medieval Venice and the Netherlands during the Renaissance came into being. It existed within the larger realist system but was real nonetheless. This logic of the West, which today extends far beyond the Western world, was not at all self-evident for most of human history. It took the traumas of the twentieth century and the hegemony of the liberal United States to finally make it plausible and practical for so many countries.

As always in international politics, the story is not simply one of good guys and bad guys. America did not share its ideas and institutions with an eager Europe and Japan simply out of the goodness of its heart. Nor did the United States strike the same happy bargain with poorer states in Latin America, Asia, and Africa; with those states the bargain was typically "don't worry about becoming democracies, just remain anti-communist and we will protect you, trade with you, and invest in your economy." All of these bargains were shaped by a new ideological threat forwarded by great power rivalry with a communist international subsystem of its own.

---

8. G. John Ikenberry, *Liberal Leviathan: The Origins, Crisis, and Transformation of the American World Order* (Princeton, NJ: Princeton University Press, 2011).

The Soviet International Subsystem

The communist Soviet Union had been an enemy of fascism and Nazism and ally to the Americans and British during World War II. Marxism-Leninism, the ideology behind the Soviet state, was "internationalist" in theory. It fundamentally rejected the liberal-democratic and free-market orientation of the West, however. The state was to own all resources on behalf of the workers, and the Communist Party was to control the state. It was the internationalism of communism that made it such an enemy of fascism, and also of Western integration. The Soviet Union included Eastern lands that Hitler coveted for Germany. Germany invaded the USSR in June 1941, betraying a non-aggression pact Hitler had with Stalin. The battles on the Eastern Front added up to the most destructive war theater in human history. Repulsing Germany's massive invasion cost the USSR an estimated 20 million people. That comes to forty Soviets for every one American killed in the war. The Soviet Union paid a much bigger price in the "Great Patriotic War" than the Western powers did.

The Soviet dictator Josef Stalin was determined to build a buffer of states between his country and Germany after the war. In 1944 and 1945, Soviet armies drove the German Wehrmacht westward and back toward Germany and did not stop at the Soviet border. They pursued the Wehrmacht through Eastern Europe, occupying Poland, Czechoslovakia, Hungary, Romania, Bulgaria, and eastern Germany itself, including the capital city of Berlin. And once the Red Army occupied a country, it stayed. The Soviets chose not to annex these states to the Soviet Union. Instead, it made them into satellite countries. Stalin's grand strategy included not only military occupation but also the installation of communist regimes in these states. He feared non-communist states on the Soviet border because he thought they would be implacably hostile to communism. Stalin could control communist parties in Eastern Europe, partly because of ideological affinity and partly because these elites lacked broad legitimacy with the people and so would always need Soviet help to stay in power. As Stalin told a Yugoslav communist leader in April 1945: "This war is not as in the past; whoever occupies a territory also imposes his own social system. Everyone imposes his own system as far as his army can reach. It cannot be otherwise."[9]

Before the Second World War, Stalin had not tried to build an expanded Soviet empire. "Socialism in one country" had been his motto since 1924. The war changed Stalin's mind, however. Between 1944 and 1948, the Kremlin manipulated events in Eastern European countries and maneuvered communist parties into power. (The one communist party the Soviets could not control was that of Yugoslavia; because its leader, Josip Broz Tito, had courageously fought the Nazis and enjoyed the support of most Yugoslavs, and so did not need Soviet support.)

---

9. Milovan Djilas, *Conversations with Stalin*, trans. Michael B. Petrovich (New York: Harcourt, Brace, Jovanovich, 1962), 114.

In other words, in 1945 the Soviets built an international subsystem of their own, parallel to the liberal one that the Americans built but based on a very different set of ideas. The Soviets described their system as a fraternal order of socialist states, but the big brother—the Soviet Union—was decidedly coercive. These countries' ruling communist parties rejected capitalism in favor of state ownership of factories and farms. They rejected voluntary international trade in favor of a forced trading system in which the USSR and its satellite states bartered goods on terms determined by the Soviet Communist Party. (Under the Marshall Plan in 1948 the United States offered the Soviet Union and all East European states aid —a huge program of grants to Western Europe to assist recovery from the war—but Stalin declined and forced the East European governments to do the same.) They rejected multi-party liberal democracy in favor of the dictatorship of the communist party. The Soviets also imposed a communist regime on northern Korea (which the Red Army occupied in 1945), and the Kremlin spent the Cold War trying to extend the influence and rule of communist parties throughout the world without bringing on world war.

As the Soviets were consolidating control over Eastern Europe, Western Europeans and Americans initially feared that in Stalin, they had another Hitler on their hands, a dictator who would not stop until he dominated the world. In the late 1940s Europe was the key. If communism spread to western Germany, France, Italy, Spain, Scandinavia, the Low Countries, and Britain as well, Moscow would thereafter dominate world politics more generally. It was not surprising that influential State Department thinkers like George F. Kennan sought to "contain" further Soviet expansion, because the industrial and raw material balance was up for grabs.[10]

Realism and the Cold War

Competing over these key areas, Russia and the United States fell into a Cold War soon after the end of the Second World War. Historians have hotly debated the origins of the Cold War, and the disagreements are only now being settled.[11] Early Western historiography blamed the Soviets for being expansionist owing to communist ideology or Russian nationalism. In the 1960s and 1970s a revisionist school of thought blamed the United States for being blind to legitimate Soviet security concerns. A post-revisionist school has taken advantage of the opening of the Soviet archives in the 1990s and is settling on a view that conflict was nearly inevitable owing to two basic facts that realists stress: there were only two great powers, and the international system (as always in the modern world) was anarchical, with no world government to settle disputes. The Soviets and Americans were

---

10. This was the origin of the "containment" policy.

11. See Melvyn Leffler, *A Preponderance of Power* (Stanford, CA: Stanford University Press, 1990).

bound to fall into serious tensions. The advent of nuclear weapons—the development of the atomic bomb by the United States in 1945 and by the Soviet Union in 1949—only made superpower relations more tense and more dangerous. In the early years, there was no possibility of Soviet compromise with the West.

Realism does not fully account for the Cold War, however, especially its severity. Think about the situation if Britain rather than the Soviet Union had been the other superpower. Britain, a fellow liberal democracy with an even longer history of economic openness than America, would have reached agreement with Washington. In that kind of world, the two superpowers would not have feared one another's political and economic regimes because they were essentially the same. The liberal international system that the Americans began building in 1944 would have been no threat to the British. In other words, we only can understand the severity of the Cold War if we take into account the wide ideological distance between the United States and Soviet Union.[12] (As we discuss later in this chapter, the Cold War only ended when that distance shrank considerably when Mikhail Gorbachev began to make the Soviet Union more liberal and capitalist.)

Besides the fundamental ideological differences, historians today also note that Stalin was incurably suspicious of everyone, probably genuinely paranoid as he got older, and so very difficult to deal with. He broke many of his promises to the Americans, which angered President Harry Truman and pushed him to take a harder line. However much Western states may have wished to extend democracy into Eastern Europe, the Soviets were even more eager to capture the industrial West for their sphere of influence. Soviet Foreign Minister Vyacheslav Molotov attested to Stalin's fetish for territory.[13] For their part, Britain and the United States acknowledged the Soviet position in Eastern Europe and made few gestures to unseat the communist regimes that Russia had installed there. As Churchill put the matter in 1946, an "Iron Curtain" ("from Stettin in the Baltic to Trieste in the Adriatic") had descended on the continent, dividing Europe in two.[14]

The American situation, then, was similar to that faced by liberal powers in past centuries. They faced rivals who were not liberal and so had to play the realist game. In the eighteenth and nineteenth centuries (see Chapters 4 and 5), Britain was relatively democratic and had growing interest in free trade, but it was operating in an international system (centered in Europe) in which the other great powers were much

---

12. On ideological distance and great-power rivalry, see Mark Haas, *The Ideological Origins of Great Power Politics, 1789–1989* (Ithaca, NY: Cornell University Press, 2005).

13. See David Holloway, *Stalin and the Bomb* (New Haven, CT: Yale University Press, 1994), 168.

14. In October 1944, however, in agreement with Stalin, Churchill had consigned Bulgaria and Romania to the Soviet sphere, preserving only Greece for preponderant British influence. The division was supposed to be 50-50 in Yugoslavia, and for a time Belgrade hovered between Eastern and Western camps.

less democratic and more closed economically. Thus the overall international system was realist and Britain had to act accordingly. In the same way, after 1945 the United States had strong interests in complete economic openness, and the liberal international subsystem it built existed within a broader realist international system. Washington would have preferred that the global system be one of free trade and open foreign investment. Indeed, during the war President Franklin Roosevelt and his cabinet explicitly opposed the ideas of "spheres of influence" by great powers in favor of an open world without great-power competition. The power and ideology of the USSR made that impossible. Ironically, it would take what we call an overbalance of power by the United States and the West to put an end to the Soviet countersystem.

Berlin and Korea

Stalin saw democracy and free markets in Western Europe as a threat but would not use war to address the threat. He found other ways, including subversion and the funding of communist parties, to limit the inroads of Western capitalism. His most audacious gambit was the Berlin Blockade of 1948–1949. At the time Germany was occupied by the victorious Allies—the Soviet Union, the United States, Britain, and France. The city of Berlin (Germany's largest) was in the middle of the Soviet zone but was itself divided among the four Allies—a miniature of Germany as a whole. Wanting all of Berlin, Stalin used troops and tanks to try to choke off West Berlin, hoping to bring the West Berliners to heel and force the Western powers out. But the Truman administration decided to push back and stand with West Berlin. Truman organized the Berlin Airlift, in which U.S. and British aircraft brought food, medicine, and all-important coal to Berlin by air (Figure 7.1). Stalin was not willing to risk all-out war, and so did not shoot down these Western planes. The Berlin Airlift went on for eleven months, until the Soviets gave in and re-opened Western land access to West Berlin.

The Cold War in Asia

In October 1949, a few months after the end of the Berlin Blockade, the world's most populous country, China, became communist as the guerrilla forces of Mao Zedong finally triumphed in that country's long civil war, defeating Chiang Kai-shek's Nationalists. Although Mao and the Soviets were to have tense relations that eventually would boil over into enmity in the 1960s, communist China was largely subordinate to the Kremlin in the 1950s. To Western governments, it appeared that communism was on the march as fascism had been in the 1930s.

Stalin sought to exploit communism's momentum and increase pressure on the West. In North Korea, dictator Kim Il Sung had been pleading with Stalin to allow him to invade capitalist South Korea, aligned with the United States.

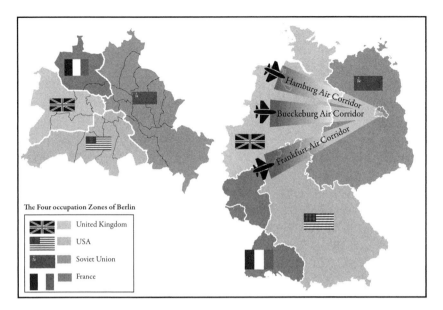

The Four occupation Zones of Berlin

🇬🇧		United Kingdom
🇺🇸		USA
		Soviet Union
		France

FIGURE 7.1 The Berlin Airlift, 1948–1949.

Soviet documents show that in January 1950 Stalin gave Kim permission, and in June more than 150,000 Northern troops invaded the South.[15] That assault was designed to swallow up the South Korean capital city, Seoul, before Truman could react. Stalin had not fully taken into account the U.S. occupation forces in Japan that were quickly transferred to Korea. For separate reasons, the Soviets were boycotting the UN Security Council, allowing the Americans to win approval for a UN action to repel the North Koreans from the South (Figure 7.2). As it was, the Korean clash was closely drawn. Stalin correctly assumed that America would not use nuclear weapons or attack Soviet interests elsewhere in the world. But U.S. and South Korean forces sustained the Pusan perimeter long enough to permit General MacArthur's massive amphibious Inchon landing (behind North Korean lines), which forced Northern troops to withdraw northward.

In October 1950, as MacArthur pushed the communists north of the 38th parallel toward the Yalu River, North Korea's boundary with China, Mao, with Stalin's encouragement, invaded North Korea with 200,000 troops. Mao wanted to reinstate something approximating the old 38th parallel division of the peninsula. The UN troops retreated back into the South. On November 9,

---

15. Vladislav M. Zubok, *A Failed Empire: The Soviet Union in the Cold War from Stalin to Gorbachev* (University of North Carolina Press, 2007), 79–80.

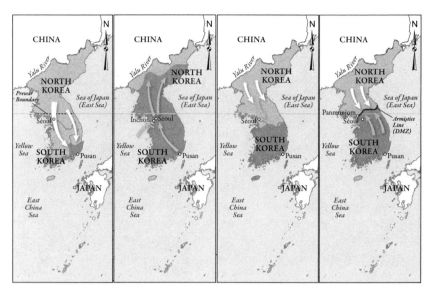

FIGURE 7.2 Territory held by UN and Communist forces at four points during the Korean War.

1950, however, Truman threatened to use nuclear weapons if China did not moderate its offensive. A military dividing line was then established close to the old 38th parallel. The war continued in a stalemate for three more years. Finally, the new U.S. President Dwight Eisenhower hinted at resumption of the Western advance with all weapons fair game if the North Korean negotiators did not sign the July 1953 armistice agreement. They promptly did so, and the Korean War effectively came to an end (although even today no peace treaty has been ratified).

> The atomic bombs that ended World War II brought about what analysts call a "nuclear revolution." These supremely destructive weapons gave their possessors the power to do catastrophic damage to enemies without defeating them in warfare first. Eventually the Americans and the Soviets reached a stable situation of nuclear deterrence, in which each side was confident that the other would not launch a nuclear strike on it because doing so would be to commit national suicide. But nuclear-armed states were greatly concerned about the spread of these weapons, and those concerns remain today. Of particular concern is the possibility that terrorist groups could acquire nuclear weapons. Because it would be difficult to pinpoint which terrorists used these weapons, and hence to retaliate against them, it is doubtful that terrorists could be deterred from using them to destroy major cities.

Limited Versus All-Out War

Clearly, during these years the United States and the Soviet Union were in a security dilemma, in which steps that either state took to make itself more secure made the other feel less secure. Security dilemmas are common in international relations, but the Soviet–American dilemma was especially acute because both superpowers had nuclear weapons. These were the ultimate weapons, capable of destroying entire cities. The Soviet Union exploded its first atomic bomb in 1949 (having gotten help from its spies in the United States). The dynamics of nuclear war and deterrence made Soviet–American relations dangerous and confusing.

The United States and the West had fought a limited war in Korea, refusing to use nuclear weapons. Did that mean that the United States would fight only limited war elsewhere? If so, the democratic future of Western Europe was in danger, because NATO was hopelessly outnumbered by Soviet troops in Europe. Europe was all-important demographically and geopolitically to the United States. The majority of West Europeans strongly preferred American hegemony to Soviet domination. But the Warsaw Pact force of 175 divisions would obliterate in purely conventional (non-nuclear) terms the less than 30 divisions that NATO had painstakingly accumulated on the central front in West Germany. NATO spoke optimistically of amassing a force of fifty divisions, which might at least theoretically have contained a Soviet offensive without resort to nuclear weapons. But the West never achieved such a force, so a purely conventional defense of Europe seemed unattainable.

In the minds of Western military planners, then, the credibility of the nuclear deterrent against a Soviet invasion depended on Western nuclear superiority. Until the late 1960s the United States enjoyed such superiority. After testing its first atomic bomb in 1949, the USSR began to build a nuclear arsenal and a fleet of rockets. But the Soviet nuclear buildup was slower than that of America. In the 1950s the Eisenhower administration openly threatened "massive retaliation"—a disproportionate nuclear counterattack against Soviet cities following an attack on Western Europe, even a conventional one. It was never clear whether the United States would carry out such a threat, but the threat allowed NATO to spend far less on conventional armaments than the Warsaw Pact did.

Following the Cuban Missile Crisis of October 1962, when President Kennedy publicly coerced Soviet Premier Nikita Khrushchev into withdrawing short-range nuclear missiles from Cuba, the Soviet Union set out on the most rapid arms buildup in history. By 1968, with a huge arsenal of intercontinental ballistic missiles (ICBMs), the Soviets had achieved nuclear equality with the United States. Now the safety of Western Europe was in doubt, because any U.S. nuclear attack on the USSR following a conventional attack on Western Europe could be met with an equal Soviet nuclear strike on the United States. Was America willing to risk New York to save West Berlin or Paris? Veteran strategist Paul Nitze reasoned that the answer was "no," and concluded that the Soviets would not in fact be deterred from launching a conventional attack. This situation points to the well-known nuclear dilemma: what you say to an enemy that you are going to do *after* he attacks you in order to deter him from attacking you—such as massive retaliation—is not in your interest to do if he *does* attack you. So how was the United States to deter an attack on Western Europe, or for that matter on other allies such as Japan, South Korea, Taiwan, Australia, or New Zealand?[16]

To support its democratic allies in Western Europe and deter a Soviet attack, U.S. defense planners decided that America had to do two things. First, it needed to increase its ability to respond to a Soviet attack with conventional weapons. In the mid-1970s the United States developed precision-guided munitions to destroy Soviet tanks and aircraft with purely conventional weapons. The AWACS (airborne warning and control system) provided strategic reconnaissance aircraft that could survey an entire battlefield and direct precision strikes on Russian conventional forces based or moving there. If these conventional tactics were effective, the United States would not have to employ nuclear bombs to defeat a Soviet ground invasion—and hence to deter such an invasion to begin with. The U.S.-NATO doctrine of "Air Land Battle" made such a response possible. Larger conventional forces, mounted during the Kennedy and Johnson administrations and endowed with greater intelligence and precision guidance, made this strategy possible.

Second, defense planners concluded that the United States must develop the nuclear capacity to hit Soviet missile sites (counterforce) and avoid Soviet cities (countervalue). That way, America could better protect itself from a Soviet nuclear retaliatory strike. After such an attack, as General Brent Scowcroft's 1983 Commission on Strategic Forces showed, the United States could respond with nuclear weapons on Soviet strategic targets (air and missile bases, command centers, submarine pens) without worrying that an all-out Soviet attack on U.S. cities would inevitably follow. The Soviets would not immediately hit American cities because their own cities were vulnerable but had not yet been hit. Also, if a crisis escalated and Russia struck U.S. airfields, missile bases, and submarine capabilities, the United States could respond in like manner without striking Soviet cities. There was no scenario in which the Soviets would be able to knock out the U.S. ability to retaliate on strategic targets. Assuming the Soviets recognized all of this, a robust NATO counterforce ability should help deter a Soviet attack on Western Europe.

By 1980 there was a standoff in European defense: neither the Russians nor the Americans could take advantage in a near-term encounter. American conventional forces were growing so that NATO could respond to a conventional attack in limited terms. If the Soviets went nuclear, they would not be able to prevent U.S. retaliation on strategic forces. But the arms race continued as the Soviets had begun installing medium-range ballistic missiles in Eastern Europe, capable of hitting Western Europe

---

16. See Thomas C. Schelling, *Arms and Influence* (New Haven. CT: Yale University Press, 1966).

but not North America. President Jimmy Carter and other NATO leaders decided to deploy medium-range missiles in Western Europe in response. Ronald Reagan, who became president in 1981, accelerated the buildup of U.S. conventional and nuclear forces and also funded research on the Strategic Defense Initiative (SDI), a missile defense system designed to render the United States invulnerable to a nuclear attack. Although its many critics dubbed the program "Star Wars" and insisted that it could never work, some analysts believe it helped push the Soviets to the bargaining table with the Americans a few years later and may have helped to end the Cold War.

Decolonization and the Third World

World politics during these years also saw the erosion and disappearance of European empires in Africa and Asia. European competition in other parts of the world was ending, and the old quest for economic monopolies and foreign territory, a quest that features so prominently in earlier chapters of this book, was over. The Second World War was the pivotal event. The United States emerged from the war more powerful than ever, but its European allies were weaker than they had been in many decades. Great Britain, France, the Netherlands, and Belgium had less material capability and less will to hold onto their empires. The United States, as discussed earlier in this chapter, was offering to protect the Europeans so that they did not need empires to be rich and secure. European weakness, in turn, helped propel nationalism and the drive for independence in Europe's overseas colonies.

Soviet–American Cold War competition quickly intertwined with this global decolonization trend. In colony after colony, many of the leaders of independence movements were communists. Mao Zedong of China and Ho Chi Minh of Indochina believed that communism was the surest route to national power and independence.[17] Many more anti-colonial leaders were not communist but did admire the Soviet Union and certain features of its regime. After all, under Stalin, communism had built the Soviet Union from a weakened hulk in 1923 to the great industrial power that defeated Nazi Germany in 1943–1945. Ironically, Stalin himself was reluctant to invest too much in these anti-colonialist admirers, thinking they were not worth the trouble. Meanwhile, the United States found itself in a dilemma: if it sided with the anti-imperialists, it would further weaken friendly governments in Western Europe (who had wanted to hold on to their empires), but if it sided with its European allies, it would damage its credibility among anti-colonial movements, who would then gravitate toward the Soviet Union.

Fatefully, the United States initially sided with its European allies and thereby made itself appear the hypocritical guardian of their backward, outdated empires

---

17. China actually was never a formal colony of any foreign state, but in the nineteenth century it was effectively divided up into exclusive economic zones by several European powers, the United States, and Japan.

and the enemy of self-government in the Third World. Indochina was such a case where the United States backed the French against Ho Chi Minh's guerrilla movement. In India and Indonesia, however, the United States sided with those seeking independence. President Eisenhower decided to support non-communist governments in Southeast Asia and assisted President Ngo Dinh Diem, a U.S. client who nonetheless enjoyed a measure of autonomy. Americans thought they were supporting a young state against a Soviet-communist threat, but to many Asians they were instead perpetuating Western imperialism against Vietnamese independence.

The problem the United States faced in the Third World became still more dire after Stalin died in 1953. Stalin's successor, Nikita Khrushchev, decided to exploit the situation throughout the colonial world and support what he called "movements of national liberation." Khrushchev positioned the USSR as the global champion of anti-imperialism.

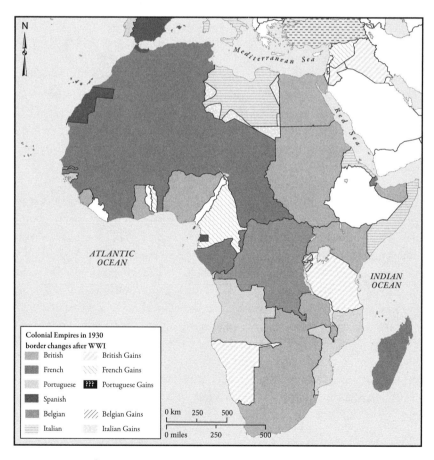

FIGURE 7.3 Africa in 1930.

FIGURE 7.4 Africa in 2000.

Between the late 1940s and the late 1960s, most independence movements succeeded. The age of formal empire was over. The effects on the world political map were dramatic, most obviously in Africa (see Figures 7.3 and 7.4).

The newly independent states formed what China's Mao Zedong called the Third World. In 1961 Indian prime minister Jawaharlal Nehru led a conference of nations that called itself the Non-Aligned Movement (NAM). The NAM professed to be tied to neither superpower; its members said that they were focused on development and avoiding dependence on the world's powerful states, and did not wish to be dependent upon either the American or the Soviet bloc. India was a democracy, but Nehru admired the Soviet Union and Soviet–Indian ties became so close in the 1960s that India's rival China, itself a communist state, openly criticized the Kremlin. Indonesia under Sukarno (up to 1965) and Cuba under Fidel Castro had close ties to the Soviet Union as well.

Thus the end of formal empires did not initially mean the beginning of global democracy and economic openness. The liberal international subsystem that the United States was sponsoring in Western Europe, North America, Japan, and Australia/New Zealand did not extend further. Instead, most of the Third World was divided into countries that ranged from communist (North Korea, North Vietnam) to authoritarian socialist (Mexico, Tanzania), to democratic socialist (India), to capitalist authoritarian (Argentina, South Korea, Zaïre). States in the first three categories tended to lean toward the Soviets or Chinese; those in the last category tended to lean toward the United States. Both superpowers enabled this dynamic by extending military and non-military aid to these regimes in hopes of keeping them out of the other superpower's bloc. They largely pursued a development strategy called *import-substituting industrialization* (ISI), which involved limiting foreign imports and subsidizing local manufacturing industry. These countries accepted foreign aid but avoided trade, especially with the West.

> Third World countries were diverse but had in common a strong desire for independence, industrialization, stability, and security. Those especially wary of becoming dependent on America and the West, such as India and Brazil, followed a strategy called import-substituting industrialization (ISI). ISI entailed protectionism, food subsidies, and government favors to new industries. The alternative was export-led growth (ELG). ELG entailed government favors to new industries as well, but the aim was to export as much as possible to the wealthy West. ISI, which typically was practiced by states that either leaned toward the Soviets or Chinese or were nonaligned, ended up a failure. Under ELG, countries such as South Korea, Taiwan, and Chile prospered, and by the late 1980s most Third World countries were beginning to imitate them and join the liberal world economy.

Scholars and politicians in the Third World also borrowed from and modified Marxist theory into what became known as dependency (*dependencia*) theory. Dependency theory came in different forms, but the essential idea was that the world capitalist economy was divided into a core and a periphery. The core comprised capitalists who enjoyed the lion's share of world wealth and were concentrated in the wealthy countries of North America, Western Europe, and Japan. The core had as its chief goal the maximization of profit or return on investment. The periphery comprised those without wealth, concentrated in Latin America, Africa, and Asia. The core invested (owned farmland and built factories) in the periphery and exploited its human and natural resources. To enrich itself, the core had to keep the costs of business in the periphery low. Hence the core recruited the governments of the wealthy countries to help it keep wages low, oppose labor unions, and act to suppress socialism in the periphery, intervening as necessary to place and keep in power dictators who would appease the core. The result, according to dependency theory, was perpetual underdevelopment and neo-colonialism in such areas. Dependency theory's general solution was for peripheral countries to break free of the global capitalist system and develop their industries via ISI. In its most general sense, this system failed.

Accordingly, other developing countries pursued a strategy of *export-led development*, which entailed selling goods to the outside world, especially the West. South Korea, Taiwan, Singapore, Chile, and other states grew rich via this strategy, as they found that participating in the liberal global economy could be lucrative. Even those Third World countries that grew by exporting, however, used government to help their industries become internationally competitive, and they did not open their economies completely to foreign imports. Still, export-led growth involved signing on to the U.S.-sponsored global capitalist economy. As a strategy for economic development, it proved superior to the discredited ISI, and most countries abandoned the latter strategy by the 1980s—most spectacularly, China. As will become clear in this next chapter, the failures of ISI, in both its communist and socialist forms, played a large role in the spread of the liberal international subsystem at the end of the Cold War. As the Cold War finally came to an end in the late 1980s, it became evident even to skeptics that the surest route to economic growth and political stability was join the network of states that were opening their economies and societies and deliberately becoming enmeshed with the world's wealthy economies.

Conclusion

The Cold War period (1947–1989) was the period in which the liberal international subsystem finally emerged in its (thus far) permanent form. Both democracy within states and open economic interaction within them was deeply institutionalized, thanks to the lessons of the horrific world wars and Great Depression and the long-term commitment of the United States to safeguarding the subsystem. The logic of the West rested upon American hegemony, and so there is an element of realism in it: had the United States not guaranteed the security of its democratic partners against Soviet attack, and their economies against economic autarky, the subsystem would not have worked. And America did these things out of self-interest, not altruism; it withheld many of these benefits from less developed countries, where democratic elections would have brought leftist, anti-U.S. governments to power.

The fact remains, however, that relations among the liberal democracies of the world after 1945 took on a distinctive quality that had only been glimpsed in earlier periods of history. Their trade became progressively more free, and their barriers to one another's investments lower. The possibility of war among them—even among ancient enemies Germany and France—became unthinkable. Fears of backsliding into a realist balance-of-power system receded into nothing. The liberal world order whose seeds were planted by the Dutch Republic in the seventeenth century and that was forecast by Immanuel Kant in the eighteenth finally emerged.

A traditional balance-of-power system persisted between the United States and Soviet Union, and between many countries outside the liberal subsystem. As we shall see in Chapter 8, it took the collapse of the USSR itself to allow the subsystem to cover the entire planet. That is the situation of the world today. The liberal international order does face challenges today, including the ongoing economic and perhaps military rise of China—a country that has embraced capitalism and export-led growth but not democracy—and diffidence within the United States itself as to whether to stay the course. In Chapter 9 we shall consider those challenges and the choices countries face in the coming years.

FURTHER READING

Gaddis, John Lewis. *The Cold War: A New History.* Harmondsworth, UK: Penguin, 2011.

Gilpin, Robert. *Global Political Economy: Understanding the International Economic Order.* Princeton, NJ: Princeton University Press, 2011.

Haas, Mark. *The Ideological Origins of Great Power Politics, 1789–1989.* Ithaca, NY: Cornell University Press, 2005.

Ikenberry, G. John. *Liberal Leviathan.* Princeton, NJ: Princeton University Press, 2012.

Leffler, Melvyn. *For the Soul of Mankind: The United States, the Soviet Union, and the Cold War.* New York: Hill & Wang. 2007.

Schelling, Thomas C. *Arms and Influence.* New Haven, CT: Yale University Press, 1966.

Smith, Tony. *America's Mission: The United States and the Worldwide Struggle for Democracy in the Twentieth Century.* Princeton, NJ: Princeton University Press, 1994.

Zubok, Vladislav M. *A Failed Empire: The Soviet Union in the Cold War from Stalin to Gorbachev.* Durham: University of North Carolina Press, 2007.

8 THE WEST'S OVERBALANCE OF POWER AND THE GLOBALIZATION OF LIBERALISM

Introduction

The Cold War continued through the late 1980s, and its legacy continues to shape world politics today. The conflict was about not simply material power, as realism holds, but ideas and ideologies—specifically, liberal democracy, exemplified by the United States, and communism, exemplified by the Soviet Union. Soviet–American competition was realist on its surface, and although the superpowers never fought each other directly, they engaged in arms races and waged proxy wars in Asia, Africa, and Latin America through clients, most notably in Vietnam. Although the liberal international subsystem, or "the West," went through many conflicts and setbacks, by the 1980s it was becoming clear to people the world over that communism was unable to compete with liberal democracy. Economic growth and technology in the Soviet Union and its bloc were lagging further and further behind those in the United States and its allies, and the West effectively achieved an overbalance of power—not simply military might, but economic and social power as well. China began to abandon state socialism (but not Communist Party rule) in 1978, and the Soviet Union began shedding communism altogether in the mid-1980s. The collapse of the USSR in 1991 meant the triumph of the liberal system foreseen two centuries earlier by Immanuel Kant; country after country embraced democracy and economic openness.

The Ideological Balance

As earlier chapters in this book make clear, world politics is not only about material things such as weapons and technology, but also about ideas—competing ideas concerning the best way to order society on both the domestic and the international levels. The Cold War that dominated world politics from 1947 through 1989 was not only a contest between two superpowers, the United States and the Soviet Union; it also was a competition between two set of ideas: liberal democracy and communism. Each set of ideas implied particular institutions and ways of life. Liberal democracy is familiar to you because it is the system under which Americans and many other people live. It entails regular competitive elections for most government decision-makers (and a set of institutions to make sure elections remain competitive, such as freedoms of the press, religion, assembly, and so on). Liberal democracy also entails freedom of commerce, or capitalism, that is, allowing individuals and corporations to own property and exchange goods and services with only enough government regulation to ensure fairness and stability.

Communism has mostly disappeared from the world, so it is less familiar to people today. It entails the control of the state and much of society by a single party. Communism teaches that capitalism concentrates power in the hands of the owning classes at the expense of the factory and farm workers and prescribes party control of the national economy: that means little or no private property, and prices and production levels set by the state. Communism in practice also means far fewer civil liberties: the state owns and controls all print and electronic media and typically prohibits all groups not under its direct control, such as opposition political parties, labor unions, private schools, and religious organizations. Today only North Korea and Cuba are fully communist countries. China is ruled by a Communist Party that exerts heavy control over many aspects of society, including the media, labor, and religion, but that allows a large degree of private economic enterprise. China, then, has a kind of hybrid domestic regime.

During the Cold War, communism and Soviet power were entangled, as were liberal democracy and American power. Where communism spread, Soviet influence tended to spread with it; where liberal democracy spread, so did American power, by and large. Both Moscow and Washington knew this and acted accordingly. Because full-blown communism collapsed in most of the world in the late 1980s and early 1990s, people today sometimes are surprised to learn that, during the height of the Cold War, the prestige of Soviet communism and the Soviet bloc was high in the Third World and even in the West itself. In the aftermath of World War II, many intellectuals in Western Europe admired the Soviet version of Marxism. French thinkers such as Jean-Paul Sartre, Albert Camus, and Maurice Merleau-Ponty favored the Soviet over the American model. In Britain the historians E. P. Thompson and Eric Hobsbawm were similar. To such observers, the Soviets had an economy that was both growing faster and distributing resources more equally and fairly than the American economy. Sartre even knew about Stalin's prison camps in Siberia—the notorious gulag—but told a British writer that it would "be wrong to speak out about injustice in a communist state" inasmuch as "to do so would be to provide ammunition for use against a cause which is that of the proletariat and thus, in the long run, of justice itself."[1]

To their credit, Camus, Merleau-Ponty, Thompson, and other European intellectuals eventually denounced the Soviet Union as the truth about its regime came to light. Among the events that changed their minds was the Soviet invasion of its satellite Hungary in 1956. That case, still vividly remembered in Eastern Europe, was one of many superpower interventions in other countries to preserve or extend influence and power by trying to alter or preserve those countries' domestic regimes and the ideas under which people lived.

Superpower Competition in Europe and the Third World

1956: Hungary and Egypt

Inspired, ironically, by the post-Stalinist reforms of Khrushchev in the Soviet Union itself, Hungary's reforming leader Imre Nagy developed an independent and open form of Marxism that appealed to Western intellectuals as well as old Bolsheviks. Nagy sought links with Western economies and states, obliterating exclusive reliance on the doctrines of Lenin and Stalin. He allowed opposition political parties to compete for influence in the government. Khrushchev and the Soviet leadership were feeling pinched at the same time by the liberalizing reforms of Wladyslaw Gomulka in Poland. On November 1, 1956, Nagy pushed too far, announcing Hungary's withdrawal from the Warsaw Pact, and called on the Western powers to recognize its status as a neutral country. Within three days Soviet tanks invaded Budapest, and soon thereafter the Kremlin installed the puppet János Kádár as prime minister of Hungary.

At this very time, Western allies Britain and France had joined Israel in intervening in Egypt to take control of the Suez Canal and overthrow Egypt's president, Gamal Abdel Nasser. Nasser had seized the canal from the private company that held it. President Eisenhower, concerned not to alienate Arab countries being wooed by the Soviet Union, acted to thwart the Anglo-French-Israeli intervention. He insisted that the three countries withdraw their forces and began to sell British pounds at a discount on world markets, driving down the value of Britain's currency. Eisenhower also flooded the floor of the Mediterranean with U.S. submarines,

---

1. Volker R. Berghahn, *America and the Intellectual Cold Wars in Europe* (Princeton, NJ: Princeton University Press), 120.

challenging the British and French invasion fleet. After several days of inconclusive fighting against Egyptians, the British and French withdrew. They did not retake the Suez Canal, and Nasser emerged from the crisis with greater prestige. British relations with the United States reached an all-time low, and Anthony Eden resigned as British prime minister, giving way to the more flexible Harold Macmillan.[2]

The crises in Hungary and Egypt added up to a success for the United States and a demonstration of Soviet perfidy and brutality for the world to see. Many Hungarians poured over the border to migrate to Europe or the United States. Those European intellectuals who did not denounce the USSR were discredited. At its heart, Russian communism was a repressive regime that, when challenged, ruled by force alone. In the aftermath, despite the challenge to NATO's unity, the Europeans sought to repair relations with Washington and to give new life to Atlantic cooperation.

Even so, in the Third World the prestige of the Soviet Union and communism (or state socialism, as it often was called) continued to be high. The main reason was that the Soviet model of industrialization seemed more relevant to the situation of most Third World countries. The United States was the world's greatest industrial power, but it had taken its free-market system the entire nineteenth century to attain that status. The Soviet Union had been a mostly agrarian society in 1917, at the time of the Bolshevik revolution, and its state-driven economy had industrialized and repulsed mighty Nazi Germany during the Second World War. In the 1950s, moreover, the Soviet economy grew faster than the American one. The official Soviet statistics reported an average annual growth of 10.1 percent in the 1950s. Historian Mark Harrison reports that the best data available show that Soviet growth averaged 7.2 percent during this period.[3] Either way, the corresponding official figure for the United States in the 1950s was only 3.8 percent.[4] Americans always had prided themselves on their technology, but even on that front the Soviets were offering a stiff challenge. In 1957 the Soviets beat the Americans into outer space by putting a satellite called Sputnik into orbit. "We will bury you," Khrushchev hectored America in 1958, meaning, "we will be at your funeral" or "we will outlive you."

Today Khrushchev's boast may sound comical, but at the time it was serious and plausible, and it resonated throughout the Third World. Even democratic leaders who would not go all the way to communism, such as Nehru of India and Arbenz of Chile, pushed state-led development over free markets. Until the

---

2. See the account in Richard Rosecrance, *Defense of the Realm* (New York: Columbia University Press, 1968).

3. Mark Harrison, "Soviet Economic Growth Since 1928: The Alternative Statistics of G. I. Khanin," *Europe-Asia Studies* 45, no. 1 (1993): 141–167.

4. Calculated using data from Angus Maddison, *Historical Statistics of the World Economy: 1–2008 AD* (dataset), The Maddison-Project, http://www.ggdc.net/maddison/maddison-project/home.htm, 2013 version.

FIGURE 8.1 Soviet premier Nikita Khrushchev with Indian prime minister Jawaharlal Nehru.
Source: STAFF/AFP/Getty Images.

FIGURE 8.2 Khrushchev with Egyptian president Gamal Abdel Nasser.
Source: SPUTNIK/Alamy Stock Photo.

1980s, the balance of ideological power was at least even, and at times it tilted toward the Soviet side. Figure 8.1 shows Khrushchev with Indian Prime Minister Nehru; Figure 8.2., Khrushchev with Egyptian President Nasser.

Berlin Again

The late 1950s and the early 1960s brought more crises between the superpowers. East Germany under communist rule would never match the vital growth of West Germany stimulated by the leadership of Finance Minister Ludwig Erhard and Chancellor Konrad Adenauer. The East Berlin riots of 1953 and the open borders to the West sucked population out. Walter Ulbricht, the East German leader, wanted to seal the border with West Berlin, but Soviet leaders told him to sort out East Germany's domestic and international problems. Historian Hope Harrison has analyzed long-secret East German archives to show that Ulbricht wore down Khrushchev, the impetuous and volatile successor to Stalin, and finally convinced him to allow Ulbricht's government to build a wall around West Berlin.[5] The first barriers were raised on August 13, 1961. President Kennedy did not try to knock the wall down inside East Germany, recognizing that East Germany could do as it liked on its own territory and also that it was advantageous to both the communist and democratic worlds that Berlin be stabilized. This meant, however, that Churchill's Iron Curtain—enclosing undemocratic puppet regimes—had become an impervious Steel Curtain as well.

The Berlin Wall in particular became an ugly symbol of the Cold War, as Ulbricht added a "strip of death" on its eastern side where guards could shoot citizens trying to scale the wall; officially, over the 29 years of the Wall's existence, 139 East Germans were killed while attempting to escape to the West. In addition, Khrushchev tried to get the Western NATO forces to leave beleaguered West Berlin, undercutting the Allied control arrangements of 1945. Intermittently Khrushchev threatened to sign a peace treaty with East Germany transferring control of the access routes to the GDR and raising the possibility that guaranteed four-power access rights might be threatened by a now-sovereign East Germany. From then on, Kennedy recognized that in any crisis, escalation might involve Berlin.

Cuba

Soviet–American struggles pervaded what was called the Third World—parts of the world divorced from the U.S.-led West and the Soviet-led East. In April of 1961 President John Kennedy, fearing the spread of Soviet influence in the Western

5. Hope M. Harrison, *Driving the Soviets Up the Wall: Soviet-East German Relations 1953–1961* (Princeton, NJ: Princeton University Press, 2005).

Hemisphere, authorized a CIA-led invasion by Cuban exile forces at the Bay of Pigs to overthrow Fidel Castro, who had seized power from the authoritarian Batista regime two years earlier. But Castro, well informed of such plans, defeated the invaders on the beach. Fearing too large an American footprint, Kennedy had not authorized air cover for the operation. In early 1962 Khrushchev decided to give arms and to increase aid to Castro. Khrushchev concluded that he could bully Kennedy and put nuclear missiles in Cuba to prevent another invasion by the United States. After all, the Soviet premier reasoned, Russia had been forced to accept U.S. nuclear missiles in Turkey and Italy that were aimed at Soviet targets.

Khrushchev misread American intentions, however. No leader in the United States could accept Russian offensive missiles in Cuba that could be aimed at one-half of the American land mass as well as at allies in Central America. On October 22, 1962, Kennedy informed the world that the missiles would have to be removed and instituted a naval quarantine (blockade) of Cuba. Russian vessels carrying missile and nuclear components went dead in the water. The U.S. Navy pressed Soviet submarines on the floor of the Caribbean to rise to the surface. On October 26, they dropped warning depth charges near Soviet submarine B-59, which was equipped—unbeknownst to them—with nuclear torpedoes. Two of the three Soviet officers on the submarine voted to send torpedoes against the American vessel dropping the depth charges. The third officer, Vasili Arkhipov, however, wanted further confirmation. He vetoed their launch and surrendered to the U.S. Navy; the world was thereby spared a much more violent conflict, possibly an all-out nuclear war.[6]

Arkhipov's courageous action did not end the crisis. Khrushchev had to remove the missiles and warheads from Cuban soil. In return, Kennedy promised not to invade Cuba. In a secret protocol, he also agreed to remove the U.S. intermediate-range missiles stationed in Italy and Turkey. Kennedy feared that Khrushchev would retaliate on West Berlin, but the Soviet leader, sensing the dangers of further escalation, held back. In the last year of his presidency, Kennedy moved to improve arms control and negotiated the Nuclear Test Ban Treaty with Moscow in 1963, which prohibited all tests of nuclear weapons except those conducted underground.

Vietnam

Dean Rusk, the Secretary of State, said of the resolution of the Cuban Missile Crisis, "we were eyeball to eyeball and the other guy blinked." In the aftermath of the crisis, American strategists were in the ascendant. If the mighty Soviet Union

---

6. Quoted in Marion Lloyd, "Soviets Close to Using A-Bomb in 1962 Crisis, Forum Told," *Boston Globe* (October 13, 2002).

would bow before the United States, no other state could stand in its way, or so it seemed to Americans. This hubris infected the way U.S. leaders thought about the rest of the Third World.

Southeast Asia was an ideological battleground during much of the Cold War. Comprising French, Dutch, British, Portuguese, and American colonies until the Second World War, Southeast Asia was conquered and occupied by Japan during the war. After Japan's defeat, the French, British, and Dutch tried to re-establish control, but in each colony—Indochina, Malaya, the East Indies—national movements declared independence. These nationalist movements contained communists and sometimes were led by them. Its strategic position made the Indochinese country of Vietnam especially important in the Cold War. In 1954, after sustaining a humiliating military defeat at the hands of the Vietnamese communists, the French left Vietnam. The country was divided into a communist North and a non-communist (but not very democratic) South. President Eisenhower feared that if South Vietnam fell to communism, all of Southeast Asia would do the same and East Asia would become a Soviet satellite like Eastern Europe. The entire world—U.S. enemies, allies, and neutrals—would conclude that America did not have the wherewithal to stand against Soviet aggression. Eisenhower sent aid and military advisors to South Vietnam, and John F. Kennedy sent even more.

Kennedy's successor Lyndon B. Johnson escalated American involvement in Vietnam several times. Johnson and his advisors, all smart, accomplished men from big business, Wall Street, and the Ivy League, believed that merely showing North Vietnam that the United States was in the game would be enough to procure restraint or even surrender. When Johnson began bombing North Vietnam in early 1965, he hit purely symbolic targets, not ones that would actually threaten the communist effort in the south.[7] Of course military and economic aid was coming to North Vietnam from both China and Russia, offsetting whatever the United States did, so it is unclear that America ever could have succeeded in its Vietnam effort. By the summer of 1968 Johnson had emplaced 550,000 troops in Vietnam. Although U.S. forces prevailed in every engagement, this superiority did not weaken the North Vietnamese's will to resist. Since the communist forces would always have plenty of equipment and logistical help, U.S. forces were in effect fighting the population of North Vietnam—in crude terms, the Vietnamese birthrate. The North Vietnamese population of 30 million increased 27 percent between 1960 and 1970, only to be slowed later by an adoption of a two-child policy by the Hanoi regime. The Americans also were fighting Viet Cong guerrillas in South Vietnam, guerrillas

---

7. Alexander George and William Simons, *The Limits of Coercive Diplomacy* (Boulder, CO: Westview Press, 1994).

who enjoyed the support of many thousands of South Vietnamese. U.S. troops often did not know who was friend and who enemy.

It is important to remember that the leaders of North Vietnam, Vo Nguyen Giap and Ho Chi Minh, were not fighting to defeat the United States, but simply to prove that the United States could not win. The struggle was political, not military. How long would Congress and the American public support and fund an unsuccessful effort that resulted in a peak of 300 draftees being killed per week? U.S. staying power in Vietnam was intrinsically limited; meanwhile, North Vietnam was not going anywhere. It would fight in place for a united Vietnam, even though as many as 500,000 Vietnamese were killed. U.S. bombing of the North Vietnamese capital of Hanoi, mining of Haiphong harbor, and even invading the North would not weaken the communist effort, for all North Vietnam had to do was wait out the United States as casualties mounted. President Johnson ultimately tapered and ended U.S. bombing and decided he would withdraw from the presidential race in 1968.

Richard Nixon became president in early 1969, having promised that he had a "secret plan" to end the war. The joke became that the plan was so secret that Nixon himself did not know what it was! The most he could do was demonstrate his toughness by carpet-bombing Hanoi and invading Cambodia to cut the invasion route to the South. Nixon hoped to coerce Hanoi into ceasing the war effort while gradually handing it over to the South Vietnamese government in Saigon. The North never wavered, and Nguyen Van Thieu, the South Vietnamese leader, had to accept that a settlement in place would allow a Northern victory as the United States withdrew, with a pledge to return captured American prisoners. For a time the administration hoped that bombing would cut off a Northern takeover of the South. Ultimately, however, under President Gerald Ford, Congress demanded a bombing halt, and the world watched as Hanoi defeated Saigon in the spring of 1975.

China as a Factor in the Cold War

Defeat in Vietnam could have crippled U.S. international relations and foreign policy from then on, but it did not. U.S. statesmen, particularly Henry Kissinger, found a way to use diplomacy to compensate for military defeats. Kissinger and President Nixon exploited tension that had arisen between Moscow and Beijing over frontiers, the tenor of foreign policy, and Moscow's refusal to share nuclear technology with China. Mao criticized Moscow's hesitancy to challenge Taiwan's position in the offshore islands of Quemoy and Matsu. Moscow, Mao reasoned, should support its effort to undermine the noncommunist Kuomintang's rule of those islands. Yet Brezhnev was hesitant to take on the U.S. Navy, which supported Chiang Kai-shek on Taiwan. Beijing and Moscow also clashed over borders, and there were military conflicts along the Ussuri River between Russia and China in 1969.

Rather than threaten the Soviets with an accelerated arms buildup, Nixon and Kissinger sought to bring in China as an antidote to Brezhnev's Russia. Mao and Zhou Enlai, his deputy, were only too glad to use their improving relations with the United States as leverage against the Soviet Union. Kissinger's tilt toward China was not excessive, however; it was designed to procure Soviet moderation, détente, and ultimately cooperation, not provoke greater conflict. In 1974, China became an ingredient in Western defense because if China were to mobilize on its northeastern frontier with Russia, it would effectively rule out a Russian invasion of the West. But the most important message was that the United States could shift between China and Russia, influencing policies in both capitals. The Nixon-Kissinger strategy was not unlike Bismarck's intermediate position between Austria and Russia, which fostered restraint by both parties in the late nineteenth century. Kissinger, Nixon, and Gerald Ford (who replaced Nixon in 1974) applied realist principles to international relations and enjoyed some success after the trauma of Vietnam. The two superpowers began to trade (U.S. sales of wheat to the Soviet Union increased sharply), started a joint project in outer space, and ratified the important Strategic Arms Limitation Treaty (SALT).

Meanwhile, in 1976 Mao died. A struggle to succeed him as head of the Chinese Communist Party ensued, and Deng Xiaoping emerged victorious. A loyal communist, but one convinced that complete state control of the economy had held China back, Deng began a series of market-based economic reforms, beginning with private ownership of farmland. "Socialism does not mean shared poverty," said Deng, asserting that communism and markets were compatible. In the 1980s Deng moved China to a version of the export-led growth strategy that countries such as South Korea and Taiwan had followed so successfully since the 1960s (see Chapter 7). In effect, China adopted the economic logic of the West (capitalism) but not the political one (liberal democracy). Still, its abandonment of state socialism foreshadowed a similar abandonment by the Soviet Union less than a decade later, and with it the global spread of the liberal international system.

Soviet Decline and Fall

During the 1970s many analysts in the West believed that the bipolar system would continue for many more decades. They were wrong. Soviet–American détente died in 1979–1980, and the Soviet communist international subsystem dissolved in 1989. The Soviet Union itself was to collapse in 1991. At the same time, the U.S.-sponsored liberal international subsystem of trading democracies went from strength to strength. Its institutions enjoyed greater success and more than tipped the balance against the retrograde Soviet Union. The West had its set-backs and conflicts, particularly in the 1970s, as the Vietnam War and economic stagnation frayed the ties between the United States and Western Europe. But the Kantian system that America and its allies set up after World War II proved durable and attractive. In the 1970s and 1980s a wave of democratization broke over U.S. allies in southern Europe, Latin America, and East Asia.

The relative success of the "logic of the West" and failure of the Soviet-sponsored communist international subsystem were accompanied by a change in the balance of ideologies: as Francis Fukuyama wrote in 1989, alternatives to liberal democracy were discredited and countries around the world began to see that they only path to wealth and stability was to join the liberal international system.[8] The West proved to have a large advantage in what Joseph Nye calls "soft power."[9] The decline of the Soviet Union paved the way for the liberal system, led by the United States, to spread rapidly and become globally dominant. It remains dominant today, although it is besieged with challenges, and Fukuyama himself acknowledges that his "end of History" pronouncement was premature, as we discuss in this book's final chapter.

Notwithstanding détente, the Soviets never intended to stop competing in the Third World, and their aid to Marxists in Ethiopia and Angola in the mid-1970s soured relations with the United States. Furthermore, there were significant elements in the U.S. Congress that never liked détente, seeing it as a deal with the devil. As early as 1974, Senator Henry Jackson and Representative Charles Vanik, both Democrats, attached an amendment to trade legislation aimed at scuttling détente. The Jackson-Vanik Amendment prohibited most-favored-nation trading relations with countries that limit emigration; the Soviet Union was making it very difficult for Soviet Jews to emigrate to Israel. Under pressure, President Ford signed it into law. In 1979 came the end of détente. First, the Senate refused to ratify the SALT II treaty, negotiated by President Jimmy Carter and Soviet Premier Leonid Brezhnev. Second, on Christmas Day the Soviet Union invaded Afghanistan in order to prop up a communist government there. In return, Carter halted U.S. exports of grain and technology to the Soviet Union and prohibited U.S. athletes from competing in the Moscow Olympics in 1980.

When Ronald Reagan became president in 1981, relations were bad and getting worse. Reagan had always opposed détente and aimed instead at a total Western victory in the Cold War. Uninterested in arms control, he openly

---

8. Francis Fukuyama, "The End of History?" *The National Interest* (Summer 1989), 3-18. See also Fukuyama's book *The End of History and the Last Man* (New York: Simon & Schuster, 1992).

9. Joseph S. Nye Jr., *Soft Power: The Means to Success in World Politics* (New York: Public Affairs, 2005).

referred to the Soviet Union as the "Evil Empire" and increased U.S. aid to anti-communist guerrillas in the Third World. On September 1, 1983, a Soviet fighter shot down a peaceful Korean airliner as it strayed accidentally over Soviet territory in the Far East. The Soviets initially claimed that the passenger plane was a spy plane, but as the U.S. released intercepted communications from the Soviet pilot to his base—asking for guidance—this claim could not be sustained. In England, Oleg Gordievsky, the Soviet KGB station chief, was asked by headquarters in Moscow to monitor meetings of the British elite and blood supplies (which would have to be increased in the event of war). The Soviet leadership regarded the autumn of 1983 as the peak of tension with the West and feared that Reagan might be planning a massive nuclear attack.[10] It was not until January 1984 that Reagan's conciliatory speech lessened tension with Moscow. By then, Brezhnev had died and been succeeded by former KGB Chairman Yuri Andropov, who perished after a year in office and was succeeded by the enigmatic Konstantin Chernenko.

In 1985 Mikhail Gorbachev, a relatively young former minister of agriculture, succeeded Chernenko. Unlike his predecessors, Gorbachev recognized that the Soviet Union had stagnated back in the 1970s and was losing the Cold War. We now know that Gorbachev was correct. Earlier in this chapter we mentioned figures from the 1950s, when the Soviet economy's growth rate was nearly double that of the United States. Those days were long gone. Between 1975 and 1985, the Soviet economy grew at an average annual rate of only 1.8 percent, while the American one grew at 3.25 percent—even taking into account the U.S. recession of 1980–1982. The gap between the superpowers only widened in the 1980s. Under Reagan's stimulus policies, the federal deficit grew but the economy did as well, at an average of 5.7 percent in 1984 and 1985; during the same period the Soviet economy averaged 0.01—an anemic growth rate. It is important to remember, too, that the Soviet economy had never come close to catching the U.S. in aggregate size. In 1984 the Soviet gross domestic product was $1,847,190,000, while the American was $4,755,958,000—over two and a half times as large.[11]

Thus the economic trends were dire for the Soviets, and Gorbachev knew it. U.S. spending on defense under Reagan was rising even more sharply. Reagan was willing to borrow huge amounts of money to outspend the Soviets. America's debt-to-GDP ratio rose to 40 percent from the prior 20 percent. Apart from the military sector (which was partly copied from the United States), Russian productivity and innovation were very low. Some Soviet consumer

10. See Oleg Gordievsky, *Next Stop Execution* (New York: Macmillan, 1995).

11. Calculated using data from Maddison, *Historical Statistics*.

products actually became *less* valuable as their raw materials were manufactured into finished goods.[12]

Then there were the deep problems with the Soviets' international subsystem, based on fraternal socialism. A huge and growing disparity had emerged between the Warsaw Pact and NATO. In 1955 the Warsaw pact had included Albania, Bulgaria, Czechoslovakia, East Germany, Hungary, Poland, Romania, and the USSR. China was aligned with the communist exemplar as well. But by 1985 Albania had left the Pact and Romania was practically gone. China had long since become a Soviet security rival and in 1978, under new leader Deng Xiaoping, began to experiment with private ownership of farmland—its first steps toward the semi-capitalist economy that it has today. As to the rest of the Third World, Khrushchev's grand strategy of bringing it under Soviet tutelage lay in ruins. India, Indonesia, Thailand, Malaysia, and even Vietnam were losing interest in a Soviet partnership. The secret was out: the Soviet model had failed.[13]

Aiming to reverse Soviet decline, Gorbachev initiated a set of deep reforms: *perestroika*, or restructuring of the Soviet economy toward more market mechanisms, and *glasnost*, or openness of the Communist Party to criticism. In other words, Gorbachev and his circle of younger communists sought to move the Soviet Union in the direction of a Western liberal democracy—if not as capitalistic as the United States, at least to a mixed economy like Sweden, open to new ideas and to the global economy. Recognizing, too, that the country could not afford an arms race with the United States, Gorbachev was willing to do business with the West—more serious business even than had been done in the 1970s. He signaled Reagan that he wanted to reduce and eventually eliminate nuclear arms, not just freeze their deployments at current levels. To the surprise of many of his critics and supporters, Reagan was open to this radical change as well. There resulted a set of new arms treaties that reduced and even eliminated some categories of nuclear weapons.

At the same time populations were becoming restive in Eastern Europe. These ancient nations compared their cultures and histories favorably to what had become a more bureaucratic, repressive, inefficient, and technically backward Russia. Poland had never been satisfied with the Soviet yoke. Hungary and

---

12. He writes: "In the later years of communism, many of the Soviet-type countries found it necessary to borrow abroad, but the capacity to repay was so limited that some of these countries soon reached the limit of their capacity to borrow or even defaulted on their loans. By Gorbachev's time, the center was simply unable to pay its bills without printing a lot of new money . . ."; Mancur Olson, *Power and Prosperity: Outgrowing Communist and Capitalist Dictatorships* (New York: Basic Books, 2000), 159.

13. See John M. Owen and Michael Poznansky, "When Does America Drop Dictators?" *European Journal of International Relations* 20, no. 4 (2014): 1072–1099.

Czechoslovakia were equally unsettled. One after another of the so-called satellite states resumed the initiative vis-à-vis Moscow. Poland's Solidarity movement, begun as a trade union in the port city of Gdansk, alarmed Poland's communist rulers, who averted a Soviet intervention by declaring martial law in 1981. In Hungary, liberals were coming to the fore. Far from suppressing these changes, Gorbachev encouraged Eastern European governments to imitate his reforms.

In East Germany, demonstrations for reform were held in Leipzig, Dresden, and other places in the state of Saxony. Gorbachev announced that, in contrast to the past, Russian military forces would not intervene to put down demonstrations or revolts from the Soviet Union.

In the spring of 1989 Hungary opened its border to Austria, allowing any citizen of any East European country who could get to Hungary to emigrate to the West. It was not until November 9, however, that the whole tottering edifice of Russian-imposed communism fell. Since East Germans could migrate through Austria, the Berlin wall served no purpose. Günter Schabowski, an East German party official, prematurely told a crowd of reporters at a press conference: "Therefore we have decided today to implement a regulation that allows every citizen of the German Democratic Republic to leave East Germany through any of the border crossings." When asked by Tom Brokaw of NBC News when the new rule would take effect, he paused, then said: "According to my information, immediately, without delay." East Berliners flocked to the Berlin Wall and began tearing it down as armed guards watched. Gorbachev did nothing to save either East Berlin or East Germany, both of which crumbled, giving way to what became the reunification of Germany, the uniting of East and West.

This was one of those rare abrupt shifts in world politics. Not only did an ugly and massive wall fall in Berlin, but the Soviet international subsystem collapsed with it. The Warsaw Pact voted itself out of existence in early 1991. Many Westerners had thought that if Germany were reunified, it would have to be neutralized and be part of no bloc. President George H. W. Bush, however, insisted that the new all-German government have the right to choose its friends and allies, including joining NATO if it wished. Gorbachev, seeing no alternative, reluctantly agreed. This choice was made easier by the willingness of Helmut Kohl, the German chancellor, to finance it, including housing for Soviet troops who had been based in East Germany.[14]

Gorbachev continued reforming the Soviet Union, to the point of giving up the Communist Party's monopoly on power in 1990. By August 1991, some party officials and military officers had had enough and attempted a

---

14. See Randolph Newnham, "The Price of German Unity: The Role of Economic Aid in the German-Soviet Negotiations," *German Studies Review* (October 1999), 421–446.

coup d'état in Moscow. The president of the Russian Republic (the largest in the Soviet Union), Boris Yeltsin, led a group of reformers in defying the coup leaders. Yeltsin climbed onto a tank outside his office and encouraged Muscovites to resist the coup. The plotters, not wanting to slaughter thousands of civilians, backed down, and Yeltsin and others seized the opportunity to abolish the Soviet Union itself. Gorbachev dissolved the Communist Party, and by the autumn fourteen Soviet republics had declared independence, including Armenia, Azerbaijan, Belarus, Georgia, Kazakhstan, Kyrgyzstan, Moldova, Turkmenistan, Ukraine, Uzbekistan, and of course Russia itself. (The Baltic republics of Estonia, Latvia, and Lithuania had declared independence in 1990.) These became independent states, free to join NATO if they wished. Estonia, Latvia, and Lithuania did so in 2004. Ukraine, Moldova, Belarus, Azerbaijan, Armenia, and Georgia held back, largely because of Russian opposition.

Globalization: The Liberal System Spreads

The collapse of communism and the Soviet Union did not just end the Cold War. It also propelled the nearly worldwide spread of liberal internationalism. The changes had begun in the late 1980s, as elites all over the Third World observed Soviet stagnation and liberal reform. In the 1990s, the changes accelerated as government after government began to adopt the ideas that animated the liberal system. They liberalized state control over their economies and began to increase exports. At the same time, the international financial institutions that lent money to troubled economies—the World Bank, the International Monetary Fund, and others—embraced the "Washington Consensus," which prescribed those same policies for borrowing countries. The third wave of democratization continued, as many countries embraced multiparty democracy at the same time. (It is significant that the United States itself ceased supporting authoritarian regimes in the late 1980s, in favor of liberal democracy, in every area of the world except the Arab Middle East. The American attraction to authoritarianism in the Cold War had been based on anti-communism; with no more communism to attract Third World elites, Washington stopped fearing that democratic elections would yield communist, anti-American governments.)[15] Figure 8.3 shows how rapidly world trade grew from the late 1980s. Figure 8.4 shows how IMF lending increased sharply in the 1990s. Figure 8.5 depicts the spread of liberal democracy across countries since 1800—note the sharp growth in the 1990s.

---

15. Owen and Poznansky, "When Does America Drop Dictators?"

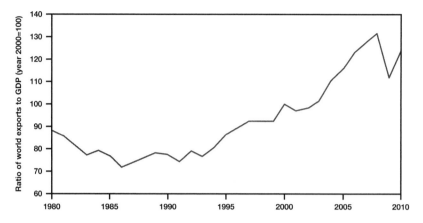

FIGURE 8.3 World trade (ratio of exports to GDP), 1980–2010.
Source: World Trade Organization.

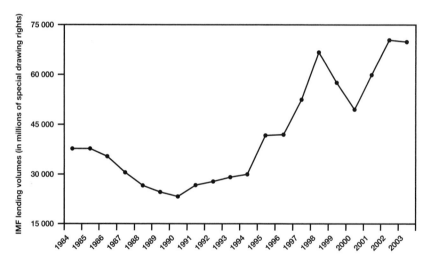

FIGURE 8.4 IMF lending 1984–2004.
Source: International Monetary Fund.

"Globalization" soon became a cliché, a word so often used that it lost its meaning. Still, something real happened in world politics after the collapse of communism. Societies became more open to one another—to ideas, capital, products, and people from other countries. The Kantian system of democracy, trade, and international institutions came to embrace most of the world; countries such as North Korea and Burma, which resisted, were notable simply because they were anomalies. By no means was war banished from the earth. But the wars

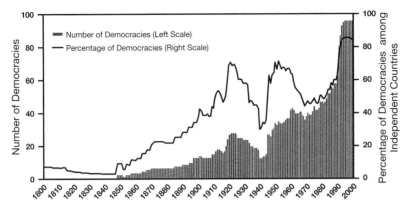

FIGURE 8.5 Number and proportion of democracies in the world, 1800–2000.
Source: After Boix, 2006.

that continued after 1990 were different. First, many have been civil wars, that is, have taken place within countries as different factions have struggled to rule or one group has tried to secede from a nation. Examples include the break-up of Yugoslavia in the 1990s and the drawn-out secession of South Sudan throughout the period. Second, many have been interventions by great powers—chiefly the United States—in small countries that push back violently against various aspects of globalization. In the 1990s Washington intervened with force in Haiti and in former Yugoslav lands in southeastern Europe to enforce human rights. In the 2000s the United States attacked Afghanistan and Iraq to eliminate authoritarian regimes that the U.S. government believed were dangerous to American interests and had been involved in attacks on the Twin Towers in New York City. The latter wars in particular are far from trivial. But the post-1990 era has been unlike previous eras in the relative absence of wars among roughly equal powers seeking to annex territory.

An Overbalance of Power

In this book's final chapter we consider challenges to the global liberal system that have emerged since the 1990s, particularly transnational radical Islamism and terrorism, and the endurance of authoritarian capitalism in China and more recently in Russia. As we shall see, the movement toward global liberalism has been interrupted and pushed back, and it is not clear what the coming decades hold.

But the significance of the rapid spread of the liberal international system since 1980 should not be underestimated. The United States and the West won the Cold War by achieving an overbalance of power in the international system. Most versions of realist theory claim that, out of the inevitable competition among states, balances of power generally emerge and that those balances are the route to stability and peace. A balance of power is said to be the surest formula for international peace because the great powers, be they two, three, or more, feel relatively secure: each knows that if another great power threatens it, enough of the other great powers will see it in their interest to resist the threatener.

But in fact, history shows that periods of balance often were times of high tension and sometimes war. The European powers were roughly balanced in 1914, yet World War I occurred. The United States and Soviet Union formed a balanced bipolar system during the Cold War, yet their relations were extremely tense at certain points, and it may have been nuclear deterrence—fear that attacking the other would lead to one's own destruction—that prevented World War III. By contrast, periods of peace typically coincide with periods when power is concentrated or is at least not divided between polar opponents seeking to undermine or destroy one another. In other words, a lasting peace usually requires an *overbalance* of power.

It is true that attempts by one great power to achieve such an overbalance by military means can trigger war, as the other great powers resist the aspiring hegemon. That is the story of World War II. But concentrations of power often come about through other means. One way is a decisive victory in a major war. The United States achieved such a victory in 1945, and in much of the world there was little or no opposition to coming together under the American hegemon.[16] Another way is when great powers decide that their competition has become counterproductive, impoverishing both by diverting investment and choking off trade.

One branch of realism, sometimes called hegemonic stability or power-preponderance theory, holds that imbalances of power are more robust than balances of power.[17] But those versions of realism ignore the social or ideational bases of overbalances. Sustaining an overbalance of power requires that the overbalance be voluntary and based on common values and interests. It could occur ideologically if all countries were of one religion or of a particular political form such as democracy. It could take place because one country peacefully sought to join another and the result was a coming together of ideologically

---

16. See G. John Ikenberry, *After Victory: Institutions, Strategic Restraint, and the Rebuilding of Order after Major Wars* (Princeton, NJ: Princeton University Press, 2001).

17. Robert Gilpin, *War and Change in World Politics* (New York: Cambridge University Press, 1981); A. F. K. Organski, *World Politics* (New York: Knopf, 1958).

similar nations, as in the European Union today. By contrast, hegemony enforced solely by military coercion is not a durable form of peace. It always inspires discontent, opposition, and a quest for alternatives that will overthrow the hegemon—in other words, attempts at balancing. Political scientist David Lake has drawn this distinction between the U.S.-led North Atlantic Alliance and the Soviet-run Warsaw Pact. The United States found it much cheaper to manage its allies than the Soviet Union did, in part because the U.S. alliance was voluntary and the Soviet was coercive.[18] When France left NATO's integrated military command in 1966, there was no hint of a U.S. or NATO invasion to bring France back into the fold. By contrast, when Hungary left the Warsaw Pact in 1956, and when Czechoslovakia did so in 1968, Soviet tanks rolled in and forced them back into the alliance.

Motives, common ideas and interests, and trust are of great importance. These are factors that realism, with its emphasis on material power and international anarchy, cannot take seriously as causes of international cooperation. If France and Germany are now so alike in economic and political terms, then they can come together and demonstrate their unity. Paris and Berlin certainly have their tensions and disagreements, but neither seeks to dominate the system. War between them has been ruled out, expectations of peaceful change have become durable, and the two can invest more long-term resources into the relationship. Other nations have joined them, creating—ultimately—an overbalance of power. The European Union is not an empire or a security threat to any state. It is merely a reflection of the achievement of social, political, and economic commonalities among particular units. (The EU is, however, a cultural and ideological threat to Putin's Russia today, as we discuss in Chapter 9.)

Another familiar example is the formation of the United States itself in the late eighteenth century. Although they might each have opted for independence, or grouped into two or more clusters, the thirteen original colonies of British North America stayed together after securing independence from Great Britain in 1783. The new nation amounted to an overbalance of power in 1787. Other territories later joined them to make the union greater and larger still. Overbalances have existed previously: The Concert of Europe, which lasted roughly from 1815 to 1848, was one such overbalance. In the late nineteenth century Bismarck's alliance system brought every major state but France within its ambit. These overbalances were grounded in commonly held ideas about conservative government and great power-dominated international order.

---

18. David A. Lake, *Hierarchy in International Relations* (Ithaca, NY: Cornell University Press, 2009).

Although the end to the Cold War was spectacular and unanticipated then, it was like other periods in world history in that it involved an overbalance of power. There is nothing inevitable about the formation and persistence of voluntary overbalances of power. Countries can dissociate themselves as Norway did from the European Union or as Britain is in the process of doing. The processes of joining and leaving are voluntary. In Chapter 9 we consider the standing of China, Russia, and other powers in relation to the U.S.-dominated overbalance of power in today's world and the future.

The overbalance that the United States achieved during the Cold War was historically peculiar in being based so heavily on democracy and trade. It also is probably the most successful overbalance in history. It empowered the groups that this book has emphasized throughout: people who want to become wealthier by selling goods abroad and who understand that sustaining their ability to do so requires that their country be open to buying from abroad as well. The Cold War overbalance also disempowered those who stood to gain from closed economies or trading monopolies and empires. It was constituted not only by international cooperation but also by international institutions constructed to perpetuate that cooperation.

Conclusion

In the 1970s the preeminent realist in the study of international relations, Kenneth Waltz, declared that bipolar systems were the most stable in international politics. Waltz built a sophisticated form of balance-of-power theory around the Soviet–American case, arguing that what mattered most was that the two superpowers had roughly equal nuclear arsenals, and hence neither could defeat the other in war.[19] Waltz was far from alone in expecting the bipolar balance of power to go on and on.

The Soviet Union did enjoy many years of growth and success. Particularly from the 1940s until the early 1970s, it showed that a non-liberal, non-democratic great power can shape its international environment so as to perpetuate itself and extend its power. For a while it bestrode much of the world like a colossus. But even as Waltz was writing his magnum opus, Soviet power was eroding, while American power in all its military, economic, and ideological aspects was increasing. The fundamental reasons for the different growth rates and power trajectories for the two superpowers cannot be captured by realism. They have to do with

---

19. Kenneth N. Waltz, *Theory of International Politics* (Reading, MA: Addison-Wesley, 1979).

differences in the ideas and institutions of the two countries: how they ordered their societies, what interests they empowered in those societies, and their relations with allies and adversaries.

Realist theory asserts that conflict, depending on the distribution of power, is a constant in international relations: it can never be reduced, only redistributed to different parts of the system. Liberal and constructivist approaches, however, argue that domestic politics (such as the degree of democracy and which domestic interests are predominant) can decisively influence the amount, duration, and location of peace. The liberal and open international economy can also affect international politics and provide a peaceful option of economic growth and trade (as opposed to military conflict and the absorption of territory). This does not mean peace for all time, since economic and domestic factors are not guaranteed to produce favorable outcomes. Highly nationalistic or ideological leaders can cause wars. Economic depressions, such as those of the 1870s and 1930s, can discredit liberal policies and lead nations to revert to territorial ambitions and empire-building. These contingencies cannot wholly be eliminated from international politics, and they may arise again. Since the ravages of World War II, the great powers have been on a more peaceful course vis-à-vis each other, and conflict has been relegated to the periphery of the system where ideological terrorism expresses itself. Even this, however, can be stanched. The Reformation ultimately did so with a compromise (more or less foreshadowed at Westphalia) to tolerate each other's religions. In the Middle East today Sunni and Shi'ite versions of Islam contend through terrorist proxies, if not national states. Compromise between them is not yet on the horizon.

FURTHER READING

Fukuyama, Francis. *The End of History and the Last Man.* New York: Basic Books, 1992.

Ikenberry, G. John. *Liberal Leviathan.* Princeton, NJ: Princeton University Press, 2012.

Keohane, Robert O., and Joseph S. Nye. *Power and Interdependence.* 4th ed. New York: Longman, 2011.

Lake, David A. *Hierarchy in International Relations.* Ithaca, NY: Cornell University Press, 2009.

Logevall, Fredrik. *Choosing War: The Lost Chance for Peace and the Escalation of War in Vietnam.* Berkeley: University of California Press, 2001.

Mandelbaum, Michael. *The Ideas That Conquered the World: Peace, Democracy, and Free Markets in the Twenty-First Century.* New York: Public Affairs, 2004.

Nye, Joseph S., Jr. *Soft Power: The Means to Success in World Politics.* New York: Public Affairs, 2005.

Olson, Mancur. *Power and Prosperity: Outgrowing Communist and Capitalist Dictatorships*. New York: Basic Books, 2000.

Owen, John M., IV. *The Clash of Ideas in World Politics*. Princeton, NJ: Princeton University Press, 2010.

Rosecrance, Richard. *The Rise of the Trading State*. New York: Basic Books, 1986.

Sarotte, Mary Elise. *1989: The Struggle to Create Post-Cold War Europe*. Princeton, NJ: Princeton University Press, 2014.

Waltz, Kenneth N. *Theory of International Politics*. Reading, MA: Addison-Wesley, 1979.

WORLD POLITICS TODAY

Introduction

At the end of the previous chapter, we left the story in the 1990s. In this final chapter, we bring it to the present day, noting both the recent advances of the liberal international order and some setbacks and current challenges. The role of agency or choice will be especially evident: nothing is inevitable, and leaders and citizens can move their countries toward more democracy, commerce, and peace or away from those things. This is true in the key states of China, Russia, India, and Brazil; of actors in the Middle East; and of people in the original liberal core states of the West.

International Relations Theory and History

The world would be simpler if one theory could explain everything. Realism claims to be such an all-purpose theory. It sees international politics always and everywhere as consisting of sovereign states (nation-states, or in some contexts city-states) dwelling in perpetual anarchy, without an overarching government to protect them or settle their disputes and punish aggression. As a result, states must always fear one another, expect the worst, and arm themselves accordingly. They should avoid dependence on one another for security or wealth, because dependence exposes them to blackmail. They should form alliances, but only temporary ones, because interests are constantly shifting. For realism, democracies are no different from other states, and international trade—which, again, should be minimal—is not a force for peace. The sure path to security is to seek and secure territory, particularly territory that provides the materials a state needs to be secure and wealthy: farmland, raw materials, and strategic locations such as ports and invasion-protected terrain. Realists claim that this theory is a universal guide to the past, present, and future of world politics and that rejecting realism means embracing utopian schemes of peace and harmony that lead to weakness and even war.

As we have made clear in this book, realism is not a universally valid theory. If we look at the past half millennium of history, we see countries, bilateral relationships, and even entire regions that do not exhibit the features and outcomes that realism expects. Realists are correct that there has been no world government and none is likely (even if it were desirable, which is doubtful). But some states have defied realist logic by seeking wealth and security through trade rather than autarky. They have embraced interdependence and achieved prosperity and power in doing so. They have given up the drive to territorial empires, seeing those as counterproductive, and have relied instead on trust, international rules, and long-term alliances. These states have tended to be liberal democracies, or (in past centuries) states moving in a liberal-democratic direction. They have had rising commercial or middle classes, people with a stake in commerce and who favor the rule of law and popular sovereignty rather than centralization under a single ruler or party. Recent studies show that states that try to conquer and hold territory tend to be authoritarian.[1]

We caught the first glimpses of these liberal democratic trading states at the birth of the modern states system in the Netherlands in the sixteenth century. England was to imitate the Dutch and in subsequent centuries become the world's leading power precisely by becoming a democratizing trading state. Later the United States was to do the same in its own way. As other states have empowered their middle classes and democratized, they have joined a kind of international club anticipated more than 200 years ago by the philosopher Immanuel Kant. A liberal international system, constructed over centuries by people across the world, has emerged within the broader global system. Liberal international relations theory, with its attention to ideas and institutions, both within and among states, explain the transformation of world politics over the centuries; realism cannot do so.

Clearly this book's 500-year story is not one of steady progress or the uniform spread of liberal democracy and peace. The ideas and policies and institutions we have analyzed have encountered pushback all along. Economic depressions, particularly those of 1873–1896 and 1929–1939, have pushed even some liberal democracies toward mercantilism and imperialism and brought general mistrust

---

1. Thorin M. Wright and Paul F. Diehl, "Unpacking Territorial Disputes: Domestic Political Influences and War," *Journal of Conflict Resolution* 60, no. 4 (2016): 645–669.

and major war. It is important to remember that the same could happen in the future, and indeed today there are significant signs that the growth and deepening of the liberal international system is halting and perhaps diminishing. The human race will never achieve a certain utopia of universal democracy and perpetual peace. But more and more countries have moved in that direction, and more and more can do so. Realism is good as far as it goes, but it does not go as far as its proponents believe, and its explanatory power has decreased over time. In this chapter we review briefly the tension between realist and liberal logics in world politics over the past five centuries and conclude with observations about the present day and an analysis of the choices available to countries in the future.

Realism Gradually Yields to Economic Links

In the year 1400, lords and peasants populated Europe, but states were not yet fully formed. Feudalism—the overarching social and economic system—reflected a decentralized Europe that did not separate people into different nation-states. Individuals were supposed to serve God, and all of Europe composed one ecclesiastical realm under the Roman Catholic Church. Kings and nobles fought wars, but their territories and loyalties overlapped; "France" and "England" were not clearly demarcated into the sovereign nation-states that we are accustomed to today. This changed, however, with the advent of Protestantism.

Martin Luther denounced the sale of indulgences— promises by the Church to get their loved ones out of purgatory and into heaven more quickly. The revenue from indulgences were used by the Church to build the magnificent St. Peter's Basilica in Rome, and on October 31, 1517, an outraged Martin Luther pounded his ninety-five theses onto the door of the Castle Church in Wittenberg, Saxony (Germany) (Figure 9.1). The Catholic Church reacted and excommunicated Luther. But he refused to yield and indeed expanded his criticisms to encompass the spiritual and political power of the Church, and Protestantism was born.

Soon, Protestants found that they needed help to withstand the suppression of the Pope and the church hierarchy. For protection, they allied themselves to local German princes, who had reasons of their own to defy Church authority, and the struggle against Catholicism became territorial in character. This was perhaps the first example of realism in modern garb because Protestant princes declared themselves sovereign over the religion of their territory. The transnational authority of the Church and the Holy Roman Empire was damaged irreparably. States began to fight one another for territorial dominance. The Thirty Years' War—a zero-sum struggle that began as a religious revolt and evolved into a battle for power and territory between the Habsburgs of Spain and Austria and the kings of Sweden, Denmark, and France—ravaged Europe from 1618 to 1648 and decided which state would adhere to which branch of Christianity.

FIGURE 9.1 Engraving of Luther nailing his ninety-five theses to the Wittenberg church door.
Source: Peter Righteous/Alamy Stock Photo.

Protestants triumphed in northern Germany, Scandinavia, England, Holland, and Switzerland, and Catholics took the South—Austria, Bavaria, Spain, France (in the Gallican church), and Italy. During this gargantuan struggle, perhaps one-fifth of the population of Germany perished.

By helping princes establish sovereignty over their territories, the religious struggle helped establish modern states and the international system depicted by realism, in which states fight and threaten war to compete for territory. After the Peace of Westphalia (1648; Figure 9.2), and even more that of Utrecht (1713; Figure 9.3), states continued to vie with one another. But even as this system of sovereign states reached an apogee, trade and economics were diluting the single-minded struggle over territory in some regions of Europe. Despite the predatory example of Louis XIV of France, some leaders understood that nations might gain from trade more than they could derive from military conflict. England, Holland, and later the young United States prospered through internal development and trade. At the end of the eighteenth century the Industrial Revolution offered another string to the bow of national prosperity: the machine age substituted factory-produced textiles for the old handwoven fabrics of the continent and India. As industry began to replace farmland and precious metals as the chief source of prosperity, territory itself lost value and capital—money used to make more money, as in industrial machinery—increased in value.

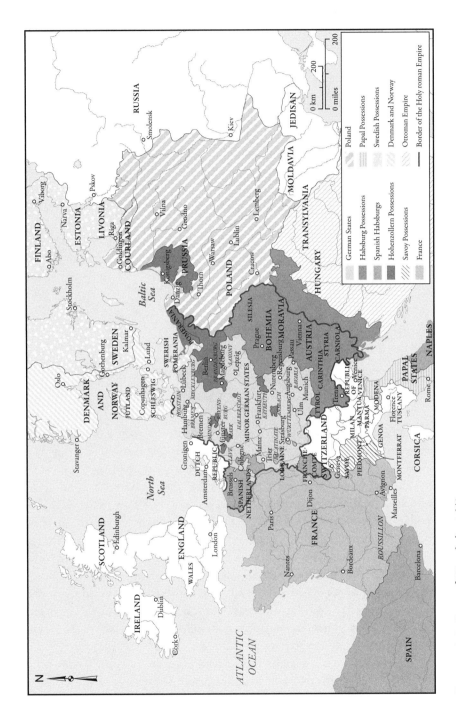

FIGURE 9.2 Peace of Westphalia, 1648.

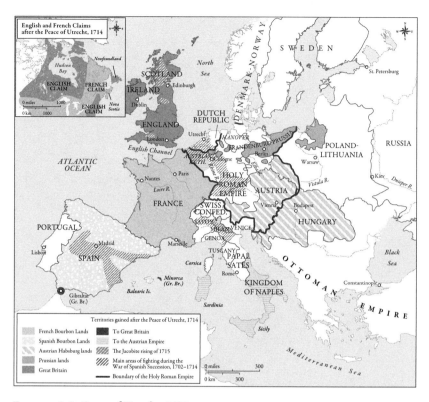

FIGURE 9.3 Peace of Utrecht, 1713.

But as we know, this massive shift in the sources of wealth did not prevent war between commercial nations. Early modern trading states built empires and monopolized the trade of their colonies. The introduction of popular regimes in France and the United States in the late eighteenth century changed the direction of politics and foreign affairs and for that reason generated a reaction among Europe's old monarchies. The young French Republic, feeling mortally threatened by those monarchies, extended its liberalism to other states through force, and Napoleon conquered much of Europe. America, on the other hand, being far away from Europe, relied on demonstration and example. In assessing other countries, both the French and the Americans asked: Was a country liberalizing or repressing its population? If it was liberalizing, it could be trusted to rely on peace and trade. If it was repressing, it was likely a predator and prone to war.

The question reverberated for the entire nineteenth century, changing the direction of politics and economics. Liberal and industrializing countries countered agricultural and aristocratic monarchies. England and France gradually became more modern, but Russia, Prussia, and Austria represented the old social order. The trouble was that neither side won. The aristocrats developed nationalism as a remedy against social change, and more liberal states sought to punish conservative nations. England and France subdued Russia in the Crimean war (1854–1856). Prussia humiliated Austria and then France (between 1866 and 1871), gaining enough prestige to satisfy Berlin's aggrieved and potentially liberal population. The net result was a bimodal international system in which industrialism and trade benefited one set of claimants, and nationalist expansion another. If economics did not work, war might become necessary to gain approval.

The liberal international subsystem was set back in the latter part of the nineteenth century. In 1873 a great depression broke out, international trade plummeted, and economic progress began a period of relative decline. Nations sought to sell their surplus wares overseas. Territory became highly valuable again, even the liberal great powers began to worry about one another's gains, and ideologies of empire gained traction. The 1880s and 1890s were years in which European states grabbed massive amounts of territory in Africa and Asia—the so-called New Imperialism.

Two disparate systems had been proceeding side by side and interacting: the peaceful trade and domestic development alternative and the militarist colonial and imperial option. But the second, realist-style system was reasserting itself. By 1890 there had been few enough converts to liberal democracy and peaceful relations. Even liberalizing societies such as Prussia-Germany and France used tariffs and mercantilism to protect their domestic industries and embraced nationalism as a social cement. After 1890 Germany sought colonies and created an Imperial Navy to reach them in face of British naval primacy. France probed Indochina and Morocco, and England, which already ruled India, took Egypt, Nigeria, and parts of Southeast Asia. By 1914 it was clear the military-territorial trend had won out, and the states of Europe eyed one another with growing fear.

The First World War was supposed to decide the issue. After Russia mobilized on July 30, 1914, Germany attacked France and Russia. But the war did not produce a decisive result. Germany—narrowly defeated in 1918—was forced to accept blame for the war and resolved on revenge. Nations should instead have learned to use economic as opposed to military means. The 1920s should have been peaceful, but they were only a prelude to another disastrous conflict. The Great Depression (1929–1939), like its predecessor that began in 1873, caused vast amounts of wealth to disappear. Under domestic political pressure from massive numbers of unemployed people, governments—starting with that of the United States—reduced foreign trade. With the economic option to wealth and security being shut down once again, some great powers began to conclude that expanding their territory was a better strategy to achieve wealth and security than was peaceful trade. In the 1930s Germany, Italy, and Japan all began to rearm and build new empires, expanding their power and threatening the liberal democracies (France, Britain, and the United States).

After the horrific Second World War (1939–1945), many believed that any kind of liberal international system was finished and that realism would return with a vengeance. Recognizing the supreme value of territory and working to make sure all great powers had enough (at the expense of small countries and colonies) appeared to some leaders the only guarantor of stability in a world of conflict. After 1945 Stalin's view that territory equals power was asserted by many political scribes and some leaders. But two factors modified this conclusion. First, because they were more transparent and held liberal ideas in common, democratic countries could more easily ally and achieve together what none could gain on its own. Second, these countries, led by the United States—which had emerged from the war as the world's most powerful country—had learned from the preceding century that free-market democracies had to cooperate to forestall more great depressions and to keep their economies open. They set up international agencies such as the International Monetary Fund (IMF), the World Bank, and the General Agreement on Tariffs and Trade (GATT) for this purpose. (The United States also created a network of alliances against the Soviet communist bloc for insurance.) The first group attracted late-coming authoritarians who saw trade as the means of advancement. Foreign trade tended to rise more quickly than GDP, and its beneficiaries were the long-term gainers in international politics and power. Territory was important, but it was not crucial in this quest, for even smaller nations like Japan, Belgium, Switzerland, and West Germany advanced, while the Goliaths—the United States and the Soviet Union—skirted the choice.

Norms and power dictated the ultimate result, and the differences between the Soviet and American blocs were painfully evident. When a Soviet ally in Eastern Europe threatened to defect and become more democratic, Soviet tanks would roll in and crush the threat. The Soviets did this three times—in East Germany in 1953, Hungary in 1956, and Czechoslovakia in 1968—and would have done so in a fourth, in Poland in 1980, had not that country's communist government declared martial law to suppress rising dissent. Meanwhile, the closest to a defection from the U.S. alliance structure was France's withdrawal from NATO's integrated military command in 1967 (not a full withdrawal from NATO itself). Washington was not pleased with Paris, but there was no question of the United States attacking France. The two superpower blocs displayed different levels of economic success as well. Later Soviet economic growth rates, based on heavy industry, turned out to be frail and inconsistent; by 1980, Soviet growth had slumped to 1 percent. The United States had faced reversals like the recession of 1973–1974 and that of 1980–1982. But the American economy rebounded, and investment in new computers made by IBM and Apple changed the workplace forever.

Most important, however, was the creation of an overbalance of power in Western hands. Not only did NATO grow in size, but the U.S. coalition including Japan, Mexico, Canada, and South Korea prospered in foreign trade. By 1990, the Western coalition in Europe and Asia dwarfed the recumbent Soviet empire, which was actually declining. In past centuries the liberal states had not been dominant but had been counterbalanced by agrarian, territory-seeking states. Now, for the first time, the liberal club of states had become predominant. This growth did not exacerbate conflict: it led instead to cooperation. The Western group was numerous and strong and it attracted states from the old Soviet bloc. Mikhail Gorbachev was the living representation of the importance of free peoples in preference to repressed Soviet citizens. Fourteen new countries emerged from the Soviet grasp in 1990, Russia among them. Russian leaders like Boris Yeltsin undoubtedly hoped that Russia might join the West or at least help dismantle it as peace transpired. But they were wrong. The Russian economic and political systems were not liberal enough to qualify for membership, and NATO was not disbanded.

The World Since 1990: Globalization and Its Discontents

Through most of this book we referred to the "liberal international subsystem," a kind of oasis surrounded by the wider realist global system. As of the 1990s, it becomes appropriate to drop the prefix "sub" and simply to refer to the liberal international system. The vision of Kant from two centuries earlier was realized as never before. Alternative strategies toward national stability, growth, and security, including communism, state-directed growth, and import-substituting industrialization, had all failed. Export-led growth, which had been practiced with success not only by the democracies of Western Europe but also by the "Asian Tigers" of South Korea, Taiwan, Singapore, and Hong Kong (then still a British colony), to say nothing of Japan, offered a surer route to development. The West's Cold War victory meant that democracy, too, looked like the winning system of government. What political scientist Samuel Huntington called the "third wave" of global democratization, which actually had begun in the 1970s, crested in the early 1990s.[2]

This was when the term "globalization" came into vogue. Globalization was (and is) best defined as the opening of national economies to movements of goods, capital, and labor to form a more and more integrated world economy. Driving globalization was the "Washington Consensus" that free markets, trade, democracy, and human rights made up the winning formula. The Washington Consensus was held to by governments not only in the West but also in the former Soviet bloc and in most countries in what had been called the Third World. The Consensus also was facilitated by international financial institutions such as the World Bank and IMF, which required borrower states to open up their economies and democratize their political systems. Former communist states such as Poland and Mongolia hired Western economists to advise them about "shock therapy," or the abrupt adoption of capitalism. Third World countries were optimistically renamed "emerging markets," and many states in Asia, Africa, and

---

2. Samuel P. Huntington, *The Third Wave: Democratization in the Late Twentieth Century* (Norman: University of Oklahoma Press, 1991).

Latin America undertook similar reforms, betting on trade rather than autarky. Figure 9.4 shows variation in global trade as a percentage of global income since 1820; note the ups and downs prior to 1945 (including serious downturns after 1873 and 1929), but also the steep climb beginning in the mid-1980s.

In geopolitical terms, the international system shifted in 1990 from the familiar Cold War bipolarity to a structure unprecedented in the preceding 500 years: unipolarity, with the United States as the sole superpower. America faced threats and worried about stability in several regions of the world. It intervened militarily in Central America, the Caribbean, southeastern Europe, the Middle East, and sub-Saharan Africa and made a serious show of force in East Asia in the 1990s. But Washington faced no real security rival, no state remotely capable of counterbalancing its colossal military power. Indeed, in the First Gulf War (1991), most countries of the world, including the Soviet Union, backed the U.S.-led effort to drive Iraqi forces out of neighboring Kuwait. The coalition cobbled together by U.S. President George H. W. Bush agreed that the Persian Gulf, which produced one-third of the world's oil and had half of the world's crude oil reserves, was a vital region and that the United States could be trusted to lead the world in keeping it safe. Near-global support for the war demonstrated just how much governments around the world were betting on the U.S.-led liberal international order.

Criticism of the United States and the post–Cold War global order was plentiful, of course. The French word for American power was *hyperpuissance* ("hyperpower"). The U.S. interventions in Somalia, Haiti, Bosnia-Herzegovina, and

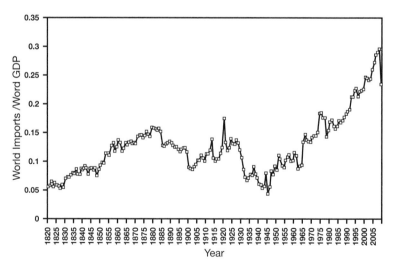

FIGURE 9.4 Trade as a percentage of global income, 1820–2005.
Source: After Chase-Dunn and Kwon, 2010.

Kosovo drew sharp criticism from various countries. Its show of naval force in the Taiwan Strait in 1996, after China fired several missiles off the coast of Taiwan, was not welcome in Beijing. Globalization, too, drew criticism from those who pointed out that while aggregate income typically rose in individual countries, the distribution of that income became more and more skewed. The IMF's policies generated protests from those who thought they were the old Western imperialism in a new guise. But a favorite slogan of British Prime Minister Margaret Thatcher in the 1980s—"there is no alternative"—kept globalization going.

Many of the same liberalizing trends continued into the twenty-first century. Figure 9.5 shows a more precise view of global trade, focusing on the post-1970 period. Note that trade increases after 1990 and then accelerates further after 2003.

Furthermore, the nearly global spread of the liberal international system was accompanied by a marked decrease in war deaths. Figure 9.6 shows that the decline in battle deaths that began after 1985 persisted after 2000. Note that battle deaths in international wars virtually disappear, and battle deaths in civil wars nearly do so as well.[3] The world is still a violent place, and civil and international wars remain a constant threat. But the data clearly show that political violence has declined.

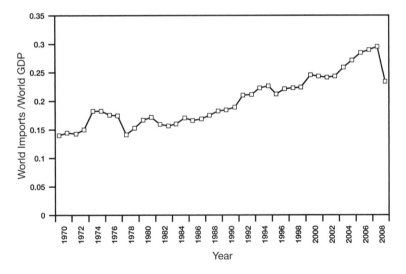

FIGURE 9.5 Trade as a percentage of global income, 1970–2009.
Source: After Chase-Dunn and Kwon, 2010.

---

3. As noted in Chapter 1, much of the decline is the result of improved medical and transportation (battlefield evaculation) technology; see Tanisha Fazal, "Dead Wrong? Battle Deaths, Military Medicine, and Exaggerated Reports of War's Demise," *International Security* 39, no. 1 (2014): 95–125.

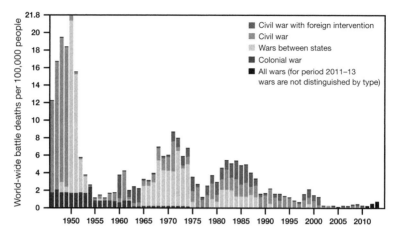

FIGURE 9.6 Rate of battle deaths, 1946–2013.
Source: After Roser, 2016.

Ideas and History

The liberal international system came into its own after the Second World War, when the balance between conflictual and cooperative ideas shifted toward the latter. At first the ideology of military expansion was deterred by nuclear weapons: too much expansion risked World War III, which might well have ended civilization. Conventional clashes still occurred in Korea and Vietnam, but the traditional battlefield in Europe remained silent. The world economy allowed another method—rising commerce—to flourish in many domains, particularly those aligned with the United States. The emerging economies first remained behind but began to prosper as raw material mining and then outsourced manufacturing arrived. Indonesia, Iran, India, and parts of Africa began to blossom. This particularly occurred as liberal or even democratic governments replaced autocracies in countries such as South Korea, Taiwan, and Chile. Some states like China and Singapore remained dominated by a single party, but they also opened themselves to trade and investment from overseas. Like Park Chung-Hee's South Korea (1963-1979), these authoritarian states sought victory on the commercial battlefield, not in landed combat.

In the longer term, mastery of technology and information made up for deficient control of territory. The central interpretation and manipulation of information influenced many nations. Those left out suffered in myriad ways and did not fully participate in decision-making for the world as a whole. A further centralization has occurred: that of access to the latest and most potent understanding of complex events. Countries cut off from the latest information cannot fully compete. Scientific advances like gene editing and cyber penetration of others' computers now exist. The number of capitals that access and manipulate exotic techniques can be counted on the fingers of one hand. If such capacities are achieved, typical measures of power become still less relevant. A country no longer need attack another to become healthier or more efficient. Some potential new techniques need to be thought through from a moral standpoint. For example, a country might simply edit the genes of its population and improve itself entirely from within. The point is that modern technology has the potential to render the conquest of territory less and less relevant.

Challenges to the Liberal International System

Neo-Mercantilism Returns to the West?

Still, it is not at all clear that the liberal international system is continuing its forward trajectory. Liberal internationalism began to encounter significant problems after 2000. The problems that hamper free trade never went away. Although neoclassical economic theory says that any state will be better off practicing free trade even if no other state does so, for political reasons any government is going to have difficulty signing up for free trade with any other country unless that other country reciprocates. One problem is that a big economy (a monopsonist) can, like Walmart, set the price for the goods its buys, and other states know this. Another is a problem we described in Chapter 5: in every country there are people—uncompetitive companies, workers, even entire industries—that stand to lose from free trade. These interests press their governments to maintain barriers to imports, and so each country is internally divided politically over foreign trade and tariffs continue or are even raised.

For these and other reasons, governments generally have trouble trusting one another when it comes to free trade. Before World War II, it was difficult for states to enter and maintain free trade agreements. Between 1850 and 1870, under British leadership, countries did move to freer trade and most-favored-nation arrangements (by which advantages extended to one nation were then offered to others). The United States, however, starting with the Morrill Act of 1861, opted for successively higher tariffs, giving itself advantages as others cut duties. By the 1870s other states raised tariffs under the prodding of the Great Depression of 1873–1896. Germany, Austria, France, and Russia increased their duties during this period, with only Great Britain resisting the temptation to limit imports.

In 1944, as the Second World War was drawing to a close, U.S., British, and other leaders took steps to help as many countries as possible practice free trade. In Chapter 7 we described how, after World War II, they designed the GATT—which became the World Trade Organization (WTO) in 1995—to overcome problems of coordination and mistrust among states. The GATT was a mechanism by which multiple governments could negotiate together, in painstaking detail, how much and when they would reduce trade barriers in various goods. The GATT had great success by sponsoring several rounds of trade talks, including the Dillon Round (1960–1962), the Kennedy Round (1962–1967), the Tokyo Round (1973–1979), and the Uruguay Round (1986–1994).

But the most recent, the Doha Round, began in 2001 and stalled in 2008, effectively ending in failure in 2015. The Doha Round foundered on disagreements between wealthy countries (particularly the United States) that did not want to lower agricultural subsidies and poorer countries that would not lower tariffs unless they did. In the aftermath of the collapse of these talks, the United States under the Obama administration negotiated separate free-trade agreements with East Asian countries (excluding China), the Trans-Pacific Partnership (TPP), and Europe entered into the Transatlantic Trade and Investment Partnership (TTIP).

But the 2016 U.S. presidential elections put the TPP and TTIP in doubt as well. In the Democratic Party the self-described socialist and anti-globalist Bernie Sanders nearly defeated the liberal-internationalist Hillary Clinton for the Democratic nomination. And Clinton was defeated in November 2016 by the Republican Donald Trump, who was openly skeptical of free trade deals, America's alliances in Europe and Asia, and democracy promotion in general. The rise of Sanders and triumph of Trump probably owed a great deal to the financial crisis of 2008–2010, which destroyed large amounts of wealth, threw hundreds of thousands out of work, and gutted the value of the chief financial asset of millions of Americans: their home. Regardless, the 2016 elections suggested that those who had lost jobs from economic openness—from free trade, from American companies investing abroad, and from immigration—were in distress and ripe for mobilization by politicians. (Most economists argued that more jobs have been lost to automation than to economic openness, but in the political realm that did not matter.) In the realm of ideas, too, liberalism seemed exhausted; internationalists in both the Democratic and Republican parties had trouble articulating why it was good for America to stay the liberal-internationalist course.

The other main center of liberal internationalism, Europe, was undergoing similar challenges and changes. The European Union has been a liberal project since its origins in the 1950s. Since the 1990s the EU had deepened its integration beyond being a mere free-trade zone into a set of countries with free movements of capital and labor. Here, too, those who find that they or their children do not have the well-paying manufacturing jobs that were plentiful until the 1980s seem to have had enough. Anti-EU and anti-American populist parties on the political right in northern Europe, and on the left in Spain and Greece, gained strength after 2010. In 2016 the British public voted to leave the EU altogether. Some voted for "Brexit" because of job losses, but others named a desire to restore British sovereignty over the laws and regulations emanating from the EU capital in Brussels as the main reason.[4]

Economist Branko Milanovic has produced a graph, the "elephant curve," that helps explain why the countries that pioneered global liberalism began to

---

4. Michael Ashcroft, 'How the United Kingdom Voted on Thursday—and Why," http://lordashcroftpolls.com/2016/06/how-the-united-kingdom-voted-and-why/, accessed on August 8, 2016.

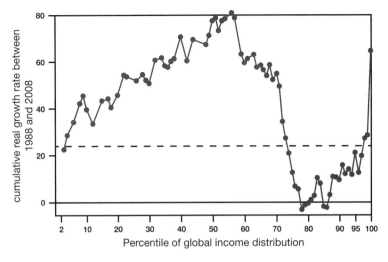

FIGURE 9.7 Income changes of the world's population by level of wealth, 1988–2008.
Source: After Lakner and Milanovic, 2016.

retreat from it (Figure 9.7). All groups have done well by globalization except the upper middle class, whose incomes fall between the 75th and 90th percentiles. These are mostly people from Russia, Eastern Europe, Latin America, and, significantly, the manufacturing sectors in North America and Western Europe. This roughly corresponds to people who voted against Clinton in the United States and for Brexit in Britain.

Neo-Mercantilism in Asia?

Then there is China, a state with great historic staying power and adaptability.[5] From 1644 until late 1911, China was ruled by the Qing dynasty, also known as the Manchus (from Manchuria). By 1750 China had crushed the smaller nations on its northern periphery. The Qing were influenced by Mongols, not their predecessor Ming dynasty. The Qing created armies like the Austrians or Ottomans. They had mobile cavalry. They wanted to solidify a multicultural empire. They killed off enemies near Mongolia. They could have expanded against Russia, which was weak (to their north), but instead they turned to the West. Their "Yuanmingyuan"— bright gardens—were a symbol of Manchu rule until they were destroyed by the British in 1860 during the Opium Wars. Chinese history was not simply a story of how to increase the power of the weakened state (through imperialism); it was

5. Odd Arne Westad, *Restless Empire: China and the World Since 1750* (New York: Basic Books, 2015).

about a society that adapted to external influences and absorbed different peoples. The Republic of China established in 1912 attempted to accelerate modernization, but it lost a civil war to the rival Communist Party, which in 1949 founded today's People's Republic of China. The mass killings of the Maoist years (1958–1962 and 1966–1976) were as important as external influences for the nonce. Only after Mao died could society move back toward a form of authoritarian-capitalist modernity.

China's troubled past, however, is not an excuse for continuing authoritarianism. It has flourished historically not when internally rigid and externally closed but when open, diverse, and willing to adapt and learn. Marxism may have been an imposed excrescence, but state-influenced capitalism was likely to be the long-term result. Today China is nationalist but not universalist. In contrast to the Maoist era, it has no doctrine (like widely accepted European versions of Marxism propagated by Lenin) to justify its expansion. Japan will not imbibe Chinese doctrines or power. It will not try itself to balance China but has strong links with the United States. China might be able to dominate the Association of South East Asian Nations (ASEAN). But ASEAN, India, and Japan are linked with the United States.

If China emphasizes economic ties, it will go further than if it stresses territorial dominance. To that end, it is pursuing the One Belt, One Road initiative to construct trade routes overland, through Central Asia, and by sea, through the South China Sea and Indian Ocean. One Belt, One Road is an impressive strategy, but brings new challenges to China. It means that China's biggest future challenger will likely be India. For economic reasons China wants to avoid a face-off with the United States. China's friends are not strong or decisive. They include Omar al-Bashir (Sudan), Robert Mugabe (Zimbabwe), and the Burmese (Myanmar) junta in Naypyidaw—all of whom are weak locally. In Africa, China is now following in the footsteps of European imperialists in terms of its relations with post-colonial states – although it is not establishing a formal empire. China does not appear to have a political plan for the Middle East.

More generally, notwithstanding its semi-capitalist economy and reliance on exports, China has not fully abandoned neo-mercantilism. China's own investors have been prevented from dumping the national currency (renminbi ["people's currency"] or yuan) and investing in foreign currencies. The Chinese central bank (People's Bank of China, or PBOC) has purchased Chinese stocks to maintain the value of the renminbi. It has also sometimes devalued the currency to maintain export competitiveness in face of declining growth.

What will be the longer-term effect of such policies? The question is more relevant because the United States, while still far and away the world's leading military power,[6] has gradually been losing its dominant economic position as other countries,

---

6. Stephen Brooks and William Wohlforth, *America Abroad: The United States' Global Role in the 21st Century* (New York: Oxford University Press, 2016).

including India, Brazil, Turkey, and Indonesia, have experienced periods of rapid growth since 1990. The Chinese economy remains the most impressive, and therein lie serious questions. Part of the story of the growth and deepening of the liberal international system over the past few centuries has been the hegemony—the power, leverage, and influence—of liberal hegemons, chiefly Great Britain in the nineteenth century and the United States in the twentieth. China's economy will soon become the world's largest. Its currency qualified for global "reserve currency" status in November 2015. The renminbi thus joined a privileged basket of currencies, including the dollar, the euro, and the yen, by which IMF assets are measured. Technically, the renminbi did not fully meet the criterion of "usability" because it was not fully convertible or freely available for investment inside of other countries. As the Chinese economy comes to equal and surpass the American, the character of the international system could become less liberal. Figure 9.8 depicts the growth curves of the two massive economies, measured in purchasing-power parity and in nominal terms.[7]

Yet, the Chinese leadership may find itself hampered if it tries to reassert economic sovereignty. In the 1960s two IMF economists, Robert Mundell and J. Marcus Fleming, determined that a country's policymakers could not manipulate its exchange rate, its interest rate, and its degree of capital mobility at the same time. If capital was fully mobile, they had to choose between managing the interest rate or the exchange rate. If they chose the interest rate, then a decline in the interest rate would lead to an outflow of currency, reducing the exchange rate.

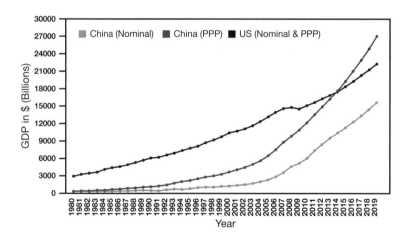

FIGURE 9.8 U.S. and Chinese economic growth since 1980.
Source: Statistics Times.

---

7. Purchasing-power parity (PPP) controls for the higher cost of living in the United States; nominal does not, and simply states the size of each economy based on the actual currency exchange rate.

If, on the other hand, they sought to manage the exchange rate, then any decline in the exchange rate (lowering the value of the currency) would lead to a departure of funds, which would also force up the interest rate. Up until now China has not permitted capital to move freely in and out of the Chinese market. Thus the PBOC could set currency values and also the interest rate.

But if, as a reserve currency, the renminbi will be mobile and capable of being invested anywhere, then China will have to choose between setting exchange rates and currency values. If China chooses to regulate its currency, its interest rates will fluctuate with world demand. A lower-valued currency will raise Chinese interest rates because the PBOC will want to prevent savers from transferring income overseas. This in turn will reduce Chinese growth. As a reserve currency the renminbi will progressively gain mobility, but this means that Chinese economic growth will be determined by events in the world economy. China will lose full economic sovereignty. Also, the increase in Chinese domestic consumption will tie Chinese growth to the purchases of a declining and aging population, again lessening the rate of China's development.

The pattern of world economic cooperation will be affected. Bjørn Lomborg has done pioneering work investigating the way states respond to one another when their situation is like what game theorists call a prisoner's dilemma. If the game is deemed likely to continue, participants will initially bet on cooperation over time. But as responses become more and more cooperative, a country that suddenly shifts to punishment strategies will be rewarded because others (under prisoner's dilemma conditions) will at least initially continue their past cooperation. It will take some time for others to understand that cooperation no longer works. Unless international institutions sustained by overbalances of power are in place to prevent such negative shifts, conflict and perhaps even war is possible.[8]

Anti-Liberal Ideologies and Terrorism

Entangled with these trends away from global economic liberalism are a rejection of liberalism and indeed a rejuvenation of anti-liberal politics within some countries and across entire regions. The most obvious region is the Middle East. Terrorism has been an ever-present reality in the Western and Middle Eastern worlds since 2001, when the Twin Towers of the World Trade Center, as well as the Pentagon, were attacked by nineteen terrorists, mostly from Saudi Arabia. Nearly 3,000 people died on 9/11, and the threat of more catastrophic terrorism led the United States and many other countries to heighten border and internal security measures at considerable cost. The U.S.-led wars in Afghanistan (beginning in

---

8. Bjørn Lomborg, "Nucleus and Shield: The Evolution of Social Structure in the Iterated Prisoner's Dilemma," *American Sociological Review* (1996): 278–307.

2001) and Iraq (beginning in 2003) would not have taken place without 9/11. The radical jihadist ideology that motivated the terrorists shows no sign of dying out in the Middle East or indeed in other parts of the world.

Yet the economy and the security apparatuses of major states adjusted to the threat of catastrophic terrorism. Only if terrorists possessed nuclear bombs would Western security have been radically affected, and this has not happened. Nuclear states have increased their control over existing weapons, and thus far terrorists themselves have been unable to make such a weapon.[9] This may change in time, and greater intelligence and concentrated effort is needed to prevent such possibilities. Homeland security operatives in many countries working together can diminish this risk. Fortunately, the technical requirements for building a nuclear bomb are high. A plutonium-239 weapon requires a massive nuclear reactor to produce the fuel. This is a large undertaking, difficult to conceal. Such weapons have to be detonated precisely by circumferential explosion to compress the core of the fuel. The process is very exacting. If a gun-type U-235 weapon is used instead, it requires a substantial concentration of highly enriched uranium (HEU)—over 50 pounds—which then must be sent at extremely rapid speeds to collide with another source of U-235 (achieving criticality). This is not easy, and predetonation or a fizzle is possible. Terrorists have not yet conquered a facility or a state where they could conduct such experiments without detection. They may be better off trying to steal an existing weapon, but this is not easy, not even in Russia, and Nunn-Lugar provisions and protections make it more difficult still. The Nunn-Lugar Program, in existence since 1991, helps secure weapons of mass destruction and the materials used to make them from the former Soviet Union.

On balance, conventional terrorism employing captive or brainwashed suicide terrorists is easier, and, as we have seen in the Middle East, it frequently occurs. It is not clear that such tactics coerce governments or peoples to do the terrorists' bidding, however. Terrorists have been able to divide some countries into separate compartments. Syria has been dismembered following the revolt against Bashar al-Assad. Lebanon is no longer coherent, and Yemen exists in limbo with feuding Sunni and Shi'ite factions. Libya is no longer a single entity with a government that controls all its provinces. The countryside must be retaken militarily by outside forces.

Radical Islamism, then, is a powerful ideology. Part of what drives it are political and economic conditions in the Middle East, where even areas that appear stable are in a precarious position. The region is in the throes of a long legitimacy crisis, in which people disagree deeply and sometimes violently over the proper system of government and source of the laws. Popular pressure for democratization and reform exists nearly everywhere, as the chain of uprisings and revolutions in

---

9. Graham Allison, *Nuclear Terrorism: The Ultimate Preventable Catastrophe* (New York: Holt, 2005).

2011–2012, often called the Arab Spring, shows. Politics remains on a knife's edge in much of the Arab Middle East. The apparent exceptions are the oil-rich sheikdoms of the Persian (or Arabian) Gulf—Kuwait, the UAE, Saudi Arabia, Qatar, Bahrain, and Oman. These sheikdoms have been able to provide a tolerable life for their small populations, and the progressive urge to reform has thus far been monetarily deflected. The 40,000 dependents of the Saudi royal family have been treated the best, but Kuwaitis have not suffered, enjoying a per capita income of $52,000 in 2015. In short, there is no correlation between democratic structure and wealth in these countries because of the exceptional revenues earned by the oil producers.[10]

But the rivalry between two Persian Gulf oil giants, Saudi Arabia and Iran, is endangering the scheme. The Saudis increased production in the 2010s, driving down prices in an attempt to bankrupt Iran. But they were unavoidably pointing the oil weapon at themselves. In addition, natural gas, solar and wind power, and considerable oil production in other countries (e.g., Russia and the United States) were reducing demand for Middle Eastern oil, lowering its price while opening up Arab states to the possibility of democratic reform. The cheaper the world oil price, the worse is the Saudi balance of trade, which in turn degrades the Saudis' ability to pay subsidies. The Saudis have hoarded previous surpluses in banks and would then have to spend their savings as the pressure for reform mounts. Even if Saudi citizens were appeased, however, conflicts with foreigners would likely increase. Hostility continued between Sunni and Shi'ite practitioners of Islam, exacerbated by the Shi'ite domination of Iraq. Two successive prime ministers of Iraq were Shi'ites: Nouri al-Maliki and Haider al-Abadi. This presented a dire challenge to Sunnis. U.S. General David Petraeus arranged a 30,000-person surge in U.S. troop strength in 2007 that brought Sunnis back to influence and power in Anbar province and Mosul through a strategy of U.S. conciliation and economic support. Remembering the Iran-Iraq War, many soldiers and citizens resented Iranian influence in their country.

But under Iranian pressure the Shi'ite-led Iraqi government refused to sign the Status of Forces Agreement (SOFA), which was the sine qua non for the retention of U.S. presence and influence there. U.S. bases were deserted, and American forces retreated to Afghanistan. The ensuing Shi'ite dominance and the return of Iranian influence led disaffected Sunnis to rebel in many parts of Iraq, not least in Anbar province. In response, ISIL (also known as ISIS, the Islamic State, or

---

10. Robert J. Barro, "Economic Growth in a Cross-Section of Countries," *Quarterly Journal of Economics* 106, no. 2 (1991): 407–443; Daron Acemoğlu and James A. Robinson, *Why Nations Fail: The Origins of Power, Prosperity, and Poverty* (New York: Crown Business, 2013); Seymour Martin Lipset, "Some Social Requisites of Democracy: Economic Development and Political Legitimacy," *American Political Science Review* 53, no. 1 (1959): 69–105.

Daesh), a radical Sunni organization, spread into Syria and Lebanon and sent terrorist tentacles into Western cities like Paris and Brussels. Even San Bernardino, California, was hit with a terrorist attack in 2015. ISIL was more effective than al-Qaeda because it acted like a state—offering protection, economic assistance, and ideological comfort to its Sunni population. More generally, the sheer brutality of the Syrian civil war forced hundreds of thousands of refugees to flee to Jordan, Lebanon, Turkey, and Europe, destabilizing those countries. The United States under President Barack Obama decided not to take the lead in ending the Syrian war, and so Iran and Russia did so, siding with the Assad government against not only ISIL but also the more moderate Syrian opposition. Overall, the Obama years saw an American drawing down in the Middle East and a reassertion of Russian power there.

Europe, where the modern states system first appeared, is again a pioneer of a new system. After the horrific world wars of the twentieth century, Western European states began to integrate by breaking down many economic, legal, and political barriers that divided them. For all of its successes, the European Union today has an uncertain future. To the EU's east, meanwhile, Russia under Vladimir Putin has been trying to return to the nineteenth century by seizing territory from Ukraine and creating fears that he will do the same in other former Soviet states, such as the Baltics or Moldova. Here is one way that ideas matter in world politics: Putin has paid a price for defying the logic of the modern international system, but his idea of Russia as a realist-style great power tells him that the price is worth paying.

As the 2010s drew to a close, Russia stood no chance of becoming economically dominant. Its economy remained small and heavily dependent on oil and gas, and hence hostage to Saudi oil policy. Competing with China, Russia chose the old Silk Road, particularly the ever-present "Stans" (Kazakhstan, Uzbekistan, Tajikistan, Turkmenistan, and Kyrgyzstan) as potential nodes in such an anti-Western collection. Nonetheless, Russia retained a large nuclear arsenal. The regime of Vladimir Putin also deeply resented the loss of Russian prestige when the Soviet Union collapsed in 1991, and what Putin regarded as betrayal and mistreatment by the West thereafter, particularly the eastward expansion of NATO. Putin reasserted Russia's military presence in the Levant by fighting on behalf of the Assad government in Syria. He also proved adept at using what leverage he had to expand Russian influence and divide Western countries both internally and against one another. By portraying Russia as taking the lead in fighting jihadist terrorism and safeguarding traditional values, and by providing support for populist, anti-EU and anti-American parties in Europe (mentioned earlier in this chapter), Putin threatened the future of the EU and with it transatlantic solidity. Liberal internationalism would suffer a serious setback were Putin to succeed and the EU and NATO dissolve.

Conclusion

All of these developments—a weakening commitment to liberal international-ism in the West, the continuing rise of non-democratic China, the persistence of extremism and ideological strife in the Middle East, and Russian nationalist resentment—show that 500-year story we have told over the preceding nine chapters does not necessarily lead to a happy ending, or an ending at all. A liberal international system with a logic of self-government, commerce, and peace has unmistakably spread over the past few centuries to cover most of the globe. But history teaches that worsening economic conditions can lead nations to restart arms races and seek new territory.

One of the central claims of this book is that history shapes international relations theory. Realism, which holds that sovereign states must fear one another and compete for territory and power, tends to flourish in times and places where states are ruled by people or coalitions that repress the interests of their people. These states see wealth and security as deriving mostly from direct control of agriculture or raw materials such as minerals and fossil fuels, and they do not trust other states to keep access to such things open. Liberalism, which holds that states can be rich and secure through the peaceful means of trade, tends to flourish in times and places where states are gov-erned by their people and a constitution that protects their rights. These states see wealth and security as deriving from international economic openness, particularly trade in goods and services. They trust one another to keep access to essential goods, such as food and energy, open. Realism claims that it is a universal theory and that liberalism and constructivism are charming illusions that do more harm than good.

Realism still captures some aspects of world politics today. Russia has behaved in a classically realist fashion in recent years, annexing territory belonging to its neighbor Ukraine (the Crimea) and threatening to take more. It is no accident, however, that Russia is not a liberal democracy. Neither is China, nor are the governments in the Middle East (apart from Israel and Tunisia). All are capital-ist (with strong doses of state control), but none recognizes the full list of fun-damental civil rights that liberal democracies do, and none allows meaningful political competition. An important question for the future is: Is there an alterna-tive to liberal democracy that can succeed over the long term in the twenty-first century? If so, that system is likely to spread, as elites in other states decide to copy it. After all, imitation of success is responsible for much of the spread of liberal democracy and the liberal international system over the centuries. The spread of a less liberal or anti-liberal regime would likely mean the retreat of the liberal international system and an expansion of a new kind of realist system.

The various Islamist and secularist-authoritarian regimes in the Middle East seem unsuitable for export to the wider world, as does Putin's regime, with its reliance on high energy prices and a formidable propaganda machine.[11] China, with its sustained economic growth and ability to adjust to changing conditions, is the most successful non-democratic regime. One key question for the future of global order, then, is whether China's market-Leninist system will continue to flourish and will inspire imitation in Asia and elsewhere. The Chinese Communist Party is betting that it can hold on to power while steering its country to ever-greater wealth and influence while avoiding war. Its bet has paid off better than many experts in the West believed that it could. But ultimately, China will have to choose between further openness, including democracy, and a retreat to neo-mercantilism and seizures of foreign territory. The historical successes of liberal democracies presented in this book imply that, to succeed over time, China will need broadened participation at home. Broadening is necessary for Beijing to have international clout. Communist leaders are not representatives of the people. The same is true of Russia and of the non-democratic states of the Middle East. There are ample forces within these countries pushing them, sometimes slowly and gently, toward democracy. History shows that the path toward peace and prosperity for all lies with those liberal-democratic forces.

History also teaches, however, that theory can shape history—theory understood as a set of ideas about how the world works or can work. Even in crisis, liberal democracy remains a beacon of hope for the disappointed and dispossessed. Ultimately, nations can fashion a world without that much conflict because they have the internal means to improve themselves. The centuries-long growth and deepening of the liberal international system was owed partly to developments in ideas, institutions, and technology. But it also was a product of countless choices made by governments, business people, militaries, and ordinary citizens. This is the final and most important way in which realism is wrong: international anarchy does not determine all of the foreign policy decisions that governments make. People have agency. This is true of those who rule China and Russia: they may choose to continue along the paths of old-style centralized realist politics at home and fear and suspicion abroad. It is true as well of the people and governments of the liberal democracies, including the United States: they can respond to the current challenges to liberalism by turning away from liberalism and toward the centralization of power at home and the quest for autarky abroad, as so many did in the 1930s. Or they may respond with the time-honored tradition of reform, continuing their historic commitments to the decentralization of power at home and peace and trade abroad. The latter will require clear thinking, consensus, and political will.

---

11. Peter Pomerantsev, *Nothing Is True and Everything Is Possible: The Surreal Heart of the New Russia* (New York: Public Affairs, 2014).

Some of that thinking will draw upon experience and history. Central banks and fiscal authorities can stimulate the global economy. Debt is not nearly as worrisome as it has been portrayed. Helicopter drops of monies can keep the engines of economics pulsating and turning, and finance can be widely spread to eliminate areas of stringency. Reliable debt repayment also strengthens liberalism and democracy, as the Bank of England underscored after 1690.[12] Some of that thinking, however, will regenerate new ideas of reform. The good news is that one of the great strengths of liberal democracies is their facility for reading and adjusting to changing economic, technological, and social conditions, both within their borders and beyond. As we have shown throughout this book, this flexibility has allowed the liberal international order itself to adapt to changes over the centuries. With their openness and institutions that reward innovation, market democracies generate, propagate, and absorb new ideas better than other kinds of countries. They are going to need those qualities in the coming years as never before. As they continue their 400-year tradition of adaptation and reform, leaders and citizens of democracies can have confidence that the long transformation of the international system will carry forward and attract more and more nations to expand the zone of cooperation and peace.

FURTHER READING

Acemoğlu, Daron, and James Robinson. *Why Nations Fail: The Origins of Power, Prosperity, and Poverty.* New York: Crown Business, 2012.

Axelrod, Robert. *The Evolution of Cooperation.* New York: Basic Books, 1984.

Brooks, Stephen, and William Wohlforth. *America Abroad: The United States' Global Role in the 21st Century.* New York: Oxford University Press, 2016.

Harrison, Ewan, and Sara McLaughlin-Mitchell, *The Triumph of Democracy and the Eclipse of the West.* New York: Palgrave-Macmillan, 2014.

Kagan, Robert. *The Return of History and the End of Dreams.* New York: Knopf, 2009.

Milanovic, Branko. *Global Inequality: A New Approach for the Age of Globalization.* Cambridge, MA: Belknap Press, 2016.

Owen, John M. *Confronting Political Islam: Six Lessons from the West's Past.* Princeton, NJ: Princeton University Press, 2015.

Rosecrance, Richard. *The Resurgence of the West: How a Transatlantic Union Can Prevent War and Restore the United States and Europe.* New Haven, CT: Yale University Press, 2013.

---

12. James MacDonald, *A Free Nation Deep in Debt: The Financial Roots of Democracy* (Princeton, NJ: Princeton University Press, 2006).

INDEX